T0320200

Waste and Environmental Policy

This book deals with the increasingly complex issues of waste generation, waste management and waste disposal that in less developed industrialised countries arouse diverse but critical concerns. It takes a socio-economic and policy-oriented perspective and provides empirical evidence at EU and regional level. The EU and Italy are taken as relevant case studies, given the disparities in environmental performance between less and more developed areas.

The rich and varied empirical evidence shows that a robust delinking between waste generation and economic growth is still not present, thus future policies should directly address the problem at the source by targeting waste generation in EU countries. Some structural factors like population density and urbanisation present themselves as relevant drivers of both waste management and landfill diversion. Nevertheless, economic and structural factors alone are not sufficient to improve waste performance. Though waste policies are to be redesigned by covering the entire area of waste management, some first signals of policy effectiveness are arising.

This work will be of most interest to students of environmental economics and environmental sciences, as well as policy makers, waste utility managers and companies in the waste management sector.

Massimiliano Mazzanti is lecturer in environmental economics and associate professor at the University of Ferrara, Italy.

Anna Montini is assistant professor in economics and lecturer in economics and environmental economics at the University of Bologna, Italy.

Routledge Explorations in Environmental Economics

General editor Nick Hanley
University of Stirling, UK

1 **Greenhouse Economics**
Value and ethics
Clive L. Spash

2 **Oil Wealth and the Fate
of Tropical Rainforests**
Sven Wunder

3 **The Economics of Climate
Change**
*Edited by Anthony D. Owen
and Nick Hanley*

4 **Alternatives for Environmental
Valuation**
*Edited by Michael Getzner,
Clive Spash and Sigrid Stagl*

5 **Environmental Sustainability**
A consumption approach
*Raghbendra Jha and
K. V. Bhanu Murthy*

6 **Cost-effective Control of
Urban Smog**
The significance of the
Chicago cap-and-trade
approach
*Richard F. Kosobud,
Houston H. Stokes,
Carol D. Tallarico and
Brian L. Scott*

7 **Ecological Economics and
Industrial Ecology**
Jakub Kronenberg

8 **Environmental Economics,
Experimental Methods**
*Edited by Todd L. Cherry,
Stephan Kroll and
Jason F. Shogren*

9 **Game Theory and Policy
Making in Natural Resources
and the Environment**
*Edited by Ariel Dinar,
José Albiac and
Joaquín Sánchez-Soriano*

10 **Arctic Oil and Gas**
Sustainability at risk?
*Edited by Aslaug Mikkelsen and
Oluf Langhelle*

11 **Agrobiodiversity, Conservation
and Economic Development**
*Edited by Andreas Kontoleon,
Unai Pascual and
Melinda Smale*

12 **Renewable Energy from Forest
Resources in the United States**
*Edited by Barry D. Solomon
and Valeria A. Luzadis*

13 **Modeling Environment-improving Technological Innovations under Uncertainty**
Alexander A. Golub and Anil Markandya

14 **Economic Analysis of Land Use in Global Climate Change Policy**
Thomas Hertel, Steven Rose and Richard Tol

15 **Waste and Environmental Policy**
Edited by Massimiliano Mazzanti and Anna Montini

Waste and Environmental Policy

Edited by
Massimiliano Mazzanti and Anna Montini

 Routledge
Taylor & Francis Group

LONDON AND NEW YORK

First published 2009
by Routledge
2 Park Square, Milton Park, Abingdon, Oxon. OX14 4RN

Simultaneously published in the USA and Canada
by Routledge
270 Madison Avenue, New York, NY 10016

Routledge is an imprint of the Taylor & Francis Group, an informa business

© 2009 Massimiliano Mazzanti and Anna Montini

Typeset in Times New Roman
by Taylor & Francis Books

British Library Cataloguing in Publication Data
A catalogue record for this book is available from the British Library

Library of Congress Cataloging in Publication Data
Waste and environmental policy / [edited by] Massimiliano Mazzanti &
Anna Montini.
    p. cm. – (Routledge explorations in environmental economics ; 15)
    1. Refuse and refuse disposal–European Union countries. 2.
Environmental policy–European Union countries. I. Mazzanti,
Massimiliano. II. Montini, Anna.
  HD4485.E85W365 2009
  363.72'8–dc22
                        2008037950

ISBN 978-0-415-45936-5 (hbk)
ISBN 978-0-203-88137-8 (ebk)

This book is dedicated to
Anna Chiara and Paolo, and
to the future of Matteo and Pietro

Contents

List of figures	xi
List of tables	xii
List of contributors	xiv
Preface	xvi
Acknowledgements	xix
List of abbreviations	xx

Introduction   1
MASSIMILIANO MAZZANTI AND ANNA MONTINI

PART I
Waste generation, waste management and waste disposal:
macroeconomic analyses of delinking and policy effectiveness   13

1   Delinking and environmental Kuznets curves for waste indicators
in Europe: evidence on municipal solid waste and packaging waste   15
MASSIMILIANO MAZZANTI AND ROBERTO ZOBOLI

2   Waste generation and waste disposal: evidence on socio-economic
and policy drivers in the EU   34
MASSIMILIANO MAZZANTI, FRANCESCO NICOLLI AND ROBERTO ZOBOLI

3   Municipal waste generation, management and greenhouse gas
emissions   72
FRITS MØLLER ANDERSEN, METTE SKOVGAARD AND HELGE LARSEN

4   The drivers of MSW generation, disposal and recycling: examining
OECD inter-country differences   91
KATIA KAROUSAKIS

PART II

Waste generation, waste management and landfill diversion: policy-oriented and regionally based analyses from Italy   105

5   Municipal waste generation, socio-economic drivers and waste management instruments: regional and provincial panel data evidence from Italy   107
    MASSIMILIANO MAZZANTI, ANNA MONTINI AND ROBERTO ZOBOLI

6   Embedding landfill diversion in economic, geographical and policy settings: regional and provincial evidence from Italy   126
    MASSIMILIANO MAZZANTI, ANNA MONTINI AND FRANCESCO NICOLLI

7   Reducing uncertainty in the monetary assessment of environmental liabilities from waste landfilling   154
    TIZIANA CIANFLONE AND KRIS WERNSTEDT

8   Separation of organic waste and composting: European policies and local choices   182
    MASSIMILIANO VOLPI

    Index   205

Figures

I.1   The income–environment relationship   2
1.1   World CO_2 emissions (million tons of C) and world GDP
       level (million 1990 international Geary–Khamis dollars)   19
1.2 CO_2 emissions intensity (fossil fuels) of world GDP and
       world GDP level (million tons of C per million 1990
       international Geary–Khamis dollars, selected years indicated)   19
1.3   Packaging waste generation per capita: EU-15   24
1.4   Municipal waste generation per capita: EU-28   24
2.1   Projected generation and landfill of municipal waste: EU-25   35
2.2   Use of landfill, incineration and material recovery as treatment
       options, 2004   36
3.1   Developments in the management of municipal waste: EU-27,
       1995–2006   80
3.2   Developments in municipal waste: EU-27   84
3.3   Developments in the management of municipal waste: EU-27,
       1980–2020   86
3.4   Generation and landfill of BMW, and landfilled BMW as a
       percentage of BMW generated in 1995, 1995–2020   87
3.5   Emission of GHG from the management of municipal waste:
       EU-27, 1980–2020   88
6.1   Per capita landfilled waste in Italian provinces, (kg, 2005)   130
6.2   Per capita incinerated waste in Italian provinces, (kg, 2005)   131
6.3   Separately collected waste share in Italian provinces, (%, 2005)   132
8.1   Evolution of composting capacity, separation of organic waste,
       separation of other waste, and estimated amount of organic
       waste in remaining waste   196

Tables

1.1	EKC analysis of packaging waste	26
1.2	EKC analysis of municipal waste	27
2.1	Literature survey of waste-related studies	40
2.2	Descriptive statistics and a summary of research hypotheses	45
2.3	Main variables (1995–2005 values)	46
2.4	MSW generation regression results, EU-25	53
2.5	MSW generation, EU-15	54
2.6	MSW generation, EU-10	55
2.7	Landfilled MSW, EU-25	56
2.8	Landfilled MSW, EU-15	58
2.9	Landfilled MSW, EU-10	58
2.10	Incinerated MSW, EU-15	59
2.11	MSW generation regression results, EU-25: Swamy random-coefficients linear regression model and dynamic analysis	61
2.12	MSW landfilled regression results, EU-25: Swamy random-coefficients linear regression model and dynamic analysis	61
3.1	Model parameters for municipal waste generation, EU-15	75
3.2	Model parameters for generation of municipal waste, EU-12	77
3.3	Composition of municipal waste, 2005	82
3.4	Key economic and socio-economic assumptions	83
3.5	Projected changes in municipal waste, population and private consumption, EU-27	85
4.1	Description and sources of the data	94
4.2	Descriptive statistics	95
4.3	Analysis of variance for all the variables	95
4.4	Parameter estimates for MSW generation	96
4.5	FGLS estimates of MSW generation	97
4.6	FGLS estimates of percentage landfilled	100
4.7	FGLS estimates of percentage of paper and cardboard recycled	101
4.8	FGLS estimates of percentage of glass recycled	101
5.1	Descriptive statistics: dependent and independent variables	111
5.2	Provincial level: base estimations and additional specifications	115

5.3   Regional level: base estimations and additional specifications   118

6.1   Descriptive statistics and research hypothesis (*provincial* data set): dependent and independent variables   133

6.2   Descriptive statistics and research hypothesis (*regional* data set): dependent and independent variables   134

6.3   Landfilled waste per capita: regional data, 1999–2005   136

6.4   Landfilled waste per area: regional data, 1999–2005   136

6.5   Other specifications with landfilled waste per capita, 1999–2005 (20 regions)   137

6.6   Specifications for landfilled waste per capita (semi-log model, balanced panel), province analysis, 1999–2005   141

6.7   Specifications for landfilled waste per capita (log-log model, unbalanced panel) provincial analysis, 1999–2005   144

6.8   Heckman two-stage regressions (probit + unbalanced panel)   146

7.1   Cost-based valuation approaches   164

7.2   Natural recoverability of NRD and human-directed restorability of natural resources and services   165

7.3   Improper or illegal waste disposal that causes NRD   169

8.1   Variables included in the model and their expected effect on composting   192

8.2   Data summary   195

8.3   Determinants of composting capacity: instrumental variable estimation   197

Contributors

Frits Møller Andersen holds a master's degree in economics from the University of Aarhus, Denmark, and is head of the Energy Systems Analysis research programme at Risø-DTU. He has been responsible for the development of several energy and environmental models used for Danish and European forecasts and scenario analyses related to energy demand and waste generation.

Tiziana Cianflone is an economist at the National Environmental Protection Agency of Italy (APAT). She received her doctorate from the University of Rome III for a thesis on 'Institution, Environment and Economic Development Policy'. Her work focuses on the economics of public choice, heritage conservation, and natural resources and environment quality.

Helge V. Larsen holds an MSc in electrical engineering and a PhD in energy modelling from the Technical University of Denmark (DTU). She is senior scientist at Risø-DTU and her specialism is the development of energy models, especially for electricity systems and the integration of wind power into the north European electricity system.

Katia Karousakis is an environmental economist and policy analyst in the Environment Directorate of the Organisation for Economic Co-operation and Development (OECD) in Paris. She holds a BSc from the University of York, UK, a master's degree from Duke University, Durham NC, and a PhD from University College London.

Massimiliano Mazzanti is lecturer in environmental economics and assistant professor at the University of Ferrara, Italy. For many years he has collaborated as research fellow with CERIS-CNR, an institute of the National Research Council in Milan, and was awarded an MSc in Environmental and Resource Economics by University College London.

Anna Montini is assistant professor in economics and lecturer in economics and environmental economics at the University of Bologna, Italy. She also collaborates as a research fellow with the National Research Council in

Milan (CERIS-DSE). She holds a PhD in political economics from the University of Siena, Italy.

Francesco Nicolli is an environmental economist with a PhD in economics awarded by the University of Ferrara, Italy, and a master's in environmental economics from the University of Birmingham, UK. His main research interests are environmental and waste-related regulation in the European framework, and applied microeconomics.

Mette Skovgaard holds a master's degree in economics from the University of Aarhus, Denmark. In her capacity as project manager at the ETC/RWM Ms Skovgaard has conducted a number of analyses of policy measures in a European context. Her special interests are policy effectiveness analysis and scenario analysis within the field of waste and resource management.

Massimiliano Volpi received his PhD in economics from the University of Milan and holds a master's in Integrated Environmental Management from IUSS, University of Pavia, in Italy. His main research interests hinge on the econometric analysis of environmental policy and technological change. He was a visiting PhD student at MERIT, Maastricht, Netherlands.

Kris Wernstedt is an associate professor in the School of Public and International Affairs at Virginia Tech University's campus in Washington DC. Since receiving his doctorate in planning from Cornell University, his work has concentrated on environmental and economic aspects of contaminated land, water resource planning, and the socio-economic dimensions of climate change.

Roberto Zoboli is full professor of economics and political economy at the Catholic University of Milan and research director of CERIS-DSE, institute of the National Research Council of Milan. For many years he has worked on issues such as innovation dynamics in firms and economic systems, environmental policy evaluation, resource efficiency analysis and trends.

Preface

This book originated from various institutional research projects and other individual pieces of research, conducted since 2003 on the topic of waste economics and policy, including waste management, the effectiveness of waste policy at EU and national levels, and the evaluation of market and non-market effects of landfill sitings. The analysis of waste has found some collocation within a research area that deals with the decoupling of major environmental pressures from economic growth, in which waste-related issues are as relevant as, for example, climate change and water supply. The sustainability of waste generation, management and disposal is key to the wider issue of the sustainability of economic development.

We would underline that the chapters in this volume are not a collection of papers associated with a single project but the product of different analyses, at the European and Italian levels, with diverse starting points, which find some convergence and complementarity in terms of their methodology and results. Much of the collaboration and complementarity among the researchers involved in this volume is ongoing and further analyses of waste management, the economics of waste and assessments of waste and environmental policy effectiveness can be expected.

Most of the research in this book has been developed co-operatively with partners from the National Research Council in Milan (specifically the Institute for the Study of Firms and Development, and Economic Systems Dynamics, now CERIS DSE), the University of Bologna (Department of Economics and Faculty of Law) and the University of Ferrara (Department of Economics, Institutions and Territory). A major stimulus for the analytical work described in this book is the collaboration between CERIS-DSE, APAT (the Italian Environmental Protection Agency), which is the data source for most of these analyses, and the European Topic Centre on Waste and Material Flows in Copenhagen. This collaboration started in 2002–3, in the form of a series of projects under the umbrella of the European Environmental Agency (EEA) focusing on issues such as resource extraction and management, waste packaging policies, EU policies for landfill diversion, methodology for the evaluation of policy effectiveness, among others. The results of these analyses are referenced and acknowledged as the inspiration for the current work. In the course of this research, several doctoral students joined the research network and the work on waste issues. They have contributed greatly to several of the papers that form the chapters of this book.

Formal and informal research networks are defining and creating a set of expertise and accumulated knowledge on waste policy effectiveness, the driving forces for reductions in waste generation and landfill diversion. This book, rather than being a conclusion, represents a departure in the direction of new investigations and better evidence in relation to the complex web of direct and indirect factors contributing to the target of reducing the economic and environmental pressures/costs associated with waste generation, collection and disposal. This task is posing increasing challenges to institutions devoted to data collection and monitoring, which are required to provide detailed and reliable data in a difficult environment in terms of data assessments, to researchers who need to define and refine economic and policy-oriented empirical models, in which the interaction and endogeneity that characterize certain key factors, the dynamic framework and the spatial/regional features of waste systems are extremely challenging issues.

It should be noted that by chance the book was being compiled at a time when the topic of waste became critical in parts of southern Italy. When the delicate balance between waste generation and disposal breaks down, owing to policy failures or inadequacies related to both waste collection and management, local environmental pressure hot spots emerge along with 'not in my backyard' attitudes and behaviour. This is an especially vexed problem with respect to the siting of landfills and incinerators. Some of chapters in this book compare the northern and southern regions of Italy, which present quite stark differences in terms of waste management performance. Some of these are income-driven; others are policy-driven. Although specific and associated with certain idiosyncratic features, the Italian analyses, which compare economic and institutional performance across regions, and the EU analyses, which focus on western countries and new members' heterogeneity in economic, institutional and social terms, are of general interest. This is, first, because they provide food for thought for local and European policy makers in the difficult environment characterized by increasingly stringent targets with respect to various waste streams, at both management and disposal levels, and even stricter waste generation policy objectives for the future. The convergence among different regions – very often with very different structural economic situations – will necessitate national or regionally based implementation of EU policies on waste and environmental issues, in order to reduce compliance costs and increase effectiveness. This is the most important and most difficult task. Robust empirical evidence on the evolution of waste systems, and interactions between waste policies and economic development, constitute the information required to eventually adjust and reshape current and future frameworks. Second, the now rather long-standing EU experience on waste policy implementation, which goes back to 1994 and in some national cases even before, might be relevant to other countries or areas of the world that are trying to introduce waste-related efforts or make them more effective. The evidence in this book on the importance of various policy drivers, structural and economic backgrounds, and other socio-economic and institutional features, in our opinion is generalizable to other areas, making the book useful to a wide audience.

M.M.
A.M.
August 2008

Acknowledgements

We acknowledge the helpful comments from participants in workshops, conferences and informal conversations. It would be impossible to identify all individually, but we would especially thank Frits Møller Andersen, Mette Skovgaard and Roberto Zoboli for their very helpful suggestions on many parts and aspects of the analyses. Roberto Zoboli made an especially large contribution, based on his very deep knowledge of innovation and waste processes, in providing economic significance to the results of the empirical analyses. We are indebted to him for what we have learnt over the years of working together on the many projects on environmental economics issues at the CERIS-DSE Institute of the National Research Council in Milan. Massimiliano Mazzanti is also intellectually indebted to Professor David William Pearce, who was very stimulating as a research supervisor. Even a few words exchanged with him were always full of valuable hints and support for young researchers.

We also thank Federico Foschini and others working at APAT in Rome for support on data-related issues. We thank Sara Fiocchi, Emanuele Gessi, Valentina Iafolla, Lorenzo Ragazzi and Cecilia Vita Finzi for their work on construction of the preliminary dataset. We are also indebted to the many other people participants in the workshops and meetings on the effectiveness of EU waste environmental policies, held between 2005 and 2008 at the European Topic Centre on Waste and Material Flows and at the European Environment Agency in Copenhagen, without whose input, comments and discussion the quality of the papers that constitute the chapters in this book would have been lower. Ultimate responsibility for their content, however, remains with the authors.

We are also grateful to Cynthia Little for her very efficient and careful revision of English style and grammar.

Massimiliano Mazzanti acknowledges financial support from the 2007 research funds for young researchers from the University of Ferrara and general funding support from the local research funds of the University of Ferrara in recent years. Anna Montini acknowledges financial support from the research funds of the University of Bologna.

Abbreviations

ACM	avoided cost method
APAT	Agenzia Protezione Ambiente e Territorio
AR	auto-regressive
BAU	business as usual
BMW	biodegradable municipal waste
C&D	construction and demolition
CBA	cost–benefit analysis
DCM	defensive (or mitigation) cost method
DEFRA	Department for the Environment, Food and Rural Affairs
DTI	Department of Trade and Industry
DWM	decentralized waste management
EAP	Environmental Action Programme
EEA	European Environmental Agency
EIONET	European Environment Information and Observation Network
EKC	environmental Kuznets curve
ELV	end of life vehicles
EPA	Environmental Protection Agency
ESI	environmental sustainability index
ETS	emissions trading scheme
EU	European Union
EUB	environmentally undesirable behaviour
EUT	Expected Utility
EUWM	environmentally undesirable waste management
FEM	fixed effects model
GDP	gross domestic product
GHG	greenhouse gas
GMM	general method of moment
ICT	information and communication technology
IIASA	International Institute for Applied Systems Analysis
IMR	inverse Mills ratio
IPAT	impact, population, affluence, technology
IPCC	Intergovernmental Panel on Climate Change

IPPC	integrated pollution prevention and control
IV	instrumental variable
kg	kilogram
LCA	life cycle assessment
LSDV	least squares dummy variable
MSW	municipal solid waste
NIMBY	not in my back yard
NRD	natural resources damage
NRDA	natural resource damage assessment
OECD	Organisation for Economic Co-operation and Development
PCB	polychlorinated biphenyls
RCM	restoration cost method
R&D	research and development
REM	random effects model
SCM	surrogate cost method
TEV	total economic value
TP	turning point
UK	United Kingdom
UN	United Nations
UNFCCC	United Nations Framework Convention on Climate Change
US	United States
VA	value added
WEEE	waste electrical and electronic equipment
WG	waste generation
WKC	waste Kuznets curve

Introduction

Massimiliano Mazzanti and Anna Montini

The chapters in this book are based on a series of papers that provide varying and complementary evidence related to the currently hot topic of waste management and waste disposal, which is becoming unavoidable in both developing and developed countries. For example, very recently, some areas in southern Italy have been experiencing a collapse in their waste management performance, which at the time of writing has still to be resolved, and is due mainly to a set of factors such as low proportion of separated waste collection, absence of serious alternatives to landfill, increasing scarcity of land in densely populated areas, failures in local policy implementation and property rights enforcement. The problem with waste management and correlated externalities resulting from landfill is that waste stock accumulates, and the process is difficult to reverse when the balance between inflows of waste generated and outflows of waste treated becomes uneven.

Waste generation and waste disposal are becoming increasingly prominent issues in the environmental arena, both in terms of policy perspectives and in the context of delinking analysis. Waste generation is increasing more or less proportionally with income, and the economic and environmental costs associated with landfill are also increasing. Thus waste management, from production to disposal, is an environmental issue no less relevant, and potentially more critical, than water scarcity or climate change. It interlinks with climate change, since incineration, recycling and landfill all result in the production of greenhouse gases (GHG). Diversion of waste from landfill (landfill diversion) is one of the options being used to reduce these emissions.

The main questions addressed in this book refer to the extent to which the diverse waste flows generated by household and economic activities are decoupled or not from the growth in income per capita. Decoupling or delinking analysis, to some extent related to the more specific realm of environmental Kuznets curve (EKC, see Figure 1 for an intuitive sketch) and to conceptual frames such as IPAT (an accounting identity used to identify the relative role of P – population level, A – affluence and T – technology for the observed change in I – impact over time and/or across countries), is the primary tool used to assess whether or not environmental performance is improving. Without any other judgements (from outside economics, from

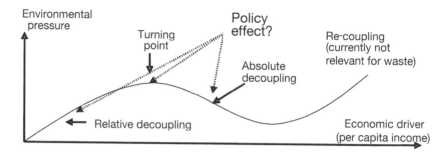

Figure I.1 The income–environment relationship

saving capital-based rules of sustainability) it should be noted that delinking *per se* cannot lead automatically, even in its absolute form, to sustainability. In other words, observing a decrease in environmental pressures – for waste, the set of externalities associated with waste generation, incineration and landfill – along the dynamics of economic growth is a positive element but does not automatically imply that sustainability will be achieved. Nevertheless, absolute decoupling is the way towards sustainable performance: increasing the environmental efficiency of economic growth by moving the environment–income relationship below critical thresholds in terms of environmental impacts.

European Union (EU) policy thematic strategies on resources and waste include reference to absolute and relative delinking indicators (EC 2003a, b; Jacobsen *et al.* 2004). The former, according to the EKC framework, is a negative relationship between economic growth and environmental impacts associated with the descending side of an inverted U shape. The latter is a positive, but decreasing in size, income–environment relationship – the ascending path – a positive, lower than unity elasticity in economic terms. No delinking is observed in the ascending part of the EKC, in case of a unitary or higher than unity elasticity. The achievement of increasing delinking experience is a prime necessity for waste, an issue that is of equal relevance in terms of environmental impact and economic costs, to climate change.

The European Environmental Agency (EEA), has often acknowledged that 'it is increasingly important to provide answers to these questions because waste volumes in the EU are growing, driven by changing production and consumption patterns. It is also important because there is growing interest in sharing best practice and exchanging national-level experience across Europe, with the common goal of achieving more cost-effective solutions to the various problems being faced' (EEA 2007: 4).

Indicators of decoupling/delinking are becoming increasingly popular for detecting and measuring improvements in environmental/resource efficiency with respect to economic activity at the level of and in connection with policy making and policy evaluation. The Organization for Economic Co-operation and Development (OECD 2002) has conducted extensive research

Income–environment relationships, dynamic trends and decoupling

The reasoning surrounding decoupling can be framed by reference to the EKC model, which describes the state of the dynamic relationship between environmental pressures and economic drivers. This model proposes an inverted U-shaped relationship between per capita income and environmental pressure. The model implies that in the first stage an increase in income leads to an increase in environmental pressure. In the second stage, above a certain level of income, the environmental pressure will decrease, as the economy is better able to invest in less polluting technology, consumers reallocate expenditure in favour of greener products, there are more awareness-raising campaigns, etc. Even policies that are aimed at reshaping the 'business as usual' trend towards more environmentally efficient and sustainable paths are likely to be implemented with an increasing strictness and effectiveness in terms of economic development. At a later stage, there might be a potential recoupling, observed for some pollutants, where environmental pressure grows in spite of increasing income. The scale effects of growth again will outweigh improvements in the efficiency of resource use and management. A recoupling could thus emerge in well organized waste management systems, if the pressures from the production of goods and final disposal economic and environmental effects are taken into account, following a life cycle approach (LCA) perspective.

In this context environmental pressure involves: waste generation, landfill or incineration. We explore how this relationship is altered by the inclusion of socio-economic and policy drivers. Drivers fall into three categories: economic, socio-economic and policy-based.

into the use of decoupling indicators for reporting and policy evaluation purposes, and the EEA's state-of-the-environment reports (EEA 2003a, b, c) use a number of decoupling or resource efficiency indicators. EEA (2006) highlights the importance of market-based instruments for achieving a stronger delinking for waste indicators.

Landfill diversion is a specific and important element of EU policy as a means to improve the use of resources and reduce the environmental impacts of waste management. Following the targets provided by Directive 1999/31/EC on Landfill of Waste, Member States are required to establish national strategies to reduce the amount of biodegradable municipal waste going to landfill. This Landfill Directive is expected to have a major effect on the design of future waste management systems and policy making.

In addition, GHG emissions have become more and more relevant in relation to waste and its disposal. The landfill of biodegradable waste produces methane, which is more harmful than CO_2 in terms of its carbon potential. In 2005, GHG emissions from waste management in the EU-15 contributed to 2.6 per cent of the total, as discussed by Andersen, Skovgaard and Larsen in Chapter 3. Countries can take positive action to combat climate change by increasing their landfill diversion. As noted by the EEA (2007), this means that effective waste management that includes high levels of recycling, and possibly incineration with energy recovery, can partly offset the emissions produced when raw materials and products are extracted and manufactured. This implies that the waste management sector could contribute to meeting the Kyoto targets. Waste policies, specific carbon-oriented policies such as the innovative EU Emissions Trading Scheme (EU ETS), renewable energy policy provisions, and innovation-oriented regulations, are major drivers of the struggle to achieve carbon reductions. Direct and indirect policy effects need always to be taken into account. If, in this book, we at times stress win–win solutions, it must be remembered that trade-offs will also arise. For example, in the field of end-of-life vehicle management and disposal, the use of plastics in automobile manufacture contributes to reducing emissions because vehicles of this construction are lighter. However, plastic poses major recycling and incineration problems, while heavier ferrous materials can be easily recovered and recycled.

There are also some interlinks with innovation-oriented directives based on the technological content of energy recovery solutions related to the incineration of municipal solid waste (MSW) and other waste flows.

The main contribution of this book is its structural integration of delinking analysis, revolving around the core income–environment relationship, with the analysis of an extended set of explanatory variables, ranging from socio-economic to geographical and structural factors, to policy levers, all of which, as we will show, play (major or minor) roles as driving forces of waste generation, recycling, incineration and landfill. The embedding of waste generation and waste disposal in the geographical, economic, social and policy environments is necessary to understand fully the complex web of links and interrelationships that characterize the waste chain, from generation to landfill, and the waste realm from both the economic and the management perspective.

Our analyses try to assess the various roles played by such factors in driving waste generation and waste disposal trends, offering a perspective that goes from the macro level (EU, OECD, Part I of this volume), to more specific investigations (on Italy, Part II) that are aimed at exploring in depth what is driving waste trends and also the wide differences between different areas (western and eastern EU members, richer and poorer parts of Italy). The important role of national environmental agencies in providing reliable and sufficiently detailed data both over time and across regions is unavoidable.

Such evidence, based not merely on the income–environment relationship, can evaluate what are the current significant factors driving waste flows, thus informing and providing food for thought to local and EU policy makers. In these chapters we mainly assess the *ex post* effectiveness (not the efficiency) of waste policies pertaining to the EU and to member states.

We note that these analyses are complementary to methods of evaluating the efficiency of waste policies, *ex ante* or *ex post*, based on cost–benefit analysis (CBA). The work by Pearce (2004) on waste policies is a good example of CBA applied to his field. We would again remark that the two directions of analysis – evaluating efficiency and effectiveness – are complements, not alternatives. Our work is on a relatively more macro-level and complements the well developed field of landfill siting optimal procedures and CBA applied to landfill and incineration siting, as alternative recycling options.

Thus it is clear that the message in this book is general: given that the EU, and even Italy as a member country, have quite well developed waste policies, their experience should inform other EU member states, newcomers or countries in other parts of the world that want to reshape current strategies or to initiate waste policies starting from a zero base. As recognized by the EEA (2007), it is important to know whether we are on track to meet the targets in the Landfill Directive, and also to know which policies work well and which are less significant. This will help in the design and refinement of future EU policy developments. To be more specific, the Sixth Environment Action Programme of the European Community puts emphasis on *ex post* evaluation of the effectiveness of current policy measures in terms of their environmental objectives. It underlines how essential it is to know what measures have been implemented in response to a given directive, what their effects are/were and whether the specific idiosyncratic economic, institutional, social and even geographical features of the national context have affected the efficiency of a set of policy instruments.

Given the emphasis on policy making, and based on currently available data, the contributions in this book focus mainly on MSW, which, if not the major component of waste in quantitative terms, is perhaps the most problematic, given its diffuseness, and is the area on which much policy effort is focused. The MSW analyses described in this book can be extended, using the methodological environment developed, to other serious waste issues, such as C&D (construction and demolition), WEEE (waste from electrical and electronic equipment) and hazardous waste, which nevertheless have some specific features related to the main sectors of production of these types of waste.

We note that MSW issues apply to the whole of society. The achievement of higher waste performance involves many actors and stages: production, aimed at reducing the weight of the waste component, consumption/household level, focusing on improving separated collection, on recovering by composting, and on consuming more and more goods associated with less packaging. Then there are the public and private waste management utilities responsible for pricing, collection and recovery. These utilities, in co-operation with public agents at the local level, need to create a favourable regulatory framework for improving waste-related performance, implementing EU and national policies by using the flexibility allowed to adapt to local economic and geographical situations.

As a final point in this introduction to the issues we address linking past, current and future scenarios, we draw attention to the Waste Framework Directive, which was under revision at the time of writing, and being voted on by the European Parliament in relation to critical facts that could shape future policy frameworks in Europe. Several of the new provisions that are being included in the directive aim at reducing landfill of waste. The list of proposals being debated at EU level is very long. The introduction of quantitative targets on the reuse and recycling of household waste, and targets for the stabilization of waste generation, are likely to emerge from these discussions. A target for per capita waste generation will be newsworthy, and the future challenge for most EU countries will be to decouple waste generation from economic growth, and to achieve stabilization, if not effective reduction.

We believe that the evidence and methodological suggestions that are provided in this book will inform about and will provide useful hints on the structuring of future waste policies, taking into account the evidence on waste–income–policy relationships, which can be generalized to most countries, alongside evidence that is related more to national and regional characterizes. This should lead to the ad hoc reshaping of regulatory interventions based on institutional, economic and socio-territorial features.

The first chapter, by Mazzanti and Zoboli, focuses on delinking trends for MSW generation and packaging waste in EU countries. The core income–environment relationship is investigated. The main message is one of no delinking: even a relative delinking is only weakly indicated by the data. They find no EKC evidence for municipal waste or packaging waste respectively for 1995–2000 and 1997–2001. The estimated elasticities for waste generation with respect to household consumption are close to unity. This chapter opens the way to the subsequent analyses, which focus on extended sets of time series data at EU level, and on regionally disaggregated data sets at country level, and exploit larger sets of explanatory variables in addition to income, and wider sets of waste indicators, including (because of its availability) waste generation.

The second chapter, by Mazzanti, Nicolli and Zoboli, updates the EU-related evidence for the 1990s and questions whether delinking has occurred overall, specifically in the EU-15 and the new member countries. This chapter provides a comprehensive analysis of waste generation, incineration, recycling and landfill dynamics, based on panel data for the EU-25, to assess the effects of different drivers (economic, structural, policy) and the eventual differences between western and eastern EU countries.

The main issue addressed is whether the Landfill Directive and other complementary waste strategies implemented at country level have been the motivation for the implementation of policies to divert waste from landfill. The authors show that for waste generation there is still no EKC trend, although elasticity to income drivers appears lower than in the past. Regarding landfill and incineration, these two trends, as expected, are respectively decreasing and increasing, with policy providing a strong driver. This demonstrates the effectiveness of policy even at this early stage of policy implementation. This is essential for an *ex post* evaluation of existing landfill and incineration directives. The eastern European countries appear to perform generally quite well, thus benefiting from their EU membership and related policies in terms of environmental performance. It can be concluded that, although absolute delinking is far from being achieved for waste generation, there are some first positive signals of increasing relative delinking for waste generation and average robust landfill diversion.

The third chapter, by Andersen, Skovgaard and Larsen, deals with waste trend forecasting and GHG net emissions deriving from the management and disposal of waste in future EU scenarios. The authors first estimate waste trends for the EU-15 and the EU-10 new entrants, and find that waste generation is linked with economic activity by non-constant trend ratios. This analysis of delinking in EU countries provides forecasts in favour of relative delinking, but it does not confirm EKC evidence, that is coherent with other econometric evidence presented in this book. Projections for 2005–20, for the UK, France and Italy show an increase in MSW of around 15–20 per cent, which, at least at first sight, may be compatible with relative delinking with respect to GDP and consumption growth.

Regarding GHG emissions, the authors show that the net effect deriving from landfill diversion and increases in incineration and recycling is associated with a reduction in emissions which, although not massive, may play some part in the overall EU strategy towards climate change.

In the fourth and last chapter of Part I Kaurosakis extends the realm of delinking oriented analyses by using OECD data sources. She deals with policy evaluation by testing a synthetic environmental policy index on country waste performances, and presents evidence on the determinants of waste generation and waste disposal. Using cross-sectional time series data from the 30 Organization for Economic Co-operation and Development (OECD) member countries, this chapter addresses the gap by examining the underlying economic, demographic and policy factors of MSW generation, landfill disposal and the paper/cardboard and glass recycled as a proportion of apparent consumption. The results complement and show overall coherence with the above analyses on the EU. Despite recent data indicating a decoupling of economic growth and waste generation in certain OECD countries, the MSW generation model suggests that, aside from GDP, urbanization also has a positive impact on the generation of municipal waste. This is discouraging, given that projections show that the share of the total population living in cities will grow at a rapid rate in the future. With regard to the disposal of MSW, this analysis has provided evidence that higher levels of GDP per capita are associated with a smaller fraction of MSW going to landfill. Then, though urbanization is associated with greater amounts of waste generated, it is managed in a more environmentally friendly way, either via incineration or via recycling. The negative sign of real landfill tax indicates that the higher the landfill taxes on waste the smaller is the proportion of waste that is deposited in landfill. This is a strict policy variable and should be encouraging for governments wanting to divert additional waste away from landfill.

With regard to the proportion of paper and cardboard, and glass, that are recycled, the main determinants of recycling are economic growth and population density. In the case of glass recycled, this is also affected by the real landfill tax. Recycling of glass and paper and cardboard, therefore, is determined more by market forces than by policy forces. Higher population densities are expected to lower the collection and recovery costs of recycling, thus increasing the economic viability of this disposal option.

The chapters that comprise Part II of the book provide various analyses, manly based on but not limited to empirical evidence for Italy and attempt, as did the chapters in Part I, to communicate very comprehensive evidence on the various interconnected phases of the waste cycle: waste generation dynamics, landfill diversion and natural resource damage occurring as a consequence of legal and illegal waste disposal, separated collection and composting. This last, for lack of data, is not investigable in quantitative terms at EU level. Here Italy shows some leadership that could usefully be extended to other countries. The study of waste generation, and even more so landfill diversion, exploits regional and provincial heterogeneity and analyses in depth the waste–economic-policy dynamics, uncovering the main causes of territorial differences in performance. This is very important, given the current situation in Italy and other EU countries, characterized by wide divergences between the environmental performance of wealthier and more policy-committed regions and generally poorer regions, with lagging and rather lax policies. The main policy target associated with average policy effectiveness at country or EU level is to achieve convergence rather than divergent trends. This could reduce the overall cost of working towards targets, where the marginal costs of recovering further waste units are steeply increasing in better-performing areas. It is important to work towards greater convergence to avoid the creation of waste hot spots in certain local areas. The authors of the chapters in this part of the book exploit a very rich source of annual data, updated by the Italian environmental agency in its report on waste, and other socio-economic information.

The first chapter in Part II, by Mazzanti, Montini and Zoboli, provides original empirical evidence on the EKC hypothesis regarding provincial waste generation. The empirical analysis uses a disaggregated panel data set based on the Italian provinces, and provides mixed evidence of an EKC relationship. The turning point occurs at very high levels of value added per capita, which characterize a very limited number of wealthy (northern) Italian provinces. The tests, using some recently adopted waste policy/management instruments, show that there is some policy-driven effect on waste generation at source, and that there is some endogeneity with respect to socio-economic drivers. To achieve delinking and to avoid increasing the gap between northern and southern Italian areas, more effective policy instruments should be implemented and the weight in waste policies should be rebalanced towards waste prevention targets and instruments, in line with the stated priorities of the EU and member countries. This chapter emphasizes the need for future policies, scrutinized by CBA analyses, that associate targets specifically with waste generation per capita, and not just the recycling and landfill stages.

The following chapter by Mazzanti, Montini and Nicolli presents a complementary analysis on landfill diversion, covering the 103 Italian provinces for the period 1999–2005. Such an extended, decentralized and recent source of data is of major interest for investigations dealing with waste processes and policy valuation, where evidence is typically scattered and high-quality data rare. The case study of Italy, a main EU member country, is valuable and offers important information on the evaluation of policies such as the 1999 Landfill Directive. Italy's problematic economic, institutional and environmental performance heterogeneity offers an interesting analysis of how economic and policy levers impact on the dynamics of landfill in such settings. Finally, as waste management and landfill policies are being implemented at a very decentralized level, this informs the policy-making processes that have operated or will operate in similar directions. Evidence shows that the observed decoupling of economic growth and landfill is driven by a mix of structural factors, such as population density and opportunity costs: local opportunity costs and landfill externalities matter in shaping waste policies and local commitment to landfill diversion. But it is not only structural factors that are relevant. If on the one hand landfill taxation is not arising as a significant driver of the phenomenon, then, even at the more coherent regional level where the tax is implemented, waste management instruments, in terms of the provincial data set, are associated with high significant negative effects on landfilled waste. Good performance in managing waste according to economic rationales helps to reduce the amounts going to landfill. In association with the features of the tariff system, the authors underline the key role played by the share of separated collection. The evolution of both the collection and the tariff systems are factors that may combine to drive a wedge between the comparative waste performance of the northern and southern regions of Italy. We can affirm that relying only on the endogenous path characterized by landfill and economic growth (the baseline environmental Kuznets curve scenario) will not assure delinking. Some policy actions are needed to affect the shape of delinking.

Cianflone and Wernstedt (Chapter 7) complement previous empirical evidence by providing a methodological chapter that discusses the natural resources damage (NRD) assessment methods that are important to signal to potential polluters the costs that will incur for site restoration, for example in landfill siting investments. The recent development of legal frameworks in the EU is leading to full cost internalization of eventual damage by whoever owns and manages sites. Landfill sites must eventually be restored to their *ex ante* environmental status, and damage must be compensated by payments to victims and community stakeholders and technical restoration interventions at the site. Nevertheless, current NRD assessment processes in Italy are fraught with uncertainties relating to technical aspects of the restoration process and to the valuation component. This creates the basis for a discussion about how to decrease the valuation uncertainties associated with *ex post* compensations determined by environmental liability schemes. The chapter provides a conceptual taxonomy of possible states of the world characterized by different features of environmental damage, in terms of uncertainty and irreversibility, that can be used for rational future evaluation processes within the implementation of liability schemes that are becoming increasingly important in the EU as a consequence of the Liability Directive. They argue that, on practical grounds, cost-based approaches that yield financial values are the most appropriate methods of estimating restoration costs. Depending on the degree of natural recoverability and human-directed restorability of the damaged resource, avoided cost, defensive cost, restoration cost or surrogate cost methods can provide estimates that are defensible from a theoretical viewpoint, as well as being practical and applicable in regulatory or adjudicated settings. To improve the application of these methods, standardization of NRD assessment techniques could adopt two straightforward protocols that would not require legal changes to the liability regime in many cases. First, a simple, transparent, prioritized list of cost-based approaches would reduce the range of choices available to NRD assessors when undertaking assessments. This could reduce the uncertainty that potential polluters face *ex ante* about the costs that the liability regime may impose if the polluters undertake EUB that results in NRD. It also would benefit the assessors. Second, for the portion of NRD that represent non-use values that are not amenable to cost-based methods, the development and application of standardized monetary estimates that could be applied through benefits transfer could decrease the range of the monetary values applicable to NRD assessment in a liability regime.

Volpi's final chapter presents some theoretical and empirical insights on a specific element of the waste filiere, composting, a field in which Northern Italy leads in the EU. Thus, this chapter offers insights for a general audience interested in how to achieve higher performances in this component of the recovery/recycling process. Composting, though judged as being economically more costly by some CBA analyses in comparison with other recovery options, has the value of reducing at source the amount of waste that is collected and generated, at household and small firm level. Volpi investigates the determinants of the diffusion of organic waste composting in the Italian regions. The analysis is based on panel data for the period 1999–2005 and studies the effects of a legal innovation that shifted attention from disposal of waste, to its separated collection and recycling, which sets clear targets for local governments (that have a monopoly on the collection of waste) for separated collection. Setting and achieving these targets has played a major role in explaining the diffusion of composting, solving a situation of institutional lock-in. The contribution also provide evidence of the interdependence between previous technological choices and the diffusion of composting and finally shows that increasing population has made it difficult to find locations for new plants.

The two parts of the book thus offer complementary analyses, at a macro-economic cross-country level, mainly focusing on the current EU situation, and at a more regional level, providing a within country perspective on Italy. The two levels provide a set of coherent and robust empirical evidence on the driving forces behind waste generation, waste management and waste disposal. In addition, this two level economic, geographical and institutional analysis, includes a wide set of diverse waste issues, covering all aspects of interest to society, policy makers and economic reasoning, from waste generation to final disposal. It offers especially interesting insights on the ex post effectiveness of policy measures and policy commitments at various institutional levels. Overall, the evidence shows that, on the one hand, just relying on market dynamics may not lead to sustainable performance in the area of waste and, on the other hand, even in presence of sustainable performance in some areas, eventual business-as-usual scenarios may cause sharp divergences in waste generation, management and disposal performance across different areas, characterized by different levels of income and policy commitment and enforcement. The endogenous links that characterize income, the environmental awareness of the public, waste management and policy commitment in general could lead to increasing gaps that will need to be targeted by national and supra-national regulatory efforts.

References

EEA (2007) *The Road from Landfill to Recycling: Common Destination, Different Routes*, Copenhagen: European Environment Agency.

——(2006) *Market-based Instruments for Environmental Policy in Europe*, Technical Report 8/2005, Copenhagen: European Environment Agency.

——(2003a) *Evaluation Analysis of the Implementation of the Packaging Directive*, Copenhagen: European Environment Agency.

——(2003b) *Assessment of Information related to Waste and Material Flows*, Copenhagen: European Environment Agency.

——(2003c) *Europe's Environment: The Third Assessment*, Copenhagen: European Environment Agency.

European Commission (2003a) *Towards a Thematic Strategy for Waste Prevention and Recycling*, COM (2003) 301, Brussels: European Commission.

——(2003b) *Towards a Thematic Strategy on Sustainable Use of Natural Resources*, COM (2003) 572 Brussels: European Commission.

Jacobsen, H., Mazzanti, M., Moll, S., Simeone, M. G., Pontoglio, S. and Zoboli, R. (2004) *Methodology and Indicators to measure Decoupling, Resource Efficiency, and*

Waste Prevention, ETC/WMF, P6.2-2004, Copenhagen: European Topic Centre on Waste and Material Flows and European Environment Agency.

OECD (2003) *Response Indicators for Waste Prevention within the OECD Area*, Paris: OECD.

——(2002) *Indicators to measure Decoupling of Environmental Pressure from Economic Growth*, Paris: OECD.

Pearce, D. W. (2004) 'Does European Union waste policy pass a cost–benefit test?' *World Economics*, 15: 115–37.

Part I

Waste generation, waste management and waste disposal

Macroeconomic analyses of delinking and policy effectiveness

1 Delinking and environmental Kuznets curves for waste indicators in Europe

Evidence on municipal solid waste and packaging waste

Massimiliano Mazzanti and Roberto Zoboli

Decoupling or delinking, that is, improvements in environmental/resource indicators with respect to economic activity indicators, is increasingly used to evaluate progress in the use/conservation of natural and environmental resources. The Organization for Economic Co-operation and Development is doing extensive work on decoupling indicators for reporting and policy evaluation purposes (OECD 2002).

Various decoupling or resource efficiency indicators are included in the European Environment Agency's state-of-the-environment reports (EEA 2003a, b, c), and a few European countries started to include indicators of delinking in official analyses of environmental performance (DEFRA/DTI 2003). Some countries are considering the inclusion of delinking targets in their major environmental policies, and the US has adopted an emissions-intensity target in its climate policy.

Delinking trends in industrial materials and energy have been scrutinized in the advanced countries for several decades.[1] In the 1990s, research on delinking was extended to include air pollution and greenhouse gas (GHG) emissions, including proposals for some stylized facts on the relationship between pollution and economic growth, which are encompassed in the environmental Kuznets curve (EKC), so called because of the similarity with Kuznets's (1955) suggestions about long-run income distribution paths.[2] The EKC hypothesis, which is the natural extension of delinking analysis, is that, for many pollutants, there is an inverted U-shaped relationship between per capita income and pollution. This hypothesis does not stems from a theoretical model, but arises from conceptual intuition, although some recent contributions show the extent to which the environmental Kuznets hypothesis may be included in formalized economic models.[3] Despite increasing applied research, empirical evidence on emissions EKC remains ambiguous. Some pollutants, mainly those identified as having a regional/local impact, seem to show a turning point (TP) at certain levels of income; but there is a degree of consensus that some critical externalities, such as carbon dioxide (CO_2) emissions and waste flows, rise monotonically with income. At best, a relative delinking may take place (Stern 2004).[4]

Research on delinking and EKC is less developed in relation to materials and waste than to pollution and GHG emissions. Although work being done by the Wuppertal Institute and Eurostat is beginning to fill the gap in material flows indicators,[5] the limited results for the waste sector are a problem from a policy perspective. EU policy thematic strategies on both resources and waste include reference to absolute and relative delinking-based indicators (European Commission 2003a, b). Since a decreasing ratio of material input with respect to an economic driver would suggest future reduced production of waste, delinking across the material-to-waste chain can be interpreted in terms of *waste prevention*, which is the stated priority of EU waste policy strategy, and which is being transposed in national legislation on waste in Europe. Following OECD (2002, 2003), waste prevention activities and policies can be monitored and evaluated using absolute or relative decoupling indicators, by addressing, in particular, the trends towards reduction at source, and reuse.[6]

This contribution is a first attempt to fill the gap by developing a quantitative analysis of delinking for two major waste flows, municipal and packaging waste, at European level. Our results indicate that European countries, characterized by high income levels and by a relatively long waste policy history, are at best experiencing relative delinking, with waste indicators increasing only slightly less than economic drivers. At European level, the elasticity of two major non-hazardous waste flows considered with respect to consumption is not significantly different from unity.

Next section discusses some conceptual and methodological issues related to delinking and EKC analysis, and reviews suggestions from the EKC empirical literature useful for analyses on waste. We then present the data sets on municipal and packaging waste and discuss key issues regarding EKC econometric analysis. Main empirical results deriving from panel data analysis at European level of different EKC specifications for waste are consequentially discussed. We end the chapter with some conclusions and policy implications.

Defining a framework for delinking analysis

The relations between delinking and EKC approaches, and some of the limitations of both, can be discussed within a simple IPAT model frame,[7] which defines total impact I (waste production) as the (multiplicative) result of the impacts of population level (P), affluence (A) – measured by GDP per capita, and impact per unit of economic activity, that is, I/GDP, representing the technology of the system (T), thus $I = P \bullet A \bullet T$. This is an accounting identity aimed at decomposing the relative role of A, P, and T for an observed change of I, over time, and/or across countries.[8]

While the effects of P and A as drivers of I are clear, the exact meaning of T is less clear cut. It is an indicator of intensity, which measures how many units of Impact (natural resource consumption) are required by an economic system to produce one unit ($1) of GDP. As a technical coefficient representing the resource-use efficiency of the system (or, in the case of its reciprocal GDP/I, its resource productivity in terms of GDP), it is the most aggregate way to represent the average state of the technology of an economy, in terms of the Impact variable. Changes in T for a given GDP, reflect a combination of the shifts towards sectors with different resource intensities (from manufacturing to services), and the adoption/diffusion in a given economic structure, of techniques with different resource requirements (inter-fuel substitution in manufacturing). If T decreases over time, there is a gain in environmental efficiency or resource productivity, and T can be directly examined in delinking analysis. In being responsive to changes of the state of technology, which will also be influenced by markets and policy actions, T is the main control variable for the system. In a cross-country setting, the interpretation of T is less clear, but delinking can re-emerge as a negative relationship between I and the level of GDP or GDP/P.

In an IPAT framework, three aspects of delinking analysis and EKC analysis emerge.

Firstly, delinking analysis or the observation of T alone, can produce ambiguous suggestions. A decrease in the variable I over time is commonly defined as absolute decoupling, even though a decrease in I does not, in itself, represent a delinking process, as it says nothing about the role of economic drivers. An environmental Impact growing less (or diminishing more) than the economic drivers, that is, a decrease in T, is generally defined as relative delinking. Therefore, relative delinking might be strong, while absolute delinking might not occur (i.e. I is stable or increasing) if the increasing efficiency is not sufficient to compensate for the scale effect of other drivers. And in certain phases, the opposite may be true. Assuming a stable Population, a negative GDP trend can push down the Impact variable (absolute delinking), as was the case in most ex-communist European countries in the 1990s, while T, the Impact per unit of GDP, might be non-diminishing (no relative delinking) or might increase (relative re-linking) because the I-specific state of the technology is stationary or worsening. Therefore, a diminishing I is always a positive environmental signal, but it might not be the result of structural gains in the I-relevant technological efficiency; whereas delinking, that is, a diminishing T, is always the result of structural or technological change, but it does not allow us to claim the environment is improving unless the change in I is considered. Only joint analysis of the I and T dynamics will provide a sound basis for suggestions related to environmental performances.

Secondly, a delinking process, that is, a decreasing I, suggests that the economy is more efficient but, in itself, does not provide an explanation for what is driving the process. In its basic accounting formulation, the IPAT framework implicitly assumes that the drivers are all independent variables. However, the evidence on the dynamics of economic systems suggests that each driver, as well as the Impact, can be reciprocally interdependent through a network of direct/indirect causation. For example, evidence suggest that population dynamics (P) depend on GDP per capita (A), and *vice versa* to an extent.[9] Similar relationships or inverse-causation effects also apply to T. Theory and evidence suggest that, in general, T can depend on GDP or GDP/P, and *vice versa* if T refers to a key resource such as energy. But we can also distinguish a relationship between changes in the P and I and T dynamics (Zoboli 1996). In particular, in a dynamic setting, I can be a driver of T, as the emergence of natural resources/environmental scarcity stimulates invention, innovation and diffusion of more efficient technologies through market mechanisms (changes in relative prices) and policy actions, including price-based and quantity-based economic instruments. The re-discovery of the Hicksian induced innovation hypothesis represents the attempt to capture the channels through which I influences T, while models that include endogenous technological change capture some of influences of both I and GDP on T. In fact, improvements in T for a specific I may also stem from general techno-economic changes, for example, dematerialization associated with information and communication technologies (ICT) diffusion, which are not captured by resource-specific induced innovation mechanisms and can be very different for given levels of GDP/P because of the different innovativeness of similar countries. In this case, a decrease in T can encompass micro and macro non-deterministic processes involving dynamic feedbacks, on which economics offers a still open set of interpretations.[10]

Thirdly, EKC analysis exactly addresses one/two of the above relationship, that is, between I and GDP or between T and GDP/P. It presents benefits and costs. Even though it may provide some empirical regularities, and has great heuristic value, it may not provide satisfactory economic explanations.[11] We recall that the EKC hypothesis is that the concentration/emission of a pollutant first increases with the economic driver, as a scale effect prevails, then starts to decrease more or less proportionally, thus it becomes de-linked from income due to a steady improvement in T. More specifically, the EKC hypothesis predicts that the environmental income elasticity decreases monotonically with income, and that eventually its sign changes from positive to negative thus defining a TP for the inverted U-shaped relationship. Here, we do not address the very different meanings of the various formulations of the EKC hypothesis, which range from a relationship between I and GDP to a relationship between T (I/GDP) and GDP/P. We simply note that if the relationship is between I and GDP, the EKC provides the same information as analysis of T. Furthermore, if I and GDP display an EKC, there should be also one between T and GDP because both P and GDP, with some exceptions, are increasing over the long run, and delinking must have occurred at some level of GDP. If, on the other hand, there is an EKC regarding T and GDP or GDP/P, this does not necessarily mean that I and GDP also show an EKC, because GDP and P might have pushed I more than the relative decoupling, that is, a decreasing T has been able to compensate. This is the case for global CO_2 emissions in the very long run (Figures 1.1 and 1.2). When relying on GDP or GDP/P as the explanatory variable, EKC suffers from the issues highlighted above for delinking analysis, but with an additional risk. The existence of an EKC could give the wrong deterministic suggestion that rapid growth towards high levels of GDP/P automatically drives environmental efficiency, that is, absolute or relative delinking, and then it can the *best policy strategy* to reduce environmental Impact. But, from the IPAT framework, it is clear that GDP or GDP/P growth by itself also implies a scale effect on I, that is, a growth in Impact at

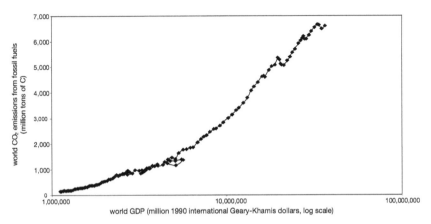

Figure 1.1 World CO_2 emissions (million tons of C) and world GDP level (million 1990 international Geary–Khamis dollars)

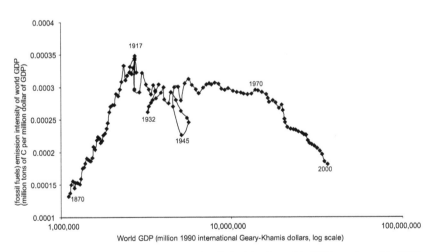

Figure 1.2 CO_2 emissions intensity (fossil fuels) of world GDP and world GDP level (million tons of C per million 1990 international Geary–Khamis dollars, selected years indicated)

each level of T (and P). In general, only if the negative effect of GDP/P on T, is consistently higher than the positive effect of GDP/P on I, will the process of economic growth lead to a negative change in I, leaving aside the effect of population.[12] *Inter alia*, this is particularly relevant for global energy consumption and GHG emissions, in the context of rapid economic and population growth in developing countries. In order to avoid a possible scale catastrophe from GDP/P and P growth in the future, the negative elasticity of T to GDP/P growth must be extremely high in developing countries, given their stationary or still increasing T.

Key issues in estimating EKC

At the econometric level, the aim of EKC analysis is to estimate a vector of coefficients, each linked to a single variable, entering as the drivers of the environmental index, using a simple reduced form equation as the conceptual model. We comment briefly on some issues related to the extensive literature developed over the last decade on EKC.[13] The focus is twofold: first, we suggest that the EKC framework, under certain circumstances, is a necessary step towards a simpler decoupling analysis. Multivariate investigations adds robustness to our results. But potential weaknesses in the EKC analysis will be thoroughly highlighted.

The EKC framework extends basic decoupling reasoning, modelling a multivariate analysis of the environment-income relationship. We refer to the EKC framework as the field of analysis for empirical work, without a particular defined theoretical model, but rooted in Kuznets's seminal work, to examine whether or not an inverted U-shape curve can be identified for pollutants and other environmental indicators. Even if EKC does not rely on a specific economic model, many theoretical assumptions related to consumption and production, are implicitly tested within the empirical context of EKC. The main economic hypotheses applying to the EKC setting are that (i) among the negative effects of income increase, we find a typical scale effect, and (ii) among the positive effects we find a composition effect concerning GDP economic activities, a technological effect, a preference-drive effect (environment being a normal/luxury good) and a market-instruments driven effect (which is integrated within the wider policy effect).

Knowing the benefits of an EKC multivariate econometric-based analysis, we need to be fully aware of the costs, and pragmatic ways of mitigating them. It is necessary to draw out the main EKC deficiencies and weaknesses. Thus, it can be seen that extending the reasoning to a more complex setting has some obvious costs and benefits.

We do not focus specifically on the more statistically oriented key issues (potential weaknesses), such as (i) differences in estimated coefficients between parametric and non-parametric models (Millimet *et al.* 2003; Baiocchi and Di Falco 2001; Galeotti *et al.* 2001); (ii) the degree of the polynomial used to proxy the environment-income relationship; or (iii) the econometric model specification used (Bradford *et al.* 2005). Less technical but possibly critical issues are: (i) the environmental performance index and economic drivers investigated; and (ii) the nature and quality of the data.

In terms of the environmental performance index, we note that careful attention should be paid to deriving policy implications. In fact, EKC studies often use different environmental indices (absolute, per capita, output based, input based, per unit of GDP). There is no general consensus over what indicators should be used, and different measures have different implications and interpretation. For example, a per capita measure reduces the chances of misunderstandings, and reduces the need for absolute measures; if we measure intensity on the vertical axis the presence of a lower bound implies that total emissions are growing at the same rate as income, in a sort of steady state equilibrium. It is obvious that the measures on the vertical and horizontal axis should be compatible with each other.[14] We note also that there is no consensus on the type and number of explanatory factors introduced as potential drivers of environmental performance. Some studies use only income variables; others include many socio-economic variables (Harbaugh *et al.* 2000) with the (correct) aim of extending the conceptual setting behind the EKC empirics; a few include policy drivers (Markandya *et al.* 2004). The choice obviously depends on data availability and research objectives.

The nature and quality of data are crucial issues. For reasons linked to data availability, the first wave of the EKC literature includes a large majority of contributions focusing on the analysis of cross-country data sets, generally from OECD and World Bank official sources. Nevertheless, first, the quality of macro data for some regions (non-OECD countries) has been questioned, and second, the exploitation of panel data sets does not allow calculation of specific country-level coefficients for the income–environment relationship.[15] The conceptual key fact is that there is no single relationship, and that many different relationships may apply to different categories of countries. In other words, the policy relevance of world-wide cross country analyses seems limited. European countries, if compared with international data sets usually exploited for EKC analyses, represent a homogeneous set of statistical units. Although the limited data variability is an intrinsic feature of such data sets, their relevance for policy-making purposes is high. Future research, as we stress in the conclusions, should focus on delinking analysis that exploits data sets including environmental and economic indicators at provincial/regional level (at national/European level). It follows that there will be a higher added value in studies based on national/regional rather than international data sets. The more that evidence is micro-based (regionally/ locally disaggregated) the more useful it will be for statistical and policy purposes. A European-level analysis, therefore, presents some value added as well as some weaknesses.

There are few EKC analyses on waste and material flows. Cole *et al.* (1997) found no evidence of an inverted U-shape EKC in relation to municipal waste.[16] Leigh (2004) provides evidence of an EKC as a waste/consumption indicator, deriving from the environmental sustainability indices (ESI). The analysis faces two potential problems: data only exist for 2001–2 and the index is based on a comparative rather than an absolute scale. Wang *et al.* (1998) found evidence of a negative elasticity, in their study of US stocks of hazardous waste as environmental impact indicators, for a county-based cross sectional data set. The nature of the pollution effect (stock/flow, hazardous/non-hazardous) seems to matter: non-hazardous and flow externalities appear to be less likely to be associated with negative elasticity, even in industrialized countries. Some authors have suggested that for stock pollution externalities the pollution income relationship difficulty becomes an environmental Kuznets shaped curve, with pollution stocks monotonically rising with income (Lieb 2004). Another structural motivation related to the lack of evidence for waste may be that the change in the sign of income elasticity of the environment/income function should occur at relatively lower income levels for pollutants whose production and consumption can be easily spatially separated, for example, by exporting associated pollution or by relocating activities (Khanna and Plassmann 2004). Although strict EKC evidence is rare, the literature underlines that waste indicators generally tend to increase with income or other economic drivers and, in general, that an inverted U-shape curve still does not fit the data.[17]

The European waste sector thus emerges as an area for further exploration of the EKC hypothesis. However, at present, waste data availability does not allow nationally focused studies nor EKC analysis including waste policy changes, since most EU waste policies were implemented in the 1990s. Nevertheless, panel data sets for municipal and packaging waste can be used for preliminary multivariate analysis. Given (1) the relative homogeneity across EU countries in terms of structural characteristics, and (2) the panel framing, which helps non-observed fixed factors to be dropped, our results, although preliminary, can be considered robust and of policy interest within a European framework.

Waste indicators and delinking: evidence for the EU

European waste policy is an extensive and evolving system of directives and regulations, on which Member States' waste legislation and policy frameworks are based. General principles and procedures for waste management have been established by horizontal legislation, that is, the Waste framework Directive, the Hazardous waste Directive and waste shipment regulation. These principles provide the basic elements on which the whole policy framework is shaped, that is, the waste management hierarchy, which puts prevention at the highest priority level, the polluter pays principle, which paves the way to economic instruments, and the requirement that waste management must not have an adverse impact on human health and the environment.

The horizontal waste legislation is complemented by more specific sets of policies: (1) legislation on waste treatment and disposal operations, such as landfill and incineration directives; (2) legislations on the management of specific waste streams. Waste treatment is generally addressed through legislative measures, including three recently adopted directives: the directive on integrated pollution prevention and control (IPPC), the Landfill Directive and the Incineration Directive. The area of specific waste streams, addresses important hazardous wastes such as oils, polychlorinated biphenyls, and batteries. Recycling and recovery targets have been set for some key complex waste flows, that is, packaging, end-of-life vehicles (ELVs), and waste electrical and electronic equipment (WEEE). Both the ELV directive and the WEEE directive explicitly include producer responsibility, on which the experience of recovery/recycling schemes for packaging and packaging waste in EU countries are, de facto, based.[18] The European Commission (EC) in 2003 launched a *thematic strategy on prevention and recycling of waste*, which proposes some innovative instruments, e.g. pay-as-you-throw mechanisms and marketable permits systems (EC 2003a). However, despite this significant policy experience, there is currently no empirical evidence on delinking even for major waste streams, such as municipal and packaging waste.[19]

Trends for packaging waste, household consumption, and GDP, which are homogeneously available for the EU-15 countries over the period 1997–2001, show waste is increasing less than the economic indicators (7.1 per cent versus 10.1 per cent of GDP, in per capita terms). Correlations between packaging waste per capita and GDP/household consumption per capita are respectively 0.36 and 0.46. The correlation between municipal waste per capita and household consumption per capita is 0.74 (from 1995 to 2000, in the EU-25, in per capita terms, waste increased 13.2 per cent while consumption increased by 14 per cent). Correlations are thus positive and significant.

In order to provide preliminary evidence on the shape of the relationship between waste generation and economic drivers, we have produced two panel databases on packaging waste and municipal waste respectively, for the European countries. In terms of packaging waste generated, we use current available information for the EU-15 for 1997–2001. Although this is a relatively short time, this panel data set may provide preliminary evidence on the existence of delinking and the current shape of the EKC for this waste indicator, and also includes some country-specific fixed effects. For municipal waste, we exploit a data set for 28 eastern and western European countries for 1995–2000; data pre-1995 are available for only some countries and the quality/reliability is generally low.[20] The two panel data matrices were produced in order to minimize missing values and the presence of observations with low reliability.

The generation of packaging waste per capita ranges from 88 kg to 214 kg in the observed countries (Figure 1.3): for 2001 Greece and Finland are the lowest ranked countries, while Ireland and France are at the top of the scale. The 2001 per capita mean value is 171 kg. For municipal waste, for 2000, (Figure 1.4), the top ranked countries are Cyprus, Norway, Iceland and Switzerland, while at the bottom are Slovakia, Poland, Latvia and Greece. The range is between 245 kg and 742 kg of waste generated per capita.

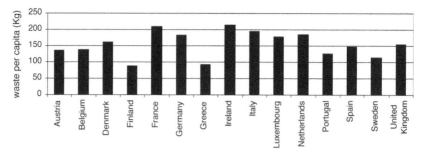

Figure 1.3 Packaging waste generation per capita: EU-15

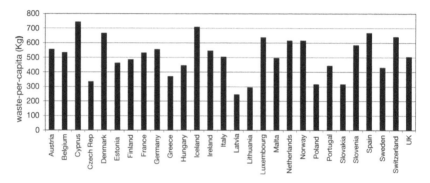

Figure 1.4 Municipal waste generation per capita: EU-28

The first methodological problem is how to specify the EKC functional relationship. There is no consensus on this point. Some authors adopt a second order polynomial, others estimate third and even fourth order polynomials, comparing different specifications for relative robustness. It should be noted that neither the quadratic nor the cubic function can be considered a fully realistic representation of the income–environment relationship. The cubic function implies that environmental degradation will tend to plus or minus infinity, as income increases; the quadratic function implies that environmental degradation could eventually tend to zero. The issue is thus unresolved. Also, third or fourth level polynomials could lead to N rather than U-shaped curves, introducing new problems for policy making related to understanding the income–environment phenomenon. The N shape is justified by a non-linear effect of the scale of economic activity on the environment, which is difficult to prove.[21] Finally, the use of the income factor only, without quadratic or cubic terms, would collapse the EKC analysis to a basic decoupling analysis.

We test the delinking hypothesis by specifying a proper reduced form, which is usual in the EKC field (Stern 2004):

$$(1) \quad \ln(\text{waste indicator}) = \beta_{0i} + \alpha_t + \beta_1 \ln(\text{consumption or GDP})_{it}$$
$$+ \beta_2 \ln(\text{consumption or GDP})_{it}^2$$
$$+ \beta_3 \ln(\text{consumption or GDP})_{it}^3 + e_{it}$$

where the first two terms are intercept parameters, which vary across countries and years. Different polynomial specifications are tested by including (i) dependent variables for waste per capita and waste in absolute terms, (ii) independent variables for household consumption or GDP per capita, thus testing the hypothesis that consumption is a more appropriate driver of waste. Rothman (1998) and Jacobsen *et al.* (2004) point out that for municipal and packaging waste the proper economic driver is household consumption and not GDP. This is a key issue on both conceptual and statistical grounds.

Thus, for each combination of the above dependent and independent variables, we estimate different specifications, including linear regressors only (delinking baseline case), linear and squared terms (EKC most usual case), and a specification with linear, squared and cubic terms. Given the panel data framework, the relative fit of fixed effects and random effects models (FEM and REM) is compared using the Hausman statistic.

Empirical results

This section sums up and comments on the results presented in Tables 1.1 and 1.2. It should be noted that, in line with our *ex ante* expectations, the economic driver that better fits (both of) the waste indicators is household consumption. Regressions concerning GDP are less robust in terms of coefficient significance and relative signs, and are not included here. This is a first result testing a crucial hypothesis on drivers, which will be relevant for future applied studies on waste delinking and EKC.

Moving to regressions that exploit consumption as the driver, cubic forms appear to perform worse than the linear or squared forms, in terms of plausibility and economic significance of coefficients. We would point out that the N shape eventually associated with the cubic forms has been raised as theoretically plausible in relation to emissions externalities; in addition, testing the N shape would perhaps be more meaningful for externalities where a TP has been reached.

Packaging waste

For packaging waste (Table 1.1), the basic specification with the linear term only, shows a significant and positive coefficient for consumption.

Table 1.1 EKC analysis of packaging waste

Dependent variable	ln WASTE /POP	ln WASTE /POP	ln WASTE /POP	ln WASTE /POP	ln WASTE /POP
Model	FEM	REM	FEM	REM	FEM
Constant	...	3.10***	...	3.13***	...
ln C	0.90***	0.78***	0.89***	0.76***	7.88***
ln C^2	...	...	0.77	0.29	5.75***
ln C^3	...	...	...	...	−2.72***
Turning point	...	...	No	No	No
N	75	75	75	75	75
F test (p value)	0.000	0.000	0.000	0.000	0.000

Note: significance at 10%, 5% and 1% is denoted by *, ** and ***, respectively; R^2 are not shown as they are not highly meaningful as fit measures in panel settings. *CIS* household consumption per capita; log waste/pop is waste per capita.

The Hausman test favours the REM: elasticities with respect to consumption are respectively 0.78 for the random effects and 0.90 for the FEM. Since the linear specification tests delinking by using econometric evidence rather than simple correlation analysis, we can see evidence of a relative delinking.

Next, the non-linear form also shows a positive and significant coefficient for the linear term, and a positive, but highly not significant, squared term. The elasticity value is 0.89 in the FEM, for both the basic case and when correcting for heteroskedasticity. Further, adding time effects to the baseline specification does not affect these results: the estimated elasticity is 0.85. Nevertheless, none of these elasticities is different from unity: and relative delinking is questionable. Finally, using absolute packaging waste production as the indicator does not change the results (absolute waste and waste per capita show a correlation of 0.35).

There are some additional statistical aspects that are worth mentioning. Estimated autocorrelation across specifications is in the range 0.2 and 0.4. Given these values and the limited number of years, this should not represent a serious problem. The Hausman test signals a better fit for the REM: nevertheless, results show only slight differences between models, with elasticities less than 1, and non-significant squared terms.

The analysis suggests that the first phase of European packaging waste policy (most national policies became operative in 1996–7, though some were in force in the early 1990s) has probably been effective in increasing environmental efficiency (slight relative delinking), although there is no evidence supporting an inverted U-shaped EKC. This confirms a mostly qualitative evaluation of the effectiveness of the first wave of packaging waste policies that more effort is needed to reverse the relationship between environmental impact and economic drivers.

Municipal waste

As far as municipal waste is concerned, preliminary econometric analysis of the full set of 28 western and eastern European countries shows limited statistical robustness. This is not unexpected, since the eastern European dataset is of lower quality and reliability. Thus, we consider only the subset of 18 western countries; the EKC regressions (Table 1.2) show that: (i) in the linear case, elasticity is 0.60; (ii) in the squared term regression, positive and negative signs respectively are associated with linear and non-linear consumption factors and statistical significance, nevertheless, is associated only to the linear factors, with estimated elasticity at 0.83. For packaging, the results do not change when correcting for heteroskedasticity and adding time effects. The cubic relationship is again not plausible if we look at the signs and coefficient levels. In all the regressions, the Hausman test favours the FEM.

In general, the analysis for municipal waste shows no evidence of a inverted U-shaped curve, suggesting only relative delinking. The squared specification presents a negative sign on the non-linear term, which never passes the statistical threshold (the t ratio is 1.172 for the regression corrected for heteroskedasticity). By adding time period effects, the squared term coefficient shows a (highest) t ratio of -1.54.

The need for further investigation, with more important and longer data sets, is confirmed when we drop two small outlier countries – Malta and Iceland – which reduces our sample to 16 countries. Then the non-linear regressions shows both terms to be significant and with the expected signs in the REM (recall, though, that the Hausman statistics favour the

Table 1.2 EKC analysis of municipal waste

Dependent variable	ln WASTE /POP	ln WASTE /POP	ln WASTE /POP	ln WASTE /POP	ln WASTE /POP
Model	FEM	FEM	FEM corrected for heter.	FEM	REM
Constant	...	...	...	...	3.12***
ln C	0.60***	0.83***	0.83***	0.30	2.20***
ln C^2	...	−0.57	−0.57	0.57*	−0.57***
ln C^3	...	...	...	−0.14**	...
Turning point	...	No	No	No	Yes
N	108	108	108	108	96
F test (p value)	0.000	0.000	0.000	0.000	0.000

Note: Significance at 10%, 5% and 1% is denoted by *, ** and ***, respectively. R^2 are not shown as not highly meaningful as fit measure in panel settings. *CIS* household consumption per capita; log waste/pop is waste per capita.

FEM). The outcome for this smaller sample is nonetheless important, since the instability of the EKC results when factors change is a key issue, and has been raised in the literature. It necessarily points the way to more detailed analyses at country level using material-specific and regionally based data sets.

Conclusion

This chapter provides a methodological perspective and econometric estimates of delinking, for waste indicators in Europe. EKC are addressed as a natural extension of delinking analysis. They confirm the hypothesis that even European countries, characterized by high income levels and a relatively long waste policy history, are at best experiencing only relative delinking, with waste indicators increasing slightly less than economic drivers. The elasticity of two major non-hazardous waste flows (packaging and municipal) considered, with respect to consumption, at the European level, is not significantly different from unity. In other words, we are a long way from seeing a reversion in the waste–consumption relationship.

It should be noted that a panel data analysis focusing on a homogenous set of countries has fewer flaws and is more informative for policy, compared to international cross section/panel analysis. The relative homogeneity characterising the European framework combined with the European framing of most waste policies, adds to the information content of the investigations, even though for our sample we provide only mean estimates. (Income elasticity is assumed to be the same for all countries at a given income level.)

For packaging waste, the absence of any delinking emphasizes that the task of the next wave of European policies, up to 2010, must be focused on achieving and increasing delinking, at least for aggregate packaging waste if not for all specific waste materials.

Obviously, in policy terms, delinking and waste–efficiency gains are the statistical counterpart of prevention because, in our case, delinking would signal a reduction in production of municipal waste and a reduction in the volume of packaging materials in the market. It would seem that the waste policies implemented in the 1990s have had low levels of effectiveness in terms of prevention at source. The various directives have generally been aimed at quantified targets, in terms of shifts between waste disposal technologies and recovery/recycling, while waste prevention, which must be the first priority in the EU waste hierarchy, has remained a policy objective with no targets. No country has introduced explicit and binding policy targets for prevention, related even to one material. Also, prevention targets are a moot point in the new revised 2004 Packaging Directive, despite its more ambitious global and material-specific targets for recycling/recovery. It would seem that, in order to avoid costly structural breaks, current waste policies have lacked the incentives for efforts to reduce waste at source and introduce innovative processes into packaging systems. In the case of packaging and municipal waste, producer responsibility policies have had some effect on recycling and recovery, but there has not been pressure to pursue the first priority, of prevention (EEA 2003a). Mechanisms of incremental recycling/recovery cost coverage have proven more effective than economic incentive instruments to reduce the amounts of packaging in the market, to the extent that a trade-off between recovery/recycling and prevention objectives can be envisaged. This comment is also applicable to single country policies.

Evaluating policies is a new complex area for further research on delinking, in which two issues are critical: first, the possibility to assess a policy-driven structural break over a short period of time; secondly, identifying the best and most comprehensive policy proxies for analysis from major directives/national polices, single instruments within the policy mix, indirect costs caused by policies. Also, the *ex post* effectiveness of waste reduction of policies, such as the landfill tax, is being debated. Landfill tax is probably too far removed from waste production to exert any effects in terms of reductions at source. Thus, in order to increase the probability of achieving a TP in the waste/income/consumption relationship, a stronger and more prevention-focused policy effort along the resource-to-waste chain is needed.

Further analysis, concerning specific packaging waste materials for Europe and/or single countries, would also be worthwhile as soon as sufficient sets of country/material data are available: different delinking processes could arise from consideration of specific countries and materials. Although preliminary, the exercise in this chapter confirms and makes more robust the perception that, on average, waste generation in Europe is not characterized by an inverted U-shaped EKC.

Notes

1 For the extensive evidence up to the early 1990s see Tilton (1988, 1991) on metals/materials, Martin (1990) on energy, and Zoboli (1995) for a selective review and discussion. For some recent thorough analyses of long run trends for energy see Ayres *et al.* (2004), Gruebler *et al.* (1999) and several works by IIASA, www.iiasa.ac.at.
2 Among the early works on pollution see Holtz-Eakin and Selden (1992), Ten Kate (1993), Selden and Song (1994) and Grossman and Krueger (1994).
3 See Andreoni and Levinson (2001), Chimeli and Braden (2005) and Kelly (2003), who find that the shape of the EKC depends on the dynamic interplay between marginal costs and the benefits of abatement.
4 The empirical literature is too extensive to be surveyed here. The main results are that water pollution seems to present a TP between $5,000 and $17,000 of per capita income, depending on the specific pollutant. For air emissions, all main externalities, except CO_2 and transport-related emissions, appear to have a TP in the range $10,000–$20,000 (Yandle *et al.* 2002).
5 See Moll *et al.* (1999), Femia *et al.* (2001), Bringezu *et al.* (2003), Eurostat (2001, 2002).
6 For an extensive discussion of delinking indicators for materials and waste and their possible adoption in policy evaluation see Jacobsen *et al.* (2004).
7 Since its formulation by Ehrlich (1971) many variants of the model have been applied to global resource dynamics, in particular through the role of population growth.

8 The equation can be derived using a model such as $I = f(P, A, T)$, assuming $\partial I/\partial P = AT$; $\partial I/\partial A = PT$; $\partial I/\partial T = PA$. Decomposition of the equation can be done on the logarithms of the variables, which makes the relationship an additive one: $\ln I = lnP + lnT + lnA$, where the elasticities related to each element, $\partial lnI/\partial ln(\bullet)$, are all equal to 1.

9 See Zoboli (1996) for an account of the positive/negative effects of population on economic growth.

10 See Jaffe *et al.* (2003) for an overview of environmental technology issues, and Zoboli (1995) for a discussion of the role of natural resource prices and price-based policies in an induced innovation hypothesis. See Carraro *et al.* (2003) for the present state of research on endogenous technological change in macro-models of energy. For a long-run structural change perspective on technological innovation and natural resources see Ray (1980) and Rosenberg (1996); for an analysis of energy systems see Gruebler *et al.* (1999) and Rosenberg (1994); for an analysis of innovation and the global environment see Quadrio Curzio *et al.* (1994) and Quadrio Curzio and Zoboli (1995, 1997). Note that, outside the neo-classical approach, the relationships between resource scarcity, economic growth and technological change were clearly defined in the 1960s by theoretical models of rent, growth and income distribution (Quadrio Curzio and Pellizzari 1999).

11 For a simple presentation of EKC and a discussion of the core hypotheses and major empirical evidence see De Bruyn *et al.* (1998).

12 If $I = f(P, A, T)$, where A is an indicator of economic development, with $\partial I/\partial A$, $\partial I/\partial P$, $\partial I/\partial T > 0$, and $T = g(A)$, with $dT/dA < 0$, then the total derivative of I with respect to A will be negative if $\partial I/\partial A < -\partial/\partial T \bullet dT/dA$, or the direct positive effect of A on I is lower than the negative effect of A on T, given the effect of T on I.

13 Good critical surveys include Stern (2004), Dinda (2004) and Dasgupta *et al.* (2002).

14 Some argue that the choice of dependent variable(s) should depend on the issue being considered. The per capita option is probably more compatible with situations where degradation derives from over-exploitation linked with population growth, whereas emissions intensity fits better with scenarios where externalities are related to industries.

15 In fact, econometric panel studies usually provide information on mean-value coefficients, since they usually rely on the assumption of different constant terms, but equal coefficients across units (FEM). We note that the superiority of heterogeneous panel data models is questioned. As an example, Baltagi *et al.* (2002).

16 They use municipal waste data for the period 1975–90 for 13 OECD countries, with environmental indicators (per capita municipal waste) monotonically increasing with income over the observed range, and find no TP.

17 Rothman (1998) argues that delinking is less likely to occur when we tackle consumption-based measures.

18 For an analysis of the economic instruments based on producer responsibility principles in European ELV policies see Mazzanti and Zoboli (2006).

19 We have only scattered evidence. Among others, Martin and Scott (2003) claim that the relationship between waste production and increased wealth is positive.

20 For municipal waste data derived from a EUROSTAT/OECD survey, the reliability is not homogeneous across countries (Eurostat 2003). For packaging waste, data are from Member States' reports to DG Environment in pursuance of Directive 94/62/EC on Packaging and Packaging Waste. For an assessment of waste data issues and methodology see EEA (2003b).

21 Shobee (2004) suggests a third-order polynomial specification as more realistic for the relationship between environmental degradation and income per capita. The issue is unresolved, with the EKC hypothesis relying mainly on empirical evidence.

References

Andreoni, J. and Levinson, A. (2001) 'The simple analytics of the environmental Kuznets curve', *Journal of Public Economics*, 80: 269–86.

Ayres, R. U., Ayres, L. W. and Pokrovsky, V. (2004) *On the Efficiency of US Electricity Usage since 1900*, Interim Report IR-04-027, Luxembourg: IIASA.

Baiocchi, G. and Di Falco, S. (2001) 'Investigating the shape of the EKC: a nonparametric approach', *Nota di lavoro* 66, Milan: Fondazione Eni Enrico Mattei.

Baltagi, B., Bresson, G. and Pirotte, A. (2002) 'Comparison of forecast performance for homogenous, heterogeneous and shrinkage estimators: some empirical evidence from US electricity and natural gas consumption', *Economic Letters*, 76: 375–82.

Borghesi, S. (1999) 'The environmental Kuznets curve: a survey of the literature', *Nota di lavoro* 85, Milan: Fondazione Eni Enrico Mattei.

Bradford, D., Fender, R., Shore, S. and Wagner, M. (2005) 'The environmental Kuznets curve: a fresh specification', *Contributions to Economic Analysis and Policy*, 4: 1–28.

Bringezu, S., Schütz, H. and Moll, S. (2003) 'Rationale for and interpretation of economy-wide material flow analysis and derived indicators', *Journal of Industrial Ecology*, 7: 43–64.

Carraro, C., Gerlagh, R. and van der Zwaan, B. (2003) 'Endogenous technical change in environmental macroeconomics', *Resource and Energy Economics*, 25: 1–10.

Chimeli, A. and Braden, J. (2005) 'Total factor productivity and the environmental Kuznets curve', *Journal of Environmental Economics and Management*, 49: 366–80.

Cole, M., Rayner, A. and Bates, J. (1997) 'The EKC: an empirical analysis', *Environment and Development Economics*, 2: 401–16.

Dasgupta, S., Laplante, B., Wang, H. and Wheeler, D. (2002) 'Confronting the environmental Kuznets curve', *Journal of Economic Perspectives*, 16: 147–68.

De Bruyn, S., Van den Bergh, J. and Opschoor, J. (1998) 'Economic growth and emissions: reconsidering the empirical basis of EKC', *Ecological Economics*, 25: 161–75.

DEFRA/DTI (2003) *Sustainable Consumption and Production Indicators*, London: DEFRA.

Dinda, S.(2004) 'Environmental Kuznets curve hypothesis: a survey', *Ecological Economics*, 49: 431–55.

EEA (2003a) *Evaluation Analysis of the Implementation of the Packaging Directive*, Copenhagen: European Environment Agency.

——(2003b) *Assessment of Information related to Waste and Material Flows*, Copenhagen: European Environment Agency.

——(2003c) *Europe's Environment: The Third Assessment*, Copenhagen: European Environment Agency.

Ehrlich, P. R. (1971) *The Population Bomb*, New York: Ballantine Books.

European Commission (2003a) *Towards a Thematic Strategy for Waste Prevention and Recycling*, COM (2003) 301, Brussels: European Commission.

——(2003b) *Towards a Thematic Strategy on Sustainable Use of Natural Resources*, COM (2003) 572, Brussels: European Commission.

Eurostat (2003) *Waste Generated and Treated in Europe: Data 1990–2001*. Luxembourg: Office for Official Publications of the European Communities.

——(2002) *Material Use in the European Union 1980–2000: Indicators and Analysis*, Working Paper and Studies series, Luxembourg: Office for Official Publications of the European Communities.

——(2001) *Economy-wide Material Flow Accounts and Derived Indicators: A Methodological Guide,* Methods and Nomenclature series, Luxembourg: Office for Official Publications of the European Communities.

Femia, A., Hinterberger, F. and Luks, F. (2001) 'Ecological economic policy for sustainable development: potential and domains of intervention for delinking approaches', *Population and Environment,* 23: 157–74.

Galeotti, M., Lanza, A. and Pauli, F. (2001) 'Desperately seeking (environmental) Kuznets: a new look at the evidence', *Nota di lavoro* 67, Milan: Fondazione Eni Enrico Mattei.

Grossman, G. M. and Krueger, A. B. (1994) 'Economic Growth and the Environment', NBER Working Papers 4634, Cambridge MA: NBER.

Gruebler, A., Nakicenovich, N. and Victor, D. G. (1999) 'Dynamics of energy technologies and global change', *Energy Policy,* 27: 247–80.

Harbaugh, W., Levinson, A. and Wilson, D. (2000) 'Re-examining the Empirical Evidence for an Environmental Kuznets Curve', NBER Working Papers 7711, Cambridge MA: NBER.

Holtz-Eakin, D. and Selden, T. M. (1992) 'Stoking the Fires? CO_2 Emissions and Economic Growth', NBER Working Papers 4248, Cambridge MA: NBER.

Jacobsen, H., Mazzanti, M., Moll, S., Simeone, M. G., Pontoglio, S. and Zoboli, R. (2004) *Methodology and Indicators to measure Decoupling, Resource Efficiency, and Waste Prevention,* ETC/WMF, P6.2-2004, Copenhagen: European Topic Centre on Waste and Material Flows and European Environment Agency.

Jaffe, A., Newell, R. and Stavins, R. (2003) 'Technological change and the environment', in K-G. Mahler and J. R. Vincent (eds), *Handbook of Environmental Economics,* Vol. I, Amsterdam: Elsevier.

Kelly, D. (2003) 'On EKC arising from stock externalities', *Journal of Economic Dynamics and Control,* 27: 1367–90.

Khanna, N. and Plassmann, F. (2004) 'The demand for environmental quality and the environmental Kuznets curve hypothesis', *Ecological Economics,* 51: 225–36.

Kuznets, S. (1955) 'Economic growth and income inequality', *American Economic Review, Papers and Proceedings,* 45: 1–28.

Leigh, R. (2004) 'Economic growth as environmental policy? Reconsidering the environmental Kuznets curve', *Journal of Public Policy,* 24: 27–48.

Lieb, C. M. (2004) 'The environmental Kuznets curve and flow versus stock pollution: the neglect of future damages', *Environmental and Resource Economics,* 29: 483–506.

Markandya, A., Pedroso, S. and Golub, A. (2004) 'Empirical analysis of national income and SO_2 emissions in selected European countries', *Nota di lavoro* 1, Milan: Fondazione Eni Enrico Mattei.

Martin, A. and Scott, I. (2003) 'The effectiveness of the UK landfill tax', *Journal of Environmental Planning and Management,* 46: 673–89.

Martin, J. M. (1990) 'Energy and technological change: lessons from the last fifteen years', *STI Review* 7 (July), Paris: OECD.

Mazzanti, M. and Zoboli, R. (2006) 'Economic instruments and induced innovation: the European policies on end-of-life vehicles', *Ecological Economics,* 58: 318–37.

Millimet, D., List, J. and Stengos, T. (2003) 'The EKC: real progress or misspecified models?' *Review of Economics and Statistics,* 85: 1038–47.

Moll, S., Femia, A., Hinterberger, F. and Bringezu, S. (1999) 'An input–output approach to analyse the total material requirement (TMR) of national economies', in R. Kleijn, S. Bringezu, M. Fischer-Kowalski and V. Palm (eds) *Ecologizing Societal Metabolism: Designing Scenarios for Sustainable Materials Management*, ConAccount Workshop Proceedings, 21 November 1998, CML report 148, Amsterdam: Centre of Environmental Science (CML).

OECD (2003) *Response Indicators for Waste Prevention within the OECD Area*, Paris: OECD.

——(2002) *Indicators to measure Decoupling of Environmental Pressure from Economic Growth*, Paris: OECD.

Quadrio Curzio, A., Fortis, M. and Zoboli, R. (eds) (1994) *Innovation, Resources and Economic Growth*, Berlin: Springer.

Quadrio Curzio, A. and Pellizzari, F. (1999) *Rent, Resources, Technologies*, Berlin: Springer.

Quadrio Curzio, A. and Zoboli, R. (1997) *The Costs of Sustainability*, proceedings of the conference 'The Fiftieth Anniversary of the United Nations and the Italian Contribution to the Earth Charter', Rome: Accademia Nazionale delle Scienze.

——(1995) *Science, Economics and Technology for the Environment*, Milan: Quaderni della Fondazione Cariplo per la Ricerca Scientifica.

Ray, G. (1980) 'The contribution of science and technology to the supply of industrial materials', *National Institute Economic Review*, 92: 33–52.

Rosenberg, N. (1996) 'The Impact of Technological Change on Resources for Growing Population', in B. Colombo, P. Demeny and M. Perutz (eds) *Resources and Population*, Oxford: Clarendon Press.

——(1994) 'Energy-efficient technologies: past and future perspectives', in A. Quadrio Curzio, M. Fortis and R. Zoboli (eds) *Innovation, Resources and Economic Growth*, Berlin: Springer.

Rothman, D. (1998) 'EKC: real progress or passing the buck? A case for consumption-based approaches', *Ecological Economics*, 25: 177–94.

Selden, D. H. and Song, D. (1994) 'Environmental quality and development: is there a Kuznets curve for air pollution emissions?' *Journal of Environmental Economics and Management*, 27: 147–62.

Shobee, S. (2004) 'The environmental Kuznets curve (EKC): a logistic curve?' *Applied Economics Letters*, 11: 449–52.

Stern, D. (2004) 'The rise and fall of the environmental Kuznets curve', *World Development*, 32: 1419–38.

Ten Kate, A. (1993) 'Industrial Development and Environment in Mexico', Working Paper Series 1125, Washington DC: World Bank.

Tilton, J. E. (1991) 'Material substitution: the role of new technology', in N. Nakicenovic and A. Grubler (eds), *Diffusion of Technology and Social Behavior*, Berlin: Springer.

——(1988) 'The New View on Minerals and Economic Growth', Working Paper 88-10, Colorado (US): Colorado School of Mines.

Wang, P., Bohara, A., Berrens, R. and Gawande, K. (1998) 'A risk-based environmental Kuznets curve for US hazardous waste sites', *Applied Economics Letters*, 5: 761–63.

Yandle, B., Vijayaraghavan, M. and Bhattarai, M. (2002) *The Environmental Kuznets Curve: A Primer*, PERC Research Study 02-01, Bozeman MT: PERC.

Zoboli, R. (1996) 'Technology and Changing Population Structure: Environmental Implications for the Advanced Countries', Dynamis-Quaderni 6/96, Milan: IDSE-CNR.

——(1995) 'Technological Innovation and Environmental Efficiency: Empirical Evidence and Explaining Factors', Dynamis-Quaderni 5/95, Milan: IDSE-CNR.

2 Waste generation and waste disposal

Evidence on socio-economic and policy drivers in the EU

Massimiliano Mazzanti, Francesco Nicolli and Roberto Zoboli

Indicators of decoupling/delinking are becoming increasingly popular for detecting and measuring improvements in environmental/resource efficiency with respect to economic activity. The Organisation for Economic Co-operation and Development (OECD 2002) has conducted extensive research into the use of decoupling indicators for reporting and policy-evaluation purposes, and the European Environment Agency's state of the environment reports (EEA 2003a, b, c) use a number of decoupling or resource-efficiency indicators. EEA (2006) highlights the importance also of market based instruments for achieving a higher degree of delinking for waste indicators.

The European Union (EU) policy thematic strategies on resources and waste, include reference to absolute and relative delinking indicators (EC 2003a, b; Jacobsen *et al.* 2004). The former is a negative relationship between economic growth and environmental impacts, associated with the descending side of an inverted U shape, according to the environmental Kuznets curve (EKC) framework. The latter, the ascending side of the U shape, may be positive but decreasing in size, income–environment relationship. This represents a positive lower than unity elasticity in economic terms. There is no delinking observed on the ascending part of the EKC if there is unity or higher than unity elasticity. Increased delinking is the primary aim for waste, which, in terms of its environmental impacts and economic costs, is no less relevant than climate change (Figure 2.1).

Andersen *et al.* (2007) recently estimated waste trends for the EU-15 and the EU-10 new entrants, and found that waste generation is linked to economic activities by non-constant trend ratios. This rather descriptive analysis of delinking in EU countries produces forecasts of increased relative delinking; it does not confirm the EKC evidence. Projections for 2005–20 for the UK, France and Italy show a growth in municipal solid waste (MSW) of around 15–20 per cent, which, at least at first sight, may be compatible with relative delinking with respect to gross domestic product (GDP) and consumption growth.

The EEA (2007: 4) argues that:

> It is increasingly important to provide answers to these questions because waste volumes in the EU are growing, driven by changing production

and consumption patterns. It is also important because there is a growing interest in sharing best practice and exchanging national-level experience across Europe, with the common goal of achieving more cost-effective solutions to the various problems being faced.

The EEA shows that countries can be categorized under three waste management groupings, based on the strategies for diverting municipal waste away from landfill, and the relative shares of landfill, materials recovery (mainly recycling and composting) and incineration. We may note that from an economic science standpoint, although costs and benefits should be evaluated for each specific situation (Pearce 2004; Dijkgraaf and Vollebergh 2004), possibly calling for better efficiency of decentralized policy implementation, at country and regional levels and from a theoretical viewpoint, a target of 50 per cent for recycling can be considered economically and environmentally reasonable (Huhtala 1997).

EEA (2007: 3) affirms that:

> The first waste management grouping comprises countries with high levels of both materials recovery and incineration, and relatively low levels of landfill. The second grouping includes countries with high materials recovery rates, medium incineration levels and medium dependence on landfill. The third group of countries has low levels of both materials recovery and incineration, and relatively high dependence on landfill.

From a waste accounting perspective, waste generation (WG), the amount of waste collected, is encompassed by three possible management options:

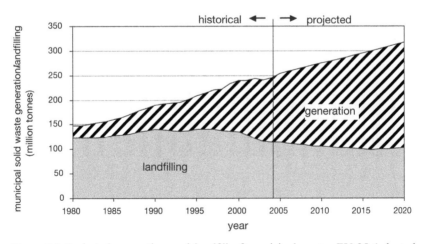

Figure 2.1 Projected generation and landfill of municipal waste: EU-25 (adapted from EEA 2007)

recycling (R) and materials recovery, including composting (C) and incineration (I), and where possible, energy recovery; incineration (with no energy recovery), landfill with the possibility of some energy recovery). Incineration is a hybrid solution; if we exclude the possibility of incineration without energy recovery, its net social benefit should be positive, giving it status within waste recovery systems in the EU, as opposed to final disposal.[1] This would mean that some (treated) amounts of waste flowing out the recycling and incineration processes would be disposed of in (regulated) landfills, which is defined as disposal even if there is the possibility of some energy recovery. The mass balance equation then would be: $WG^2 = WR(C + R + I) + L$, or $WG = WR(C + R) + I + L$.

Landfill is still the predominant treatment option for the EU's municipal waste. However, there are significant differences across countries in dependence on landfill. Figure 2.2 shows that several countries have already achieved very low landfill rates. These are countries that have not only substantial levels of incineration but also good levels of materials recovery. In general, there seem to be two strategies for diverting municipal waste from landfill: aiming for high levels of materials recovery combined with incineration, or materials recovery that includes recycling, composting and mechanical/biological treatment (EEA 2007).

The environmental impacts of landfill are massive (Pearce 2004; El Fadel *et al.* 1997; Eshet *et al.* 2004). Although at the top of EU environmental waste hierarchy, it should not be taken by default as the best economic practice in all situations; its costs and benefits are influenced by economic and technological factors. For examples of economic assessments of different

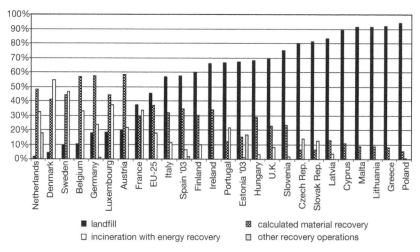

Figure 2.2 Use of landfill, incineration and material recovery as treatment options, 2004 (adapted from EEA 2007)

waste disposal strategies see Pearce (2004) and Vollebergh and Dijkgraaf (2004), among others. In the long run, waste generation reduction at source, through the imposition of policy targets in terms of waste generated per capita, is probably the most effective and most efficient answer to the problem. Given the potentially high costs in the short run, the first phase of policy implementation at EU level has focused on landfill diversion and increased shares of recycling/recovery, including incineration. There is a need to analyse empirically whether these policies have been effective in changing the endogenous relationship between economic growth and waste trends. In other words, given that waste policies are motivated by the various negative externalities arising at different stages of the life cycle (at source, at disposal level), *ex ante* cost–benefit analysis would provide indications of the most effective option to pursue and the right level of tax to impose. *Ex post* effectiveness analysis would assess the short and long-run effects of policies on the ultimate target: to drive down the waste Kuznets curve (WKC). In the absence of effective policies, we can expect a somewhat linear positive relationship between waste generation and growth, with landfill diversion being affected only by market prices and opportunity costs (of land).

This chapter provides empirical evidence on delinking trends for MSW. The main motivation and contribution of this chapter is the total lack of robust and up to date empirical evidence, for the vast region of the EU, relating to economic and policy drivers for waste dynamics. EU waste policies, although they have been in place for some time, and are one of the pillars of the EU's environmental policy, have not been empirically examined. Empirical evidence on Kuznets curve dynamics for waste is scarce, and research on delinking for materials and waste is far less developed than research into air pollution and greenhouse gas emissions. These limited research results could become a serious problem from a policy perspective.

Analyses that exploit highly disaggregated cross-country panel data on waste are even scarcer. Recent studies are single-country case studies that use regional, provincial or municipal data. In spite of the significant environmental, policy and economic relevance of waste, there is very little empirical evidence on delinking even for major waste streams, such as municipal, packaging and other waste. Analyses of policy effectiveness are also scarce and are dominated by studies of waste management optimization schemes and evaluations of externalities. Economic analyses have predominantly focused on cost–benefit assessments of relative waste site externalities (fixed and variable) and on the acceptability to local communities, with or without compensation, aimed at achieving Kaldor–Hicks Paretian improvements for society as a whole (Gallagher *et al.* 2008). The focus on cost–benefit analyses and landfill siting decisions prevails in part owing to the lack of reliable country-level and within-country data (Pearce 2004).[3]

Our first objective in this study is to provide new empirical evidence on WKC and policy effectiveness for a policy relevant region, that is, the EU, in which we disentangle the socio-economic and policy factors. The WKC is relevant for assessing the effects of socio-economic and structural factors in the BAU scenario and the additional role of policy levers in explaining the eventual delinking between environmental pressure and growth. Without policy action we would expect lower level or even no delinking, which has been the situation characterizing the waste sector so far. A secondary objective is to identify differences between the EU-15[4] and the new entrants to the EU with respect to waste drivers, delinking trends and policy effects, as a result of actions taken as a consequence of the 1999 Landfill Directive[5] and the early policy actions taken by some countries, such as Germany.[6]

Although complete delinking is far from being achieved – especially for waste generation – there are some positive signals, with a quite significant role of the EU waste policies implemented in the late 1990s and early 2000s, for diverting waste away from landfill and towards incineration and recycling. This is not to overlook other important socio-economic and technological factors (research and development, R&D). Policies interact with socio-economic, economic and other factors within a scenario of endogenous development in which vicious or virtuous circles drive regions' and countries' performance in relation to waste.

The chapter is structured as follows. The next section presents recent evidence on WKC, in order to highlight the urgent need to intensify research in this area to enable policy evaluation. Then we define the conceptual framework and the empirical model. A discussion about the original data set used in this study and comments on the empirical results regarding waste generation, incineration, and landfill and recycling options follows. The final section concludes.

Waste indicators, EKC and delinking: recent evidence

Following the pioneering work of Grossman and Krueger (1994), the World Bank (1992) and Holtz-Eakin and Selden (1992), interest in the so-called EKC has increased.[7] The EKC hypothesis is that, for many pollutants, the relationship between per capita income and pollution shows an inverted U shape, following the original and more famous Kuznets hypothesis, which over time has been considered in its original and adapted forms. Most investigations have focused on major air emissions, although evidence related to other externalities, such as local atmospheric and water emissions and waste, is accumulating. A decoupling of income growth and CO_2 emissions is not (yet) apparent for many important world economies (Vollebergh and Kemfert 2005); where it is observed, it is a relative rather than the absolute delinking assumed by the EKC hypothesis (Fischer-Kowalski and Amann 2001).

The EKC studies include few theoretical works[8] although some contributions have tried to establish some foundation for the empirics of EKC. These studies generally try to explain EKC dynamics as a preference based on the type of technological externality and on policy factors; some are worthy of further comment. Andreoni and Levison (2001), for example, is a seminal work suggesting that EKC dynamics may quite simply be technologically micro-founded, and not strictly related to growth and externalities issues. Chavas (2004) provides a dynamic theoretical scenario motivating EKC.

At the more macro-economic level, Brock and Taylor (2004) integrate the EKC framework with the Solow model of economic growth. They show that this revised model generates an EKC relationship between flows of polluting emissions and income per capita, and stock of environmental quality and income per capita, the resulting EKC being either an inverted U shape or strictly declining. Chimeli and Braden (2005) integrate the EKC into a model of total factor productivity. Low levels of income involve high values of discount rates, which are obstacles to the adoption of a pollution abatement policy. Only when the discount rate falls, as a consequence of growth, it is possible to implement measures for reductions in emissions, leading to an inverse U-shaped income–pollution pattern.

Notwithstanding the increasing relevance of theoretical studies on EKC, it is the quantitative side of the analysis that has dominated and still provides scope for research improvements at the margins. In fact, with some exceptions which we comment on below, studies using macro-panel data generally assume slope homogeneity across countries, and employ the classic fixed or random effects estimators or the more recent panel co-integration approach.

At the technical/econometric level, recent research has explored parametric and semi-parametric specifications and heterogeneous panel estimations or Bayesian procedures (Cole 2005; Mazzanti, Musolesi and Zoboli, forthcoming). We can summarize the advances and possible research steps in stating that improvements are still possible through a focus on: (i) slope heterogeneity in panel settings; (ii) dynamic specifications (GMM – general method of moment, Kiviet LSDV – least squares dummy variable correction); (iii) single-country panel data sets where within-country heterogeneity is exploited at regional level; (iii) specific time series at national or state/regional level, provided data are available over sufficiently long periods. We argue that future empirical efforts should concentrate on using newly constructed, more heterogeneous and longer data sets at country level or samples of countries in homogeneous, relevant areas, rather than cross-country international data sets, which may produce results that are too general, with important aspects being hidden within average figures from the econometric analysis (Brock and Taylor 2004).

In general, although some recent works have cast doubt on the very foundations of EKC results, by stressing their contingency on the empirical model and specifications used (Harbaugh *et al.* 2002; Stern, 2004, 1998), we (and other authors) believe that the EKC setting is a frame that can generate useful insights for the understanding of ecological-economic dynamics and for policy evaluation (Copeland and Taylor 2004).

We briefly review the evidence on waste delinking and waste management/ policy evaluation, for the most part from a chronological perspective. See Table 2.1 for a summary of the main works. This survey complements that presented in Chapter 1.

Table 2.1 Literature survey of waste-related studies

Author(s), (publication year)	Countries / geo. focus	Time period	Waste typology	Panel / cross-section data	EKC evidence	TP (per capita)
Andersen et al. (2007)	EU-15 and EU-10 countries	Pre-2000	Waste and material flows	Model allowing for trendwise changing coefficients	Waste generation linked with economic activities by non-constant trend ratios, WKC reasoning	–
Beede and Bloom (1995)	36 countries	Various years (several case studies)	Solid waste	Cross-section and time series	MSW generation positively associated, but inelastic, with respect to per capita income	–
Berrens et al. (1998)	US, county level (3,141 counties)	1991	Hazardous waste	Cross-section	Negative elasticity; inverted U shape	$20,253 and $17,679
Cole et al. (1997)	OECD countries	1975–1990	MSW	Panel	No evidence of an inverted U shape	No TP
Fischer-Kowalski and Amann (2001)	OECD countries	1975–1995	Landfilled waste and waste generated	Panel	Absolute decoupling for landfilled waste but not for waste generated	–
Johnstone and Labonne (2004)	OECD countries	1980–2000	MSW	Panel	Positive elasticities, but lower than 1	–

(Continued on next page)

Table 2.1 (continued)

Author(s), (publication year)	Countries / geo. focus	Time period	Waste typology	Panel / cross-section data	EKC evidence	TP (per capita)
Karousakis (2006)	OECD countries	1980–2000 (4 years)	MSW	Panel	MSW increases monotonically with income, elasticity around 0.42-0.45	–
Mazzanti and Zoboli, (previous Chapter)	European countries	1995–2000	Municipal and packaging waste	Panel	Neither absolute nor relative delinking (elasticity close to unity)	No TP
Mazzanti et al. (Chapter 5)	Italy	1999–2005	MSW	Panel	Relative delinking; weak sign of absolute delinking (some richer provinces)	$24,000–$27,000
Leigh (2004)	International data	2001–2002	Waste/consumption indicator	Cross-section	Evidence of EKC	$29,447
Seppala et al. (2001)	5 industrial. countries	1975–1994	Direct material flows	Panel	No evidence of delinking	No TP
Wang et al. (1998)	US, county-level data	1992	Hazardous waste	Cross-section	Evidence of EKC	$23,000 (1990 US$)

Some evidence based on cross-country regression analysis of data from the 1980s was presented in the World Bank (1992) report, which gave birth to the EKC literature. No WKC were found.

One of the earliest WKC studies was by Cole *et al.* (1997), who found no evidence of an inverted U shape in relation to municipal waste.

Fischer-Kowalski and Amann (2001) analysed the richer OECD countries and found that the intensity of materials input with respect to GDP, for all countries, shows a relative, but not absolute delinking, with materials growth over 1975–95. They note that absolute delinking holds for landfilled waste, but not for waste generated. This suggests, as can be seen from the descriptive analyses, that the evidence for waste generation and waste disposal varies, depending on improved performance in waste recovery. A study by Johnstone and Labonne (2004) uses a panel database of solid waste in the OECD countries to provide evidence on the economic and demographic determinants of rates of household solid waste generation, regressed over consumption expenditure, urbanization and population density. They find positive elasticities, but lower than 1, in the range 0.15 to 0.69. For a group of European countries Mazzanti and Zoboli, in the previous chapter, find neither absolute nor relative delinking. Using European panel data sets, they find no WKC evidence for municipal waste or packaging waste, respectively, for 1995–2000 and 1997–2000, and estimated elasticities for waste generation with respect to household consumption were close to unity.

Few WKC studies have included waste policy analyses. Kaurosakis (2006, and Chapter 4 of this book) deals with policy evaluation, and presents evidence on the determinants of waste generation and the driving forces behind the proportions of paper and glass that are recycled, and the proportion of waste that goes to landfill. The panel database is for 30 OECD countries. MSW increases monotonically with income. Urbanization exerts an even stronger effect on waste generation, while the time-variant policy index is not significant.

Other studies have investigated policy action, but at the level of single countries, exploiting the richness of regional data, which, at the same time, allows moderate generalization of results. Mazzanti *et al.* (Chapter 5) find some WKC evidence and some signals of the effectiveness of waste management instruments in driving waste generation reductions in Italy, where economic, policy and structural geographical differences are of primary interest in explaining trends.

Some studies focus on specific evaluation of the Landfill Directive, the main driver of regulatory actions in the EU, and the reason for the introduction in 1996 in the UK of the landfill tax (a rare case of a real environmental tax informed by an evaluation of marginal external costs). This group of studies, due to the lack of data when they were undertaken, provide interesting but only qualitative assessments. They include Morris *et al.* (1998), which offers insights on the potential and expected contribution of the directive to sustainable waste management. Burnley (2001) provides updated analyses highlighting some operational weaknesses and debating some preliminary assessments. Martin and Scott (2003) stress that the UK's landfill tax, which was intended to promote a transition away from landfill, towards recovery, recycling, reuse and minimization of waste, has failed to change the behaviour of domestic waste producers in a significant way. They stress that the available evidence shows that there are data on reasonable progress towards recycling, but not reuse or minimization of waste.

Outside the EU countries, analyses are rare. Taseli (2007) provides an assessment of the effects of the EU Landfill Directive in Turkey, a potential new entrant to the EU which can be compared with some of the EU-10. Taseli's study highlights the huge difficulties encountered by these countries in achieving the directive's targets even in the long run, and provides a clear analysis of the EU framework. Outside Europe, studies on landfill diversion and waste generation have flourished, especially in Far East settings, where the value of land is especially high and population density is reaching or has reached world peaks (Lang 2005; Ozawa 2005; Yang and Innes 2007). Population density and policies emerge as complementary drivers of stronger delinking for both waste generation and landfill, and also more active recycling.

Thus the literature on waste determinants and WKC analyses underlines that generally waste indicators tend to increase with income or other economic drivers, such as population, and, in general, an inverted U-shaped curve does not fit the data.

A decreasing trend (negative elasticity) can be found for the industrialized countries where waste management and policies are more developed. Nevertheless, there is a risk that WKC trends (absolute delinking) will be associated with a few rich countries or areas, and will work to divide countries in terms of waste performance indicators. Another structural reason for the lack of evidence on waste may be that the change in sign for income elasticity of the environment/income function occurs at relatively lower income levels for pollutants, whose production and consumption can be easily spatially separated, for example by exporting associated pollution or by relocating activities. This will likely be more difficult for waste flows.

The literature survey highlights the necessity and value of in-depth investigation of the driving forces and policy effectiveness in relation to waste. Our aim is to bring together the different pieces of the puzzle: WKC analyses and policy effectiveness studies, and an extensive evaluation of waste drivers. We should stress that the general value added of delinking analysis is not (only) to show whether economic drivers produce decoupling effects, but more to assess whether and to what extent there are additional factors that influence the core relationships, which increases the explanatory power of the model proposed. Our work allows a greater degree of generality, since it focuses on a homogeneous and policy-relevant regional area; most existing studies analyse circumscribed local situations, with the focus on specific waste streams and waste management instruments, unit based pricing, etc. (Sterner and Bartelings 1999; Ferrara and Missios 2005). Micro-based and locally focused analyses should be seen as complementing macro-based analyses in the understanding of waste trends with reference to socio-economic and policy issues.

The empirical model and the data

In order to verify the delinking relationships between waste indicators (from generation to disposal) and economic, socio-economic/structural[9] and policy drivers, we refer to the established EKC framework. Although, as we noted above, some theoretical based works have emerged in recent years, the EKC model derives from stylized facts proposed for the relationship between pollution and economic growth, which became known as the environmental Kuznets curve because of their similarity with Simon Kuznets's suggestions on long-run income distribution patterns. The EKC hypothesis, which is a natural extension of delinking analysis, holds that, for many pollutants, there is an inverted U-shaped relationship between per capita income and pollution.

The main methodological problem, related to the use of this delinking-related framework for the analysis in this chapter, is how to specify the WKC functional relationship. Some analyses are based on second-order polynomials, others estimate third and even fourth-order polynomials, comparing different specifications for relative robustness. Third or fourth-level polynomials could lead to N-rather than U-shaped curves, introducing new problems for our understanding of income–environment phenomena for policy making. N shapes are not relevant here, given that evidence is that even bell shapes are extremely rare.[10]

Here we test our hypotheses by specifying the proper reduced form usual in the EKC field (Stern 2004; Cole 2005; Cole *et al.* 1997; Dinda 2005):[11]

$$
\begin{aligned}
(1) \ \ln(\text{waste indicator}) = {}& \beta_{0i} + \alpha_t + \beta_1 \ln(\text{consumption}^{12})_{it} \\
& + \beta_2 \ln(\text{consumption})^2_{it} + \beta_3(\mathbf{X})_{it} \\
& + \beta_4(\mathbf{Z})_{it} + e_{it}
\end{aligned}
$$

where the first two terms are intercept parameters, which vary across countries and years. X refers to all other structural and socio-economic drivers that are added to the baseline specific in order to correct for the omission of relevant variables. Z is a vector of policy-related variables (see Tables 2.2 and 2.3 for a description of the variables).[13] In order to mitigate collinearity flaws, when highly correlated to each other, variables included in vectors X and Z are tested separately.

To test the hypotheses discussed below, we exploit information on waste collected, waste landfilled and waste incinerated in the European countries in 1995–2005 (Eurostat sources). The standard WKC specification includes variables to control for intra-country heterogeneity. These fall into two main groups: socio-economic/structural variables and policy indices.

Table 2.2 Descriptive statistics and a summary of research hypotheses (EU–25, 1995–2005)

	Min	Max	Mean	Acronym	
Dependent variables					
MSW collected/generated (kg/capita)	239.00	753.00	484.70	MSW-GEN	
MSW landfilled (kg/capita)	9.00	659.40	283.95	MSW-LAND	
MSW incinerated (kg/capita)	0.00	396.60	73.47	MSW-INC	
Independent variables					
1 Economic drivers					*Hypothesized correlation*[a]
Final consumption household expenditure (€/inhabitant – at 1995 prices and exchange rates)	900.00	21,000.00	8,103.27	C	+G eventual inverted U shape +I −L
Gross domestic expenditure on R&D (% of GDP)	0.19	4.25	1.37	RD	+I −L
2 Structural and socio-economic variables					
Population density	16.70	1276.00	174.80	DENS	+G
Urban population (% of total)[b]	50.60	97.20	71.36	URBPOP	−L ? I
Household size	1.9	3.4	2.62	SIZE	−G
Single households (%)	10.12	38.30	25.04	SINGLE	+G
Age index or 'elderly ratio' (population aged over 60: population 20-59 years)	0.3	0.5	0.358	OLDNESS	? G
Value added at factor cost, share of manufacturing	9.10	36.30	18.54	VAMAN	−G
3 Policy variables					
Decentralized waste management policy drivers (dummy)	0	1	0.24	DECPOLIND	? G, L, I
Incineration Directive (dummy: years/country where directive is ratified)	0	1	0.24	INCDIR	−G +I −L
Landfill Directive (dummy: years/country where directive is ratified)	0	1	0.27	LANDIR	−G +I −L
Waste strategy policy index (range 0–1)	0.00	0.95	0.34	POLIND	
Landfill strategy policy index	0.00	0.25	0.09	LANDPOLIND	

Note: All values in non-log format.

[a]The sign of the hypothesized correlation is shown as well as the level at which it is most relevant (*G* Generation, *L* Landfill, *I* Incineration). The element (?) means that the hypothesis is ambiguous either because opposing forces may be influencing the link or because economic and other scientific theories do not provide clear insights.

[b]Given their high correlation, population density and urban population are used alternately.

Table 2.3 Main variables (1995–2005 values)

Country	C	MSW–GEN	MSW–LAND	MSW–INC
Austria	12,700–14,500	438–630	204.7–112.6	54.3–147
Belgium	11,400–13,000	456–464	218.4–43.4	162.8–154.9
Cyprus	6,900–8,800	600–739	599.6–653.1	0–0
Czech Rep.	2,100–2,800	302–289	301.9–208.7	0–36.7
Denmark	13,400–15,600	567–737	96.4–38.3	294.1–396.6
Estonia	1,100–2,300	368–436	365.3–274.1	0–0.1
Finland	9,700–13,200	414–468	267.9–275.8	0–40.7
France	11,200–13,500	476–543	213.6–195.7	178.3–183.5
Germany	13,300–14,500	533–601	245.3–88.8	97.1–147.9
Greece	6,100–8,200	302–438	311–380.5	0–0
Hungary	1,700–2,800	460–459	346–361.8	31.9–29.1
Ireland	7,300–11,300	514–740	398.1–443.9	0–0
Italy	8,800–9,900	454–542	422.2–296.4	23.9–62
Latvia	1,000–2,000	263–310	246.7–243.2	0–3
Lithuania	900–1,900	424–378	424.4–340.2	0–0.1
Luxembourg	16,300–21,000	592–705	160.6–126.7	312.2–252.5
Malta	4,900–5,100	338–611	311.2–542.8	0–0
Netherlands	10,100–12,300	549–624	157.5–9	138.5–207.5
Poland	1,600–2,500	285–245	279.5–225.9	0–1.2
Portugal	5,500–6,900	385–446	200.3–278.1	0–98.5
Slovakia	1,400–2,200	295–289	168–227.8	28.2–34
Slovenia	4,600–6,000	596–423	456.6–329.7	0–0.6
Spain	6,900–9,000	510–597	308.4–317.5	24.3–34.9
Sweden	10,500–13,000	386–482	136.1–23.3	148.6–242.1
UK	9,200–12,500	499–584	414–374.9	45–48.9

The first group controls for socio-economic factors that might differ among countries, such as population density, urban population degree, household size, share of manufacturing in the economy. The data derive mainly from Eurostat structural indicator data sets. As far as the construction of policy indices is concerned, we exploit the country fact sheets available at EIONET[14] and public information on the ratification of the landfill and incineration directives.

Below we provide specifications for the three waste indicators investigated,[15] highlighting the factors and hypotheses that are linked with the three different levels of the waste chain, from generation to disposal. A concise discussion of the main hypotheses and, where necessary, the variables used in specific regressions is provided for each level (Table 2.2 and Table 2.3).

Waste generation

This level of analysis provides direct evidence regarding the usual WKC hypothesis on the waste generation–income relationship. Waste generation reduction or in other words waste prevention is the ultimate objective of any

social policy targeted towards waste flows, though, with a very few exceptions, explicit national policy actions (targets in terms of waste generated per
capita) do not exist. Although waste prevention is at the top of the EU's
waste agenda, no actions oriented towards waste prevention have been included
in the formal directives issued so far. Waste management (separated collection) and landfill diversion policies have generally prevailed in, if not dominated, the field, probably based on the presumed relative lower implementation
and compliance costs.

We can analyse the various research hypotheses that can be formulated at
this level of reasoning. Regarding economic drivers, a WKC-oriented structure
of the model allows the estimation of an eventual TP for waste generation.
As some recent studies have shown, this is generally not observed for the more
affluent areas within specific countries. The TP hints at GDP/consumption
level beyond which the relationship, in this case between waste production
and income, becomes negative. Econometric and descriptive empirical evidence shows that there is at best only relative delinking. We aim to provide
new evidence based on official data for the EU.

We also test various hypotheses on the possible effects exerted by socio-
economic and structural variables. Waste generation/collection is ultimately
affected by a diverse set of factors. We refer the reader to Table 2.2.

First, population density (or urban population)[16] is likely to impact positively on waste generation. Only economies of scale spurred by urbanization
could invert the trend and reduce collections where density is higher.

Household related features may also have an effect at this level. In fact, we
would expect that the larger the size of the household the smaller the amount
of waste generated per capita. However, even a positive link could be plausible
in the case where collection schemes, and waste management at the household
level (composting), are poorly developed. Accordingly, more single households
should drive up waste generation.

Second, we use the age index as a control variable. From a socio-economic
point of view, we believe that any outcome is possible. Opposing forces may
play a role: on the one hand, older people can be expected to produce less
waste than younger ones, but older people may also be less accustomed and
committed to the collection and recycling of waste. However, the opportunity costs of time are lower for older people, and waste collection actions
require time. Thus the sign of the relationship is highly unpredictable. Interaction with data on education level would be interesting, but that should be
the subject of a micro-based study. Also, tests for the factors related to age
would probably be more robust at the micro level of analysis. In the present
analysis we use them as controls and tools to mitigate the problems of
omission of relevant variables. Some of these socio-economic variables capture more than one of the structural/institutional elements characterizing a
country.

Third, we include in our analysis two types of *policy proxies*. The first is
related to the European Landfill and Incineration Directives, and their

effective implementation in the EU member states. These proxies are built as dummy variables that take the value 1 in a given year between 1995 and 2005 if the country has incorporated the directives into national law. We expect implementation to be positively correlated with delinking performance. The second group is more country-specific. To begin with we exploit a *decentralized waste management index* that reflects the degree of waste policy decentralization across countries. Decentralization may be beneficial for waste performance based on the greater flexibility and specificity in policy implementation, which may account for local idiosyncratic cost and benefit elements related to waste policies (Pearce 2004).[17] However, although decentralization may improve the efficiency of policy implementation in the EU, it may also have some drawbacks in terms of factors related to local rents and their exploitation by public and private agents. In principle, rents in the environmental arena are neither good nor bad. It is their effects on the static and dynamic elements, such as value creation and innovation, that matter. *Waste markets*, including landfill and even recycling, may be associated to rents, which might lock in a local system in a less than optimal equilibrium (Mazzanti and Zoboli 2006). This unresolved hypothesis calls for more research in the future.

Finally, we consider an environmental policy index. This is a proxy for national policies over the time period examined. It captures all possible information regarding national implementation of waste related policies (MSW, BSW, packaging waste, end-of-life vehicles), independent of the Landfill Directive. We used the country studies available at EIONET as our information source. This index is extremely comprehensive with regard to Landfill Directive-related variables,[18] and also captures some of the waste prevention features of national policies.[19] It should be noted that all other proxies vary across countries, and over time.

The importance of policy proxies in the waste arena is crucial, and a major contribution of this chapter. Their relevance is based on the fact that many European policies were enacted only recently, and their inclusion in a WKC framework could be a sort of *ex post* evaluation of effectiveness. Both structural indicators and policy variables may be important drivers of WKC shapes; their omission could overestimate the *pure* economic effect.

The specification that we test, then, is:

$$(2)\ \ln(\text{MSW generation per capita}) = \beta_{0i} + \alpha_t + \beta_1 \ln(\text{C})_{it} + \beta_2 \ln(\text{C})_{it}^2 \\ + \beta_3 (\text{X})_{it} + \beta_4 (\text{Z})_{it} + e_{it}$$

where X includes the above-mentioned socio-economic/structural factors (DENS or URBPOP, SIZE, SINGLE, OLDNESS, VAMAN) and Z is the policy levers (DECPOLIND, INCDIR, LANDIR, POLIND). We refer the reader to Table 2.2 for a synthesizing summary of the covariates related to the level of waste generation.

Landfill diversion

The second level of the empirical model focuses on the disposal stage of the waste chain. The economic driver here is hypothesized to impact on land-filled waste, following a bell shape. In fact, on average, even though some countries are increasing their share of landfill, and heterogeneity is striking across Europe, shares of landfilled waste and landfill per capita have been constantly decreasing since the mid 1990s. Therefore, we can expect to find a negative relationship, not a bell shape. From an EU average viewpoint, the period 1995–2005 may already be at the right hand, descending side of the inverted U-shape relationship for the relationship between landfill and eco-nomic growth. In the future, tests for N-shaped curves may become relevant. For example, following a decade of strong landfill diversion, Italy saw a slight increase in landfilled waste per capita in 2006, compared with 2005.

   In terms of the socio-economic and structural factors, we note that population density and urbanization are negatively related to landfilled waste. Both the opportunity costs linked with the higher value of land in densely populated and urban areas (value of land, of commercial activities crowded out by landfill sites, and other public investments), and the higher externality costs that arise in more densely populated areas, *ceteris paribus*, should drive down the use of landfill as a disposal option and provide a real investment opportunity linked to its rents compared with other market rents (Andrè and Cerda 2000). Never-theless, since the opportunity costs and environmental costs will vary across regions (EU-15 versus EU-10) this hypothesis must be scrutinized, case by case. We cannot distinguish any other factors that have an impact on landfill trends from a socio-economic point of view. The role of a country's R&D investments is expected to correlate negatively with landfill diversion because of the expected role of R&D activity as a driver of incineration dynamics. The technological content and innovation dynamics associated with incineration are stronger than those relative to the management of landfill sites.

   The core factors we test at this level are the policy levers, a crucial test in our analysis. By exploiting both binary indices and the continuous synthetic index (both of which vary over time and across countries)[20] we can verify the extent to which the policy actions that have characterized Europe in the last decade, primarily the 1999 Landfill Directive, have affected the waste–income relationship. Since the synthetic policy index also captures the gen-eral commitment of a country over the period, the econometric investigation takes account of some early actions that occurred before 1999 as well as the effective ratification of the Directive.

   The tested specification is then:

$$(3)\ \ln(\text{MSW landfilled per capita}^{21}) = \beta_{0i} + \alpha_t + \beta_1 \ln(C)_{it}$$
$$+ \beta_2 \ln(C)^2_{it} + \beta_3(X)_{it}$$
$$+ \beta_4(Z)_{it} + e_{it}$$

X (DENS or URBPOP) and Z (DECPOLIND, INCDIR, LANDIR, POLIND) usually refer to the socio-economic and policy variables linked to this stage of the investigation, as summarized in Table 2.2.[22]

Incinerated waste

The WKC-like relationship assumes a different flavour here. In fact we can expect that incineration, at least in the EU-15 (the analysis is carried out for the EU-15 due to lack of data, most Eastern EU countries show incineration levels close to zero), is positively related to economic growth in recent years. This is evident from descriptive analysis and is obviously linked with the trend towards landfill diversion. Nevertheless, the non-linearity of the relationship could assume an exponential or a bell-shaped dynamics. We consider the latter to be more plausible, given that incineration to some extent is associated with diminishing marginal returns and increasing external costs. Thus the interpretation is different with respect to the usual EKC shape for waste generation and landfill: it is related to the fact that there are other possible residual options, such as recycling and composting. The increasing role of these options in most countries should lead to and make compatible scenarios of landfill diversion and increasing, but not exponentially so, incineration, independent of the source of the delinking dynamics for waste generation. As many applied studies have shown, in the waste arena corner solutions are seldom (never) the optimal strategies, given the increasing marginal costs (financial and social) of landfill, incineration and recycling.

Thus we cannot formulate a clear hypothesis. The resulting sign is ambiguous, depending on the chosen alternative (if any) to landfill disposal. If we assume that densely populated areas will move away from landfill, the opportunity costs and environmental costs of incineration should represent a relatively better scenario. If instead the country moves away from landfill primarily towards recycling options, incineration and population density/ urbanization degree may be negatively linked.

A crucial factor that we test here is R&D intensity, exploited as a country-specific effect. Though there may be some outliers, that is, countries showing high R&D/GDP shares and low incineration, eventually, because their focus on recycling strategies is stronger, on average we would expect to find a dynamic strong correlation between a country's technological intensity and its level of incineration. The example of Germany may represent a paradigmatic case in Europe. We test whether this anecdotal fact may represent a general statistical regularity. Given its correlation with economic drivers, R&D is tested as an alternative explanatory factor. Eventual non-linearity is tested to account for a diminishing marginal effect of R&D on incineration technology strategies.

The argument around policy levers is similar to that presented for landfill diversion. At this stage we can expect a specific and robust link between implementation of the Incineration Directive and incinerated waste dynamics. The inclusion of both an endogenous driver, such as R&D, and a policy lever allows a compelling assessment of the relative strengths of endogenous and exogenous drivers.

The specification for incinerated waste is then:

$$(4a)\ \ln(\text{MSW incinerated per capita}) = \beta_{0i} + \alpha_t + \beta_1 \ln(\text{C})_{it}$$
$$+ \beta_2 \ln(\text{C})_{it}^2 + \beta_3(\text{X})_{it}$$
$$+ \beta_4(\text{Z})_{it} + e_{it}$$

or

$$(4b)\ \ln(\text{incinerated waste per capita}) = \beta_{0i} + \alpha_t + \beta_1 \ln(\text{RD}/\text{GDP})_{it}$$
$$+ \beta_2 \ln(\text{RD}/\text{GDP})_{it}^2 + \beta_3(\text{X})_{it}$$
$$+ \beta_4(\text{Z})_{it} + e_{it}$$

X (DENS or URBPOP) and Z (DECPOLIND, INCDIR, LANDIR, POLIND) usually refer to the socio-economic and policy variables.

Empirical analyses

Methodological issues and estimation procedures

All the analyses are conducted in three consequential steps: (i) a traditional baseline specification, including only the main economic driver; (ii) the specification with the structural drivers introduced as control variables; (iii) testing the significance of the different policy indexes. All regressions are estimated by both fixed and random effects, and the best specification is selected following the Hausman test. Specifications are tested in the EU-25 setting and in the two sub-samples, the EU-15, and new incoming countries (EU-10), where it is statistically meaningful and/or data availability allows it. At every level, the variables included in the vectors X and Z are inserted separately to mitigate any collinearity flaws. Only the more robust results are shown.

We also tested the extent to which random coefficient models and dynamic models add insights. First, we test the relevance of the Swamy random-coefficients linear regression model, before focusing on two different types of dynamic models, GMM and LSDV correction. With this further level of analysis we aim to test whether models that take account of aspects omitted from the simple FEM and REM analysis (such as dynamics and slope heterogeneity) confirm our results.

MSW generation

EU-25

The analyses (Table 2.4) do not show overall WKC evidence for MSW generation. The linear term shows a significant and positive coefficient for consumption, with an elasticity ranging from 0.114 to 0.230 across specifications.[23] The EU-15 and EU-25 analyses are similar, but with a higher elasticity (around 0.70–0.80) in the case of the former. These elasticities are slightly lower than found in previous analyses of Europe using waste data for the 1990s (Mazzanti 2008), and also would seem to imply a more active delinking process for the EU-10 countries.[24] In general, then, there is evidence of a relative delinking in the relation. This result is interesting and partially confirms our expectations of only a relative delinking, but with some positive signals in terms of currently lower elasticities.

The introduction of socio-economic controls does not change the results. The analysis provides evidence of relative delinking, and an elasticity equal to 0.72 in the sub-sample EU-15. The most significant and robust control variables are population density or share of urban population, and share of manufacturing[25] in total economic activity. Share of manufacturing has a negative sign, which is in line with our expectations: richer and more services-oriented economies produce more MSW. This questions the assumption of relatively better environmental performance associated with services that has primarily been addressed when we consider pollution-related issues. Structural and sector related composition effects could show, for a theme like waste (MSW includes commercial and business derived waste), counter-intuitive results. Population density (or urban population) impacts positively on waste generation: scale effects prevail over possible economies of scale in waste prevention and waste management/collection activities.[26] The other factors are never significant.

To sum up, socio-economic structural factors provide some useful hints and some food for thought in terms of waste management strategies, although they do not impact on the core relationship. Household-related variables seem not to have any great influence, which may be an indication that policy efforts have more weight on post-collection actions, such as recycling and landfill operations. Household behaviour and household characteristics, on average at least, are not correlated, either negatively or positively, to amounts of waste collected.

Next we exploit our policy proxies, adding them to the set of explanatory factors. Neither the effect of the Landfill Directive nor the environmental policy index is statistically significant.[27] This means that the efforts so far have not promoted a stronger delinking between waste collection and domestic consumption.[28] The results are the same for analyses of the smaller samples. Overall, policy levers appear to have only a marginal, if any, impact on waste generation. This reflects the absence of waste prevention-oriented policies, and the marginal or negative effects of landfill policies on waste

Table 2.4 MSW generation regression results, EU–25

Model	FEM	FEM	FEM	FEM	REM	FEM	FEM	FEM
C	0.230***	0.163***	0.117**	0.158***	0.188***	0.114*	0.118**	0.164***
Dens	0.629***	...	...	...	...	...	...	...
Urbpop	...	4.263***	1.760***	42.580***	0.290	1.760***	1.761***	1.777***
Vaman	...	...	-0.280***	...	-0.319***	-0.284***	-0.285***	-0.291***
Size	...	...	...	0.117	...	...	...	...
Oldness	...	...	...	0.120	...	...	...	...
Decpolind	...	...	...	...	-0.015	...	...	...
Polind	...	...	...	...	...	0.002	-0.0005	...
Landdir	...	...	...	...	...	...	...	...
Incdir	...	...	...	...	...	...	...	-0.022
N	275	275	264	275	264	264	264	264

Note: ... means not included. Significance at 10%, 5% and 1% is denoted by *, ** and ***, respectively. F test shows overall significance for all regressions; R^2 presents reasonably high values for panel settings.

generation. All this points to the need for waste policies targeting waste reduction at source, which so far have been lacking; policies related to waste disposal were perceived initially to be less costly.

Comparing EU-15 and EU-10

As far as MSW generation is concerned, we may robustly subdivide the analysis between EU-15 and EU-10. Some comments were anticipated above. We here comment on more specific differences, if any (Tables 2.5, 2.6).

We first note that the relationship regarding the core economic driver is different between the two sub-samples: the average EU-25 evidence is driven by the (majority) of western countries. In fact, Tables 2.5 and 2.6 highlight, as already noted, that while the EU-10 are showing a bell-shape dynamic, consistent with absolute delinking – given a quite low TP – EU-15 countries are still generating an – unsustainable – waste growth that is not decoupled from[29] economic trends. This interesting and partly counter-intuitive result deserves more future investigation, as the explanations may be diversified. Eastern countries may benefit, in joining the EU having to comply with strict environmental law at a relatively low income level, and /or some waste management practices in relatively more important rural areas may underestimate waste collection in such countries.

Also perhaps counter-intuitively, it seems that the above observed positive relationship between population density/urbanization and waste generation is mainly driven by EU-10 countries. EU-15 could have reached economies

Table 2.5 MSW generation, EU−15

Model	FEM	FEM	FEM	FEM	REM	FEM	FEM
C	0.772***	0.816***	0.787***	0.825***	0.811***	0.776***	0.830**
C^2	a	...	...	...	...	...	...
Dens	0.254	...	...	...	...	...	...
Urbpop	...	−0.203	−0.059	−0.004	−0.234	0.009	0.002
Vaman	...	...	0.092	...	...	...	...
Size	...	...	...	0.279**	0.357***	0.292**	0.279**
Oldness	...	...	...	0.340**	0.348**	0.289*	0.345**
Decpolind	...	...	...	...	0.018	...	...
Polind	...	...	...	...	...	0.001	...
Landdir	...	...	...	...	...	...	−0.001
N	165	165	165	165	165	165	165

Note: ... means not included. Significance at 10%, 5% and 1% is denoted by *, ** and ***, respectively. F test shows overall significance for all regressions at 1%; R^2 presents reasonably high value for panel settings.
aSignificant at 10% if included, though the observed associated TP is well above the observed range (€136,000), confirming the low statistical and economic significance of the estimated quadratic form. All regressions given this evidence are estimated without the quadratic term.

Table 2.6 MSW generation, EU−10

Model	FEM	FEM	FEM	FEM	FEM	FEM
C	5.490***	4.760***	5.820***	5.630***	6.320***	5.680***
C^2	−0.365***	−0.315***	−0.383***	−0.361***	−0.413***	−0.362***
Urbpop[a]	13.250***	12.550***	13.320***	13.660	13.130***	12.980***
Vaman	...	−0.150***	...	...	...	...
Size	...	...	0.120	...	...	...
Oldness	...	...	−1.694***	−1.390***	−1.720***	−1.690***
Polind	...	...	...	−0.129*	...	...
Landdir	...	...	...	...	−0.025	...
Incdir	...	...	...	...	...	−0.087***
TP	1,845	1,911	1,970	2,435	2,103	2,610
N	110	110	110	110	110	110

Note: ... means not included. Significance at 10%, 5% and 1% is denoted by *, ** and ***, respectively. TP in consumption per capita (€). F test shows overall significance for all regressions at 1%; R^2 presents reasonably high value for panel settings, [a]DENS is less significant and links with less significance of the regression.

of scale and efficiency level in waste management that counterbalance the scale effect of population density relative to waste collection trends.

Finally, moving to other explanatory forces, we may note that the insignificant effects we find for SIZE and OLDNESS derive from quite different dynamics in the groups: household size and the elderly index correlate positively with waste generation in western countries (the latter effect being somewhat counter-intuitive but possibly explained by a stronger pro-environment commitment of young generations). EU-10 instead present a more expected negative sign that may derive from the stronger correlation between elderly ratio and rural areas, where waste generation is intrinsically lower.

Finally, eastern EU countries also present negative and quite significant coefficients associated with POLIND and INCDIR. Those policy-related effects may be consistent with what we affirmed above: the decoupling trend is present even for waste generation.

Landfilled waste

EU-25

The analysis relative to landfilled waste, reported in Table 2.7, shows evidence of a WKC, which, given the scenario in recent years, is as expected. The diversion of waste from landfill in the EU began on average around 1995 (slightly before in some cases). Thus our data register only the downward-sloped part of the relationship, and the TP. This is also associated with the already mentioned relatively better performance of the EU-10 in waste generation. Further investigation is needed to confirm this possible difference.[30]

Table 2.7 Landfilled MSW, EU–25

Model	FEM	REM	REM	REM
C	3.382**	3.658***	4.156***	3.390***
C^2	−0.242***	−0.248***	−0.260***	−0.236***
Urbpop[a]	−3.694**	−1.554**	−1.714**	−1.340**
Decpolind	...	0.576**	...	...
Landdir	...	...	−0.324***	...
Polind[b]	...	...	...	−0.632***
TP	1,083	1,595	3,610	3,951
N	275	275	275	275

Note: ... means not included, [a]DENS is less significant. [b]If a specific index relating only to landfill policy is included the results do not change. The correlation between the two is 0.81. Significance at 10%, 5% and 1% is denoted by *, ** and ***, respectively. *TP* in consumption per capita (€). F test shows overall significance for all regressions at 1%; R^2 presents reasonably high value for panel settings.

The introduction of socio-economic/structural variables does not alter the previous results, and again shows a trend towards absolute delinking in relation to waste disposal in Europe. Other factors that are significant are density and degree of urbanization (EU-25/EU-15, respectively positive and negative signs).[31] The latter shows a stronger statistical significance associated with a negative sign. In our view, it is a structural factor associated with economic rationales: the significance of density and urban population, positively correlated with waste generation, is as expected, and shows that where opportunity costs are higher (in urban areas, densely populated areas) and disamenity/external effects affect more people, landfill diversion is stronger. For example, landfill studies have flourished in situations where the value of land and population density are particularly high, such as in Asia (Lang 2005; Ozawa 2005).[32] The size of the coefficient and its statistical significance are also high. These factors could explain the degree of delinking and landfill diversion in the endogenous scenario without policy interventions.

Finally, our analysis shows that the policy levers tested, that is, the policy indices, the Landfill Directive and the Incineration Directive, are highly significant and negatively correlated with landfill diversion. These results are confirmed for both sub-samples. The main relationship persists in terms of type of specification and level of significance, while the TP becomes slightly higher. This is an important result because it underlines the high level of effectiveness of European policy, an additional lever to those mentioned above, in terms of diverting waste from landfill. Policies help in the efforts to *tunnel through* the BAU endogenous delinking trend driven by mere economic drivers.

In terms of the other environmental policy proxies analysed, the decentralized waste management (DWM) index (taking three values, low/medium/high) is significant at 1 per cent and has a positive coefficient. This seems to suggest that the more that waste management is decentralized within countries the more difficult is diversion from landfill. The interpretations remain open, but the evidence is not strongly counter-intuitive: in DWM systems (Italy being an example) there are often incentives for the local waste management actors (municipalities) to increase waste disposal in terms of landfill or recycling, depending on which produces the higher rents in the local market. Since landfill rents are often very high, DWM could favour distort dynamics. This is not to suggest negative effects from DWM overall. We would underline that this variable is time-invariant, capturing only cross-country heterogeneity.

We would also point out that from a statistical viewpoint (and unlike the policy index) policy dummies appear not to be affected by endogeneity issues, being positively, but not highly, correlated with income variables (below 0.10). Early movers are likely to be the wealthier countries, Germany being an example.[33] We note that, as far as the POLIND index is concerned, the results are confirmed by the two-stage instrumental variable regression which uses consumption as a driver of the index in the first stage, and then includes the predicted values of POLIND in the specification analysing waste indicators. In this case, POLIND is highly and negatively related to landfilled MSW per capita. This potential endogeneity, which characterizes only this more comprehensive index capturing the overall waste policy commitment and action of a country, does not undermine this evidence and is dealt with.

Comparing EU-15 and EU-10

As for waste generation, data availability on landfill allows an investigation of EU-15 and EU-10 taken separately (Tables 2.8 and 2.9). The evidence showing landfill diversion – a bell-shape curve – is associated with both EU-15 and EU-10, with plausibly different TP, higher in the former case. The most striking difference is related to the URBPOP factor, that also presented opposite signs when we commented on waste generation.

Here we find that the negative effect of URBPOP and DENS on landfilled waste, then arising as a crucial factor of landfill diversion,[34] turns into a positive effect as far as the EU-10 group is concerned. There, urbanization seems to undermine landfill diversion. The very plausible motivation may be that in a first stage of development, though experiencing as we find here good performance in terms of waste collection and landfill, those countries may suffer from (rapid) urbanization dynamics, often concentrated in few big cities.

The economic reason may relate to the lower opportunity costs (lower land values) in the EU-10 compared with the EU-15. If so, the expected reduced divergences in land values may endogenously help in the future the landfill diversion performance of eastern countries.

Finally, the significant and robust evidence showing that all tested policy levers are crucial explanatory factors of landfill diversion is confirmed without great differences in both EU-15 and EU-10 countries.

Table 2.8 Landfilled MSW, EU–15

Model	FEM	FEM	REM	FEM	FEM
C	65.090**	42.130***	48.960***	61.520***	55.940***
C^2	–3.530***	–2.330***	–2.690***	–3.270***	–2.960***
Urbpop	–21.010**	...	–6.650**	–20.720***	–20.750**
Dens	...	–2.390**	...	...	...
Decpolind	...	...	0.689*	...	...
Landdir	...	...	...	–0.375***	...
Polind[a]	...	...	...	...	–0.160***
TP	10,092	8,440	8,958	12,169	12,699
N	165	165	165	165	165

Note: ... means not included. [a]If a specific index relating only to landfill policy is included the results do not change. The correlation between the two is 0.81. Significance at 10%, 5% and 1% is denoted by *, ** and ***, respectively. TP in consumption per capita (€). F test shows overall significance for all regressions at 1%. R^2 presents reasonably high value for panel settings.

Table 2.9 Landfilled MSW, EU–10

Model	FEM	FEM	REM	REM
C	6.490***	4.490**	7.890***	5.800***
C^2	–0.449***	–0.313**	–0.522***	–0.386***
Urbpop	12.400***	...	10.840***	12.860**
Dens	...	1.390***	...	...
Landdir	...	...	–0.215***	...
Polind[a]	...	..	...	–0.240***
TP	1,376	1,303	1,914	1,831
N	110	110	110	110

Note: ... means not included. [a]If a specific index relating only to landfill policy is included the results do not change. The correlation between the two is 0.81. Significance at 10%, 5% and 1% is denoted by *, ** and ***, respectively. TP in consumption per capita (€). F test shows overall significance for all regressions at 1%. R^2 presents reasonably high value for panel settings.

Incinerated waste

In this case we drop all the observations for countries with missing or zero values for the period analysed.[35] The result is a sub-sample composed of the EU-15 countries, less Ireland and Greece.[36] Missing data are often in fact very low values because incineration is a relatively new disposal option. In the first regression in Table 2.10 we observe the joint significance of the linear and quadratic terms for consumption (model 4a). This is due to the presence of an outlier, Luxembourg, which has very high income and a relative low level of incinerated waste. It is the only country with a consumption level that is in line with the TP, which appears coherently quite high. If we exclude Luxembourg from the data set, the quadratic term loses

Table 2.10 Incinerated MSW, EU-15[a]

Model	REM	REM[b]	FEM	FEM	REM	FEM	FEM
C	20.293***	1.676***	22.450***	24.287***	19.328**	...	...
C^2	-1.014**	...	-1.143***	-1.269***	-0.965**	...	...
Urbpop	0.651	...	0.111	0.252	1.157	4.451***	1.192***
RD	...	...	...	...	...	1.414***	3.623***
Decpolind	...	...	...	...	-0.868***	...	...
Incdir	...	...	0.076*	...	...	...	...
Polind	...	...	...	0.380***	...	...	0.151*
TP	22,168	/	18,409	14,319	22,348	/	/
N	137	126	137	137	137	137	137

Note: ... means not included. Significance at 90%, 95% and 99% is denoted by *, ** and ***, respectively. *TP* Consumption per capita (€). [a]Greece and Ireland are discarded, since they show only 0 values over the period. The panel is unbalanced for some years where Portugal also shows 0 values. [a]Excluding Luxembourg. F test shows overall significance for all regressions. R^2 presents reasonably high value for panel settings.

its significance and the relation becomes linear, with an elasticity greater than 1 (1.67).[37] This first step allows us to state that, in the period analysed, the trend for the European countries, based on the range of waste disposal options, is towards incineration. The TP has a different meaning here. Since incineration is neither a bad nor a good thing (Dijkgraaf and Vollebergh 2004), we would expect that a future decreasing trend might be explained by diminishing returns: ultimately, all waste recovery options, including recycling, are subject to non-increasing returns to scale and, for incineration (similar to landfill), to the problem of land scarcity (incinerator siting).

The other covariates are not relevant: DENS and URBPOP show positive but not significant coefficients.

The introduction in the regression of the environmental policy index and the incineration directive dummy gives important results. Both indicators are statistically significant at 1 per cent and 10 per cent respectively, but in this case they are positively correlated with the amount of waste incinerated, which is to be expected based on the analysis of landfill trends. It confirms our assumptions in relation to European policies. This is a trend that is common to all the countries analysed. The index of decentralized policy actions, on the other hand, shows a negative effect on incineration dynamics. On average, then, our regressions show that where waste policy is more decentralized, incineration is undermined and landfill is preferred. The fact that landfill diversion is not favoured by the decentralization of policy is a result worth noting, given the relevance of decentralization in many EU scenarios, such as Italy, Germany and Spain.

Finally, we test the model (4b) with share of R&D on GDP, the technological proxy, included as an alternative to consumption. (The two are strongly correlated.) R&D is significant and positively correlated with incinerated waste. This result is expected and underlines the importance of R&D in this field, which is characterized by innovative technologies, rapid change and major economies of scale. In the analysis (which excludes Luxembourg), as in the previous case, only the linear term is significant, and the R&D coefficient is significant and positively correlated with incinerated waste (30.24). The TP is smaller than before, but also the only country with a consumption value bigger than the TP is Luxembourg. The inclusion of R&D in the regression, which is positive and highly significant, reduces the elasticity of the relationship (1.17).

It should also be noted that if, R&D and policy factors are inserted together, the R&D effects prevail, decreasing the importance of policy.[38] This is very interesting evidence and could be interpreted as indicating that, overall, innovative dynamics (and landfill diversion), rather than policy levers, are spurring incineration.[39]

Model extensions: slope heterogeneity and dynamic models

In this section we provide evidence from the random coefficient and dynamic panel models. Because of the small amount of data on incineration, we focus on and present only the main specifications for landfill and waste generation.

First, we perform the Swamy random-coefficients linear regression model, including a test of parameter constancy.[40] The aim is to test our previous results for the presence of heterogeneity among slopes of different individuals. We estimate the previous EKC model (model 1) but considering the coefficient β as $\beta_i = \beta + \xi_i$, with $i = 1, \ldots, N$[41].

Second, based on the dynamic analysis, we estimate the dynamic effect with a traditional GMM. The estimated model becomes:

$$(5)\ \ln(\text{waste indicator}) = \alpha \ln(\text{waste indicator})_{t-1} + \beta_1 \ln(\text{C})_{it}$$
$$+ \beta_2 \ln(\text{C})_{it}^2 + \beta_3 (\text{Z})_{it} + e_{it}$$

Here Z refers to the policy variables and α is the coefficient of the lagged dependent variable. We include in our results, for every estimation technique, only the basic EKC specification (referred to as *step 1*) and a further specification including policy indicators.

Table 2.11 shows the results for MSW-GEN. We can see that accounting for slope heterogeneity generates an increase in the elasticity of the relationship. As before, the policy drivers are not significant. In the GMM estimations the scenario is similar: the relationship is still monotonically increasing. The main difference from the previous models is the significance of the policy index.[42] Thus some differences emerge with additional models, but the core evidence on delinking is unaffected.

As far as landfilled waste is concerned, Table 2.12 shows that the results of the FEM and REM are confirmed. The random-coefficient model shows the same pattern as before: the turning point is low and the Landfill Directive dummy is highly significant and negatively correlated with the amount of waste landfilled. The policy index retains its explanatory power, but only in the non-quadratic specification. Interestingly, the indexes POLIND and LANDPOLIND[43] show different significances, with the latter associated with a high significance related to landfill features of waste strategies which increase the relevance of the policy factor.

The introduction of dynamics leads to a monotonically decreasing relationship between landfilled waste and consumption. This is logical when we consider that in all the previous specifications the TP occurs in relations to low levels of consumption. In the EU, for landfilled waste, we are observing

Table 2.11 MSW generation regression results, EU–25: Swamy random–coefficients linear regression model and dynamic analysis

Model	REM	GMM–Diff one step	GMM–Diff one step
C	0.714***	0.129***	0.159***
MSW–GEN (−1)		0.817***	0.784***
POLIND01	−0.116	...	−0.140***
Slope test	0.000	...	...
Sargan test	...	0.000	0.000
N	275	250	250

Note: ... means not included. Significance at 10%, 5% and 1% is denoted by *, ** and ***, respectively.

Table 2.12 MSW landfilled regression results, EU–25: Swamy random–coefficients linear regression model and dynamic analysis

Model	REM	REM	REM	GMM–Diff One Step	GMM–Diff One Step
C	2.221***	0.674***	0.682***	−0.123***	−0.398***
C²	−0.173***	...	...	...	...
MSW–LAND (−1)	...	...	...	1.190***	0.495***
LANDDIR	−0.182***	...	...	...	...
POLIND	...	−0.043**	...	...	−0.033**
LANDPOLIND	...	...	−0.143***	...	...
Slope test	0.000	0.000	0.000	...	...
Sargan test	...	...	...	0.000	0.000
TP	605	...	...	...	...
N	275	275	275	250	250

Note: ... means not included. Significance at 90%, 95% and 99% is denoted by *, ** and ***, respectively. TP in Consumption per capita (€).

the descending part of the inverted U relationship. Furthermore, in the dynamic models, the variables for both landfill policy index and the presence of a landfill directive are highly significant and negatively correlated with the amount of waste landfilled.

Conclusion

This chapter set out to establish a sound framework to analyse delinking for diverse waste related trends, within a WKC conceptual environment that encompasses the policy evaluation stage. This study has provided new evidence on waste generation and disposal delinking, exploiting a rich and up-to-date EU-based data set that allows various analyses of the relative roles of economic drivers in the waste process, including economic drivers, structural socio-economic drivers and policy factors. The core WKC hypothesis was tested and its robustness confirmed by the inclusion of explanatory variables.

First, the results show that in terms of waste generation there is no WKC trend, though elasticity to income drivers appears lower than in the past, pointing to the presence of a current relative delinking. For the EU-10 there are some stronger signs of delinking, although further investigation is needed to provide a more robust validation. There are no landfill or other policy effects that seem to be providing backward incentives for waste prevention, a result that calls for the introduction of waste policies targeted at the sources of waste generation. It confirms the current lack of policy emphasis, at EU level, on landfill diversion.

Second, we provide evidence confirming that landfill and incineration, as expected, are significantly decreasing and increasing respectively, along an endogenous cycle of economic development, but with policy effects driving these trends significantly: the policy dummies linked with EU directives, and the comprehensive policy index we defined, are negatively correlated with landfill waste across specifications. Some additional factors, such as urbanization and population density, among others, appear to be playing a role. In the absence of policy, delinking for landfill seems to be driven by the increasing opportunity and environmental costs associated with waste disposal. As far as incineration dynamics are concerned, they seem to be explained relatively more by R&D, an income-related country-specific factor, rather than by policy levers.

Thus, this study found that there are socio-economic and policy factors that are impacting on waste trends, confirming that EKC analyses cannot rely on an approximate environment–income relationship. It should also be noted that the effects of policy may in part be endogenous in terms of economic indicators, which is particularly relevant in the waste arena.

To sum up, although complete delinking is far from being achieved, especially for waste generation, some positive signals are emerging, with a quite significant role played by EU waste policies implemented in the late 1990s and early 2000s to divert waste away from landfill and towards incineration and recycling. However, the role of other socio-economic and technological factors (R&D) should not be overlooked. Policies interact with socio-economic and economic factors within a scenario of endogenous development in which vicious or virtuous circles drive the performance of countries and regions in relation to waste.

Overall, our evidence supports the claim that, in order to pursue a more sustainable dynamic of waste generation and disposal, the weight of policy actions should be rebalanced towards the former. Although waste prevention at source is at the top of the EU's waste policy agenda, efforts so far have been biased towards disposal and recycling. In addition, only a few countries/regions (Hungary, Italy and the region of Flanders) have implemented physical per capita targets (tonnes/capita) or delinking benchmarks (waste cannot grow more than the share of GDP annually). Waste prevention targets and innovative benchmarking at policy implementation level can all be used to shape waste policies in the future. In the EU framework, country and regional decentralized implementation is playing a major role in achieving overall objectives.

Policies may have contributed to creating and sustaining markets and rents associated with waste management and disposal options, but there is a risk that EU waste policies and the dynamics of the waste system will become locked into some specific actions, with lower weight being assigned to waste prevention activities included as policy principles but never effectively implemented. The current higher costs of such a strategy may work to lower the targeted achievement costs, at all stages of the waste filiere, in the future.

Notes

1 The objectives of the Packaging Directives are fixed in terms of total recovery, including shares of incineration and recycling (EEA 2005).
2 If we include the possibility of waste prevention/reduction through the implementation of *closed loops* strategies in household and production processes, WG can be considered the net output of total waste generated by economic growth, and the proportion integrated in economic processes before collection. Note that, across countries, there is no common legal definition of waste. It is possible that waste flows recovered by closed-loop integration may fall outside some core definitions of waste flows as materials with no value for the economic agents that *produce* them. It is clear that market evolution and the introduction of policy may change the economic notion of waste, which may not be in line with the legal understanding. An example here is the issue of construction and demolition waste: the industry claims and has lobbied for permission to reuse certain materials in the same or nearby construction sites, rather than being forced to dispose of often valuable materials in specific landfills.
3 We may cite among others Powell and Brisson (1995), Miranda *et al.* (2000), Eshet *et al.* (2004), Brisson and Pearce (1995), Dijkgraaf and Vollebergh (2004). Caplan *et al.* (2007) show how economic evaluation techniques can inform the landfill siting process, while Jenkins *et al.* (2004) present a sound and very interesting econometric analyses of the socio-economic factors that explain the level of monetary compensation paid to landfill host communities.

 4 Hereafter we use EU-15 to refer to the group of western EU member countries, EU-25 for the total EU countries after the new entries in 2006, mainly eastern European countries, which we refer to as the EU-10.
 5 The Landfill Directive pursues two approaches: first, to introduce stringent technical requirements for landfills; second, to divert biodegradable municipal waste (BMW) from landfills by setting targets for the landfill of BMW in 2006, 2009 and 2016. Even more ambitious targets for the post-2016 period have been proposed by the European Parliament. The targets are based on the quantity generated in 1995, and the main implication of this approach is that there is an absolute limit placed on the quantity of biodegradable municipal waste (in tonnes) that can be landfilled by the specific target dates (EEA 2007). The Incineration Directive (Directive 2000/76/EC on the Incineration of Waste) is an ancillary and complementary piece of EU waste policy strategy.
 6 To date, the Landfill Directive has been effective in terms of improving waste treatment standards (closing landfills) and increasing capacities of alternative waste treatment. It has had less effect on diversion in Germany and the Flemish region, which embarked on a policy of diversion several years before the directive was adopted, and which are among the initiators/supporters of the Landfill Directive. In the EU-10, EU accession has been a major driver of increased diversion.
 7 We refer to Cole *et al.* (1997), Dinda (2005), Stern (2004), Andreoni and Levinson (2001), Copeland and Taylor (2004) and Galeotti (2007) for major critical surveys and discussion of the theoretical underpinnings of delinking and EKC studies, which so far have analysed air (mainly CO_2) and water emissions, with a limited focus on waste streams. A full critical survey of this vast and growing literature is beyond the scope of this study.
 8 Copeland and Taylor's (2004) seminal paper surveys the literature and presents a model in which sources of growth, increasing returns to abatement, income and threshold effects are the main drivers of EKC.
 9 We define such factors as structural since, with respect to waste trends, they are a set of exogenous potential drivers that are influenced by the historical, institutional and cultural development of the country, and also are relevant to waste management and disposal, influenced by idiosyncratic geographical aspects (population density).
10 Cubic specifications for waste are not conceptually or empirically relevant, and in fact, as expected, they are not significant.
11 This panel data model refers to a baseline fixed effects model (FEM) with fixed effects and time dummies.
12 All analyses are carried out specifying consumption as the main economic driver, since it is the most plausible in waste dynamics, given its strict link with MSW. The results do not change if we use GDP. We took household expenditure (consumption) per capita as the main economic driver, based on the hypothesis that consumption is a better independent variable for waste collection and disposal (Rothman 1998; Jacobsen *et al.* 2004).
13 The model is based on a framework derived from the EKC literature. All variables are specified in logarithmic form, using per capita values, to provide elasticity values and to smooth the data. Except where it is unfeasible, logarithmic transformations are used for all covariates.
14 EIONET is a partnership agency of the EEA and its member countries; it is fundamental to the collection and organization of data for the EEA.
15 Waste generation, incineration and landfill disposal. Waste generation data are measured by waste collection, the observable factor. We do not present the results for recycling (although they are available) because recycling is only calculated as a residual (MSW generation–MSW landfilled–MSW incinerated). Outputs also emerge as a 'residual' with regard to other analyses.

16 These variables are used alternately, given their high correlation.

17 Fredriksson (2000) studies the pros and cons of decentralization versus centralized management options regarding the siting of waste facilities. Decentralized systems are theoretically preferable, although they may have some drawbacks.

18 Thus, in any given year, each country is associated with an index value, where 1 is the maximum potential value (assuming the presence of all the policies considered). We differentiate between the presence of a strategy (low value) and an effective regulatory policy (high value). The latter is assigned a bigger weight (0 for no policy, 1 for strategy only, 2 for a policy). Prominent examples of overall environmental policy performance indices set up, for several countries, based on a synthesis of diverse policy performances, can be found in Eliste and Fredrikkson (1998). Cagatay and Mihci (2006, 2003) provide an index of environmental sensitivity performance for 1990–5, for acidification, climate change, water and even waste management.

19 Though specific waste prevention targets/actions do not exist, (landfill-related) policy variables can be included even at this level of analysis. We can hypothesize that the backward effects of landfill policies and waste management actions on the amounts of MSW generated are not significant. Nevertheless, since our synthetic policy index also captures the variety of waste measures implemented by a country in addition to landfill diversion actions, some effects may emerge.

20 This is not always the case when using policy indexes. Therefore we can exploit both fixed effects and random effects specifications.

21 We decided to exploit data in per capita rather than share terms (percentage of landfilled waste over total waste), given that policy targets are fixed in per capita terms and data are available, and also because of the difficulty involved in coping with fractional variables defined over shares. This would have been an option had the data not been expressed in tonnes per capita terms or been deficient.

22 For landfill diversion and incineration we test two stage regressions, including as a covariate the predicted values for waste generation in specifications (3) and (4), and replacing the economic driver. This accounts for the unchained and consequential nature of waste flows from generation to disposal. Results do not change; the significance of the predicted values reflects the significance of consumption in model (2), with elasticities around unity or even higher.

23 Table 2.4 presents only linear specifications. The overall results are the same for quadratic specifications that do not provide evidence of EKC, except the linear term has a negative coefficient and the quadratic term has a positive one. This is due to the nature of the data, and captures the effect of the low-income countries (Lithuania, Czech Republic, Slovakia, Poland and Slovenia), which registered a reduction in total MSW collected in the period studied. This slight anomaly generates a downwardly sloped relationship between MSW collected and consumption in the first phase. This trend does not appear in the EU-10 and EU-15 sub-samples.

24 This may be interpreted in terms of the (observed even in other contexts) delinking occurring in some east European countries (Hungary among others), which may be driving the general empirical picture. Even the EU-25 quadratic analysis shows a U-shaped curve affected by the delinking occurring in low-income eastern countries. Bluffstone and Deshazo (2003) present a case study of an eastern country process of coping with the challenges of EU waste management regulations.

25 There are no EUROSTAT data on manufacturing share for Greece.

26 Following a hypothesis sometimes tested in the EKC literature (Torras and Boyce 1998), we verified whether income inequality is associated with waste generation. Since inequality is negatively related to income drivers (-0.39), its effect is similar to that of an income driver – the richer and more equal the country the more waste it generates.

27 Although, when implementing a two-stage regression, estimating the fitted values of POLIND in the first stage (covariates URBPOP, C) and using those values as covariates in a second-stage regression with MSW generation as the dependent variable (without C), POLIND emerges with a positive sign. This signals the potential endogeneity of policy commitment with regard to income levels. Where income is higher, generation of MSW is obviously higher, given that there is no delinking evident in the EU, and waste policy actions are stronger/more extensive.

28 The underlying correlation between the dummies for landfill and incineration directives is 0.66.

29 We underline that dealing with socio-economic driver no clear hypothesis is definable. The hypothesis listed in Table 2.2 derives from a survey of economic, sociological, and waste-related discipline studies, and represents the current consensus on the possible links between waste trends and the set of explanatory factors we here capture with great richness. Counter-intuitive not highly expected results may sometime emerge from the presence of idiosyncratic features in specific country or regional situations. We should remember that econometric analysis provides evidence in terms of statistical regularities associated with a defined set of units, in our case countries.

30 The evidence may be driven by the effective good performance of those countries that are experiencing a period of economic growth that began in the late 1990s and is associated with the implementation of environmental policies (a requirement of joining the EU) proposed by the richer EU countries. We could claim that, from a development point of view, the EU-10 countries have more opportunities to be more efficient, at the same level of income, since their growth is embedded in a scenario characterized by a rich set of environmental policies that cannot be avoided, as they (among other aspects) are prerequisites of entry to the EU by those countries.

31 These become positive for the EU-10. This may imply that there is a different influence or level of opportunity cost linked with urbanization. Urbanization in the EU-10 is in its infancy and opportunity costs in terms of land and land prices are 'biting' less than in the EU-15, while scale effects have a negative impact on the environment through landfilling.

32 We would also refer to the *Journal of Environment and Development*, issue March 2008.

33 Recent studies have focused on analysing the drivers of environmental regulation, by defining endogenous factors (Cole *et al.* 2006; Alpay *et al.* 2006). Efforts aimed at setting up environmental policy indices for climate change, waste and other areas show that the developed countries' environmental regulations are more stringent. Consistent with EKC reasoning, policies may emerge endogenously – especially if correlated with income factors on both the supply and demand levels (Cagatay and Mihci 2006). Regarding (paper) waste, there is evidence of higher demand for waste management and environmental policies in the more developed, wealthier countries (Berglund and Soderhol 2003). At the micro level, Callan and Thomas (1999, 2006), who study the drivers of unit pricing adoption at municipal level, provide evidence of policy (economic instrument) endogeneity with regard to demographics, fiscal capacity and socio-economic determinants. Those studies, though showing robust evidence on MSW (policy) drivers, suffer from the cross-sectional and local nature of data that allows limited generalisation.

34 Similar very robust evidence is found in the work on Italy of Mazzanti *et al.* (forthcoming). Italy being in any case quite representative of the EU-15 situation, the result provides further insights into this possible difference between low-income and high-income countries within the EU.

35 Some regressions were carried out using a semi-log model to deal with the large number of zero values. The panels are unbalanced, given that we have missing

values. The semi-log specifications are not shown, but we comment on the results for comparison.
36 The result is an unbalanced panel, since data on Portugal and Finland, for instance, are missing for the years between 1995 and 1998.
37 The somewhat high values of the coefficients in the incineration regression may be driven by the nature of the variable, which is not discrete and shows some substantial jumps from one year to another, at least in this initial phase of expansion. In some countries, sudden changes and breaks in the total figures series occur when a big plant starts up or closes its operations.
38 Even in a two-stage regression as implemented above, the POLIND coefficient vanishes in terms of significance.
39 As anticipated, semi-log specifications for the EU-25 provide the following evidence: consumption levers are associated with weak EKC evidence; and a linear specification presents higher robustness. URBPOP is a driver of incineration, while landfilling, urban and population density favour incineration (Milan, which has closed its landfills and moved to incinerators, and the region of Lombardy). R&D is significant for the two policy factors POLIND and INCDIR.
40 Where the null hypothesis of the test is slope-equal among all individuals.
41 This mean that the slope is free to move among individuals and years.
42 It should be noted that here and below the use of a Kiviet LSDV correction (Kiviet 1995) as an alternative to GMM produces less significant results. See Bruno (2005) for a recent and thoughtful discussion, and comparisons of different dynamic panel models.
43 Which is a sub-specification of POLIND, which is more general: it accounts only for waste strategies related to landfill diversion. In previous regressions LAND-POLIND was not afforded separate comment, given that we observed no differences in terms of its statistical significance. (The correlation is in fact high: 0.81.)

References

Alpay, S., Caliskan, A. and Mahmud, S (2006) 'Environmental policy performance, economic growth and trade liberalization: a cross-country empirical analysis', Ankara: Department of Economics, Bilkent University, mimeo.

Andersen, F., Larsen, H., Skovgaard, M., Moll, S. and Isoard, S. (2007) 'A European model for waste and material flows', *Resources, Conservation and Recycling*, 49 (4): 421–35.

André, F. and Cerda, E. (2004) 'Landfill construction and capacity expansion', *Environmental and Resource Economics*, 28: 409–34.

Andreoni, J. and Levinson, A. (2001) 'The simple analytics of the environmental Kuznets curve', *Journal of Public Economics*, 80 (2): 269–86.

Arellano, M. and Bond, S. (1991) 'Some tests of specification for panel data: Monte Carlo evidence and an application to employment equations', *Review of Economic Studies*, 58: 277–97.

Beede D. and Bloom D. (1995) 'The economics of municipal solid waste', *Land economics*, 71: 57–64.

Berglund, C. and Soderholm, P. (2003) 'An econometric analysis of global waste paper recovery and utilization', *Environmental and Resource Economics*, 26: 429–56.

Berrens R., Bohara, A., Gawande K. and Wang, P. (1998) 'Testing the inverted U hypothesis for US hazardous waste: an application of the generalized gamma model', *Economic Letters*, 55: 435–40.

Bluffstone, R. and Deshazo, J. R. (2003) 'Upgrading municipal environmental services to EU level: a case study of household willingness to pay in Lithuania', *Environment and Development Economics*, 8: 637–54.

Bringezu, S., Schütz, H. and Moll, S. (2003) 'Rationale for and interpretation of economy-wide material flow analysis and derived indicators', *Journal of Industrial Ecology*, 7: 43–64.Brisson, I. and Pearce, D. (1995) 'Benefit Transfer for Disamenity from Waste Disposal', CSERGE Working Paper 6, London: University College London.

Brock, W. and Taylor, S. (2004) 'The Green Solow Model', NBER Working Papers 10557, Cambridge MA: NBER.

Bruno, G. S. F. (2005) 'Approximating the bias of the LSDV estimator for dynamic unbalanced panel data models', *Economics Letters*, 87: 361–6.

Burnley, S. (2001) 'The impact of the European Landfill Directive on waste management in the United Kingdom', *Resources, Conservation and Recycling*, 31: 349–58.

Cagatay, S. and Mihci, H. (2006) 'Degree of environmental stringency and the impact on trade patterns', *Journal of Economic Studies*, 33: 30–51.

——(2003), 'Industrial pollution, environmental suffering and policy measures: an index of environmental sensitivity performance', *Journal of Environmental Assessment Policy and Management*, 5: 205–45.

Callan, S. and Thomas, J. (2006) 'Analyzing demand for disposal and recycling services', *Eastern Economic Journal*, 32: 221–40.

——(1999) 'Adopting a unit pricing system for MSW: policy and socio-economic determinants', *Environmental and Resource Economics*, 14: 503–18.

Caplan, A., Grijalva, T. and Jackson-Smith, D. (2007) 'Using choice question formats to determine compensable values: the case of a landfill-siting process', *Ecological Economics*, 60: 834–46.

Chavas, J. P. (2004) 'On impatience, economic growth and the EKC: a dynamic analysis of resource management', *Environmental and Resource Economics*, 28: 123–52.

Chimeli, A. and Braden, J. (2005) 'Total factor productivity and the environmental Kuznets curve', *Journal of Environmental Economics and Management*, 49: 366–80.

Cole, M. (2005) 'Re-examining the pollution–income relationship: a random coefficients approach', *Economics Bulletin*, 14: 1–7.

Cole, M., Elliott, R. and Fredrikkson, P. (2006) 'Endogenous pollution haves: does FDI influence environmental regulations?' *Scandinavian Journal of Economics*, 108: 157–78.

Cole, M., Rayner, A. and Bates, J. (1997) 'The EKC: an empirical analysis', *Environment and Development Economics*, 2: 401–16.Copeland, B. R. and Taylor, M. S. (2004) 'Trade, growth and the environment', *Journal of Economic Literature*, 42: 7–71.

DEFRA (2005) *A Study to Estimate the Disamenity Costs of Landfill in Great Britain*, London: DEFRA.

DEFRA/DTI (2003) *Sustainable Consumption and Production Indicators*, London: DEFRA.

Dijkgraaf, E. and Vollebergh, H. (2004) 'Burn or bury? A social cost comparison of final waste disposal methods', *Ecological Economics*, 50: 233–47.

Dinda, S. (2005) 'Environmental Kuznets curve hypothesis: a survey', *Ecological Economics*, 49: 431–55.

EEA (2007) *The Road from Landfill to Recycling: Common Destination, Different Routes*, Copenhagen: European Environment Agency.

——(2006) *Market-based Instruments for Environmental Policy in Europe*, Technical report 8/2005, Copenhagen: European Environment Agency.

——(2005) *Effectiveness of Packaging Waste Management Systems in Selected Countries: An EEA Pilot Study*, EEA report 3/2005, Copenhagen: European Environment Agency.

——(2003a) *Evaluation Analysis of the Implementation of the Packaging Directive*, Copenhagen: European Environment Agency.

——(2003b), *Assessment of Information related to Waste and Material Flows*, Copenhagen: European Environment Agency.

——(2003c), *Europe's Environment: The Third Assessment*, Copenhagen: European Environment Agency.

El-Fadel, M., Findikakis, A. and Leckie, J. (1997) 'Environmental impacts of solid waste landfill', *Journal of Environmental Management*, 50: 1–25.

Eliste, P. and Fredrikkson, P. G. (1998) 'Does Open Trade result in a Race to the Bottom? Cross-country Evidence', Washington DC: World Bank, mimeo.

Eshet, T., Ayalon, O. and Shechter, M. (2004) 'A Meta-analysis of Waste Management Externalities: A Comparative Study of Economic and Non-economic Valuation Methods', Haifa: Israel, mimeo.

ETC/RWM (2007) 'Environmental Outlooks: Municipal Waste', Working Paper 1/2007, Copenhagen: European Topic Centre on Resource and Waste Management.

European Commission (2003a) *Towards a Thematic Strategy for Waste Prevention and Recycling*, COM (2003) 301, Brussels: European Commission.

——(2003b) *Towards a Thematic Strategy on Sustainable Use of Natural Resources*, COM (2003) 572, Brussels: European Commission.

Eurostat (2003) *Waste Generated and Treated in Europe: Data 1990–2001*, Luxembourg: Office for Official Publications of the European Communities.

Ferrara, I. and Missios, P. (2005) 'Recycling and waste diversion effectiveness: evidence from Canada', *Environmental and Resource Economics*, 30: 221–38.

Fischer Kowalski, M. and Amann, C. (2001) 'Beyond IPAT and Kuznets curves: globalization as a vital factor in analyzing the environmental impact of socioeconomic metabolism', *Population and the Environment*, 23: 7–47.

Fredriksson, P. (2000) 'The siting of hazardous waste facilities in federal systems', *Environmental and Resource Economics*, 15: 75–87.

Galeotti, M. (2007) 'Economic growth and the quality of the environment: taking stock', *Environment, Development and Sustainability*, 4: 427–54.

Gallagher, L., Ferreira, S. and Convery, F. (2008) 'Host community attitudes towards solid waste infrastructures: comprehension before compensation', *Journal of Environmental Planning and Management*, 51: 233–57.

Garrod, G. and Willis, K. (1998) 'Estimating lost amenity due to landfill waste disposal', *Resources, Conservation and Recycling*, 22: 83–95.

Gawande, K., Berrens, R. and Bohara, A. (2001) 'A consumption-based theory of the WKC', *Ecological Economics*, 37: 101–12.

Grossman, G. M. and Krueger, A. B. (1994) 'Economic Growth and the Environment', NBER Working Papers 4634, Cambridge MA: NBER.

Harbaugh, W., Levinson, A. and Wilson, D. (2002) 'Re-examining the empirical evidence for an environmental Kuznets curve', *Review of Economics and Statistics*, 84: 541–51.

Highfill, J. and McCasey, M. (2001) 'Landfill versus "backstop" recycling when income is growing', *Environmental and Resource Economics*, 19: 37–52.

Holtz-Eakin, D. and Selden, T. M. (1992) 'Stoking the Fires? CO_2 Emissions and Economic Growth', NBER Working Papers 4248, Cambridge MA: NBER.

Huhtala, A. (1997) 'A post-consumer waste management model for determining optimal levels of recycling and landfill', *Environmental and Resource Economics*, 10: 310–14.

IVM (2005) *Effectiveness of Landfill Taxation*, IVM Institute of Environmental Studies, Amsterdam: Vrije Universiteit.

Jacobsen, H., Mazzanti, M., Moll, S., Simeone, M. G., Pontoglio, S. and Zoboli, R. (2004) *Methodology and Indicators to measure Decoupling, Resource Efficiency, and Waste Prevention*, ETC/WMF, P6.2–2004, Copenhagen: European Topic Centre on Waste and Material Flows and European Environment Agency.

Jenkins, R., Maguire, K. and Morgan, C. (2004) 'Host community compensation and municipal solid waste landfills', *Land Economics*, 80: 513–28.

Johnstone, N. and Labonne, J. (2004) 'Generation of household solid waste in OECD countries: an empirical analysis using macroeconomic data', *Land Economics*, 80: 529–38.

Karousakis, K. (2006) 'MSW Generation, Disposal and Recycling: A Note on OECD Inter-country Differences', paper presented at Envecon 2006, Applied Environmental Economics conference, 24 March, London: Royal Society.

Kiviet, J. F. (1995) 'On bias, inconsistency and efficiency of various estimators in dynamic panel data models', *Journal of Econometrics*, 68: 53–78.

Lang, J. C. (2005) 'Zero landfill zero waste: the greening of industry in Singapore', *International Journal of Environment and Sustainable Development*, 4: 331–51.

Leigh, R. (2004) 'Economic growth as environmental policy? Reconsidering the environmental Kuznets curve', *Journal of Public Policy*, 24: 27–48.

Lieb, C. M. (2004) 'The environmental Kuznets curve and flow versus stock pollution: the neglect of future damages', *Environmental and Resource Economics*, 29 (4): 483–506.

Martin, A. and Scott, I. (2003) 'The effectiveness of the UK landfill tax', *Journal of Environmental Planning and Management*, 46: 673–89

Mazzanti, M. (2008) 'Is waste generation delinking from economic growth?' *Applied Economics Letters*, 15: 287–91.

Mazzanti, M., Montini, A. and Zoboli, R. (forthcoming) 'Waste generation, economic drivers, and the EKC hypothesis', *Applied Economics Letters*.

Mazzanti, M. and Zoboli, R. (2006) 'Economic instruments and induced innovation: the European Directive on End-of-life Vehicles', *Ecological Economics*, 58: 318–37.

Mazzanti M., Musolesi, A. and Zoboli, R. (forthcoming) 'A panel data heterogeneous Bayesian estimation of environmental Kuznets curves for CO_2 emissions, *Applied Economics*.

Miranda, M. L., Miller, J. and Jacobs, T. (2000) 'Talking trash about landfills: using quantitative scoring schemes in landfill siting processes', *Journal of Policy Analysis and Management*, 19: 3–22.

Morris, J., Phillips, P. and Read, A. (1998) 'The UK landfill tax: an analysis of its contribution to sustainable waste management', *Resources, Conservation and Recycling*, 23: 259–70.

OECD (2002) *Indicators to measure Decoupling of Environmental Pressure from Economic Growth*, Paris: OECD.

Ozawa, T. (2005) 'Hotelling rule and the landfill exhaustion problem: case of Tokyo city', *Studies in Regional Science*, 35: 215–30.

Pearce, D. W. (2004) 'Does European Union waste policy pass a cost–benefit test?' *World Economics*, 15: 115–37

Powell, J. and Brisson, I. (1995) 'Benefit transfer for disamenity from waste disposal', CSERGE working paper, London: University College London.

Price, J. (2001) 'The landfill directive and the challenge ahead: demands and pressures on the UK householder', *Resources, Conservation and Recycling*, 32: 333–48

Rothman, D. (1998) 'WKC, real progress or passing the buck? A case for consumption-based approaches', *Ecological Economics*, 25: 177–94.

Seppala, T., Haukioja, T. and Kaivo-Oja, J. (2001) 'The EKC hypothesis does not hold for direct material flows: EKC hypothesis tests for DMF in four industrial countries', *Population and the Environment*, 23: 217–38.

Stern, D. (1998) 'Progress on the environmental Kuznets curve?' *Environment and Development Economics*, 3: 173–96.

——(2004) 'The rise and fall of the environmental Kuznets curve', *World Development*, 32: 1419–38.

Sterner, T. and Bartelings, H. (1999) 'Household waste management in a Swedish municipality: determinants of waste disposal, recycling and composting', *Environmental and Resource Economics*, 13: 473–91.

Swamy, P. A. (1970) 'Efficient inference in a random coefficient regression model', *Econometrica*, 38: 311–23.

Taseli, B. (2007) 'The impact of the European Landfill Directive on waste management strategy and current legislation in Turkey's specially protected areas', *Resources, Conservation and Recycling*, 52: 119–35.

Torras, M. and Boyce, J. (1998) 'Income, inequality and pollution: a reassessment of the environmental Kuznets curve', *Ecological Economics*, 25: 147–60.

Vollebergh, H. and Kemfert, C. (2005) 'The role of technological change for a sustainable development', *Ecological Economics*, 54: 133–47.

Wang, P., Bohara, A., Berrens, R. and Gawande, K. (1998) 'A risk-based environmental Kuznets curve for US hazardous waste sites', *Applied Economics Letters*, 5: 761–3.

World Bank (1992) *Development and the Environment*, World Bank report, Oxford: Oxford University Press.

Yang, H. L. and Innes, R. (2007) 'Economic incentives and residential waste management in Taiwan: an empirical investigation', *Environmental and Resource Economics*, 37: 489–519.

3 Municipal waste generation, management and greenhouse gas emissions

Frits Møller Andersen, Mette Skovgaard and Helge Larsen

The increase in municipal waste generation and the environmental effects of waste management have led to the development of an extensive European Union (EU) waste policy. One of the overall aims of the Sixth Environmental Action Programme (EAP) (2002–12) is to decouple the use of resources and the generation of waste from the rate of economic growth, and to significantly reduce the volume (i) of waste generated and (ii) of waste disposal. The EU Landfill Directive (1999/31/EC), which aims to reduce the negative environmental effects of waste disposal, sets long-term targets for landfilled biodegradable municipal waste (BMW). In 2007 greenhouse gas (GHG) emissions from the landfill of BMW accounted for 2.6 per cent of total GHG emissions in the EU-15 (EEA 2007).

Andersen *et al.* (2007) presented a European model for waste and material flows, linking amounts of waste to the development of economic activities, based on analyses of past trends. Using an updated version of this model, and incorporating projections for economic development based on a scenario developed for DG TREN (European Commission 2006), we estimate municipal waste generation from 2005 to 2020. The estimation of the model is based on Eurostat data on municipal waste generation, and economic and socio-economic data for the period 1995 to 2006.

In this chapter we present a baseline scenario for the management of municipal waste in the EU, and an outlook for meeting the targets of the Landfill Directive for BMW. We also estimate GHG emissions from the management of waste. GHG emissions from landfills are mainly methane (CH_4), which is produced by the fermentation of the biodegradable parts of the waste. The Intergovernmental Panel on Climate Change guidelines (IPCC 2006) are used to calculate GHG emissions from landfills. The methodology for the estimation of GHG emissions is based on Skovgaard *et al.* (2008).

Next section presents the model equations and then we summarize the results of the estimations for municipal waste generation. A description of European waste policy and municipal waste management for the period 1995–2006 follows. Then we present some assumptions related to the calculation of GHG emissions and baseline projections for municipal waste, waste management and GHG emissions. The final section provides a short summary and conclusions.

A model for waste generation

The Projection of European Waste Amounts (PEWA) model for the generation of six waste streams in the 27 EU member states was developed on the basis of econometric analyses of past developments. The model links categories of waste to economic and socio-economic variables. Omitting country and waste indices, a general equation for the generation of waste can be written as:

$$(1) \log(w) = \alpha_0 + \alpha_1 \cdot \log(A) + \alpha_2 \cdot \log(P) + \tau \cdot T + \delta \cdot D$$

where w is a waste stream, A is an economic activity, P represents socio-economic variables such as population or number of households, T is time, D represents dummy variables, and lower case letters are equation parameters that are estimated or determined *a priori*.

If the amount of a given waste stream is related to different economic activities – for example, glass for recycling may come from domestic sources and from manufacturers of glass containers (two economic activities A_1 and A_2) – a weighting for these activities is included as $(\log(A) = s \cdot \log(A_1) + (1 - s) \cdot \log(A_2)$. If the amount of waste generated by each of the activities is known, the weighting (s) can be set *a priori*. Alternatively, an implicit weighting of activities can be estimated.

Equation (1) indicates that if the economic activity increases by 1 per cent, the waste generated will increase by α_1 per cent. If the socio-economic variable increases by 1 per cent, waste increases by α_2 per cent, and annually the amount of waste increases by τ per cent. δ represents shifts in the amount of waste, and is included mainly to correct for breaks in the data or statistical outliers.

For individual waste streams the choices of economic activity and socio-economic variables are based on theoretical considerations, and a number of parameter restrictions may be imposed due to empirical problems. As a result of multicollinearity between explanatory variables, it is not always possible to obtain reasonable unrestricted estimations of α_1, α_2 and τ. Restricting $\alpha_1 = 1$ and $\alpha_2 = 0$ equation (1) reduces to a trendwise change in the waste coefficient, that is, the amount of waste per economic activity changes annually by τ per cent. Restricting $\alpha_1 = 0$ and $\alpha_2 = 1$, equation (1) reduces to a trendwise change in the waste per socio-economic variable, for example number of households. Restricting $\alpha_2 = (1 - \alpha_1)$, equation (1) reduces to:

$$(2) \log\left(\frac{w}{P}\right) = \alpha_0 + \alpha_1 \cdot \log\left(\frac{A}{P}\right) + \tau \cdot T + \delta \cdot D$$

that is, the amount of waste per capita or number of households is related to economic activity per capita or number of households. Finally, restricting $\alpha_1 = 1$, $\alpha_2 = 0$ and $\tau = 0$, equation (1) reduces to an assumption of constant waste coefficients. This assumption is imposed in many macro-economic analyses of waste generation, for example Brunvoll and Ibenholt (1997), which develops a model for waste generation by Norwegian manufacturing, and also Andersen *et al.* (1998) and Andersen and Larsen (2006), who describe models of waste generation in Denmark.

Estimation results for MSW

Figures for private consumption, population and number of households are from Eurostat. Data on generation of municipal waste are taken from the Structural Indicators published by Eurostat. Time series for municipal waste are available for each country for the period 1995 to 2006. For most countries, this is also the case with economic and socio-economic figures. However, for some countries not all statistics are available, which limits the choice of explanatory variables.

We assume that the economic activity driving the generation of municipal waste is private consumption. More specifically, we expect the three household consumption categories of food (01), beverages (02) and clothing and footwear (03), will be the main drivers. Thus the economic activity variable in equation (1) is private consumption in categories 01–03. Although other categories of private consumption also contribute to the generation of municipal waste, for some countries detailed consumption statistics are not available and in those cases total private consumption is used as the activity variable.

In terms of socio-economic variables, municipal waste is mainly related to the number of households. The number of members in a household does affect the generation of municipal waste, but, for many waste fractions, additional household members add only marginally to the waste generated. For example, the amounts of food and packaging waste from a household comprising four persons are not much larger than the amounts generated by a household of only two persons. Thus the socio-economic variable in equation (1) in most cases is number of households. For a few countries we do not have complete data on number of households; in those cases we use population. Both number of households and population were tested for equation (1) and, overall, number of households provided better estimates. The main difference from including number of households or population in equation (1) is a decrease in the size of the trend coefficient (τ). Historically, household size has shown a decreasing trend, that is, number of households has increased more than population.

The estimation results for the equations chosen for the model are presented in Tables 3.1 and 3.2 and expose some estimation problems. The equations explain most of the changes in the amounts of municipal waste,

Table 3.1 Model parameters for municipal waste generation, EU–15

Country	No of obs.	Act. Var.	Constant α_0	Activity α_1	Household α_2	Trend τ	Dummy δ	Dummy δ_1	R^2	DW
AT	12	detail	-1.809 (2.44)	0.359 (1.04)	$1-\alpha_1$	0.014 (0.004)	-0.157 (0.03)		0.96	1.04
BE	12	detail	-0.757 (0.25)	0.462 (0.13)	$1-\alpha_1$		-0.036 (0.02)		0.83	1.89
DE	12	detail	-0.681 (0.39)	1	–	-0.009 (0.004)	0.008 (0.03)	0.050 (0.02)	0.87	1.55
DK	12	detail	-1.739 (0.51)	0.531 (0.52)	$1-\alpha_1$	0.011 (0.009)	-0.044 (0.04)		0.94	2.58
FI	12	detail	-0.775 (0.38)	0.423 (0.20)	$1-\alpha_1$		0.104 (0.02)		0.86	0.88
FR	12	detail	-2.559 (0.09)	1	–	0.009 (0.001)			0.98	1.59
ES	12	detail	-0.054 (0.55)	1	–	-0.011 (0.005)	-0.134 (0.04)		0.89	1.30
GR	12	detail	-1.724 (0.85)	0.977 (0.44)	–	–	-0.157 (0.05)		0.92	1.42
IE	12	detail /pop	-0.932 (0.15)	0.633 (0.15)	$1-\alpha_1$	–	-0.170 (0.03)		0.98	1.85
IT	12	detail	-1.658	0.488	$1-\alpha_1$	0.010	0.008		0.97	2.14

(Continued on next page)

Table 3.1 (continued)

Country	No of obs.	Act. Var.	Constant α_0	Activity α_1	Household α_2	Trend τ	Dummy δ	Dummy δ_1	R^2	DW
LU	12	detail	-1.253 (0.39)	0.271 (0.13)	$1-\alpha_1$	0.011 (0.003)	(0.02)		0.94	1.63
NL	14	detail	-1.395 (0.23)	0.942 (0.13)	$1-\alpha_1$				0.96	1.51
PT	9	detail	-1.131 (0.19)	0.777 (0.11)	$1-\alpha_1$		0.075 (0.02)		0.97	1.23
SE	12	detail	-1.181 (0.37)	0.648 (0.21)	$1-\alpha_1$		-0.104 (0.02)		0.95	1.88
UK	12	detail	-0.337 (0.22)	0.348 (0.12)	–		-0.021 (0.04)	0.050 (0.02)	0.97	1.22

Note: Standard errors in brackets.

Table 3.2 Model parameters for generation of municipal waste: EU–12

Country	No of obs.	Act. Var.	Constant a_0	Activity a_1	Household a_2	Trend τ	Dummy δ	Dummy δ_1	R^2	DW
BG no act data	12	pop	0.826 (0.59)	—	1	-0.015 (0.006)	0.160 (0.05)		0.93	1.26
CY	12	aggr. pop	-2.310 (0.33)	0.844 (0.14)	$1-\alpha_1$				0.93	1.00
CZ	12	detail	-0.697 (0.17)	0.413 (0.19)	$1-\alpha_1$		0.216 (0.02)		0.87	2.32
EE	12	detail	-0.28 (0.11)	0.50 (0.14)	$1-\alpha_1$		0.11 (0.05)		0.63	1.80
HU	12	aggr.	-0.086 (0.17)	0.149 (0.09)	$1-\alpha_1$		0.107 (0.03)	0.015 (0.02)	0.87	2.25
HU^alt.	*12*	*aggr.*	*0.664 (0.96)*	*1*	*—*	*-0.023 (0.009)*	*0.212 (0.08)*	*0.047 (0.04)*	*0.43*	*1.43*
LT	11	aggr.	-0.256 (0.22)	0.197 (0.13)	$1-\alpha_1$		0.303 (0.07)	0.098 (0.04)	0.90	2.44
LV	7	aggr.	-1.712 (0.16)	0.908 (0.27)	$1-\alpha_1$		0.211 (0.10)		0.71	0.92
MT	12	aggr.	-5.661 (0.32)	0.578 (0.21)	$1-\alpha_1$	0.045 (0.007)	-0.171 (0.03)		0.99	2.70
PL	12	aggr.	-0.869 (0.29)	0.300 (0.14)	$1-\alpha_1$		0.295 (0.04)	0.142 (0.03)	0.91	2.58
PL^alt.	*12*	*aggr.*	*2.166 (1.16)*	*1*	*—*	*-0.035 (0.01)*	*0.297 (0.09)*	*0.097 (0.06)*	*0.80*	*2.31*
SI	12	detail	1.865 (1.07)	1	—	-0.032 (0.01)	0.231 (0.07)	0.071 (0.07)	0.91	1.14
SK	10	detail	-1.936 (0.51)	0.529 (0.29)	$1-\alpha_1$	0.014 (0.005)	-0.010 (0.05)		0.77	1.16
RO	8	aggr.	-0.416 (0.18)	0.367 (0.14)	—		0.100 (0.06)		0.55	2.89

Note: Standard errors in brackets.

with R^2 values above 0.9. However, for some countries, the Durbin–Watson (DW) statistic reveals considerable autocorrelation. The DW statistic central value is 2.0, and varies between 0 and 4. Extreme values of the DW statistic indicate a misspecified model. Low values indicate a missing long-term explanatory variable, and high values indicate that the equation does not explain short-term variations. For our projections, very low values of the DW statistic are especially problematic.

In the equations and estimated coefficients (standard errors in brackets), for the 15 old member states, the EU-15, detailed activity (private consumption of food, beverages, clothing and footwear) and (with the exception of Ireland) number of households are used as the explanatory variables. For Ireland, data on households are available only for 1998–2007; therefore we preferred to use population rather than number of households for our estimates. For most EU-15 countries the restriction $\alpha_2 = (1 - \alpha_1)$ is accepted. That is, the amount of waste per household is explained by the categories of private consumption per household. For many countries, the coefficient of the activity variable is considerably lower than 1.0^1 and, in general, the assumption of constant waste coefficients is not supported by the estimations. For Germany, France and Spain the coefficient of the activity variable was restricted to 1.0, but for different reasons. For Germany, private consumption is almost constant, while for France it develops almost trendwise – implying multicollinearity with the trend variable. For Germany and France, free estimation of α_1 with $\tau = 0$ gives an estimate of α_1 close to 1, and for France also a very low DW statistic. Including a trend in the equation implies an α_1 close to zero. Therefore, restricting $\alpha_1 = 1$ and estimating τ appears a reasonable solution. For Spain, free estimation gives an α_1 coefficient considerably larger than 1, which is difficult to interpret. Nevertheless, the assumption of constant waste coefficients is not supported, as we find significant coefficients related to the time trend. That is, waste coefficients show trendwise changes.

For the 12 new EU member states (EU-12) data are more incomplete, which raises a number of estimation problems. For Bulgaria and Cyprus, data on number of households are available only for 1999–2006; thus we use population as the socio-economic variable. Also there are no data on private consumption for Bulgaria, which implies that the equation reduces to a trendwise change in municipal waste per capita.

For most of the other new member states, total private consumption is chosen as the activity variable, and the restriction $\alpha_2 = (1 - \alpha_1)$ is imposed. For most of these countries the estimated trend coefficient is not significant, and in the chosen equation the restriction $\tau = 0$ is imposed. For some countries the estimated α_1 is quite low, implying that the projected growth in waste generation is very low. For Hungary and Poland, two large countries that are responsible for most of the municipal waste in the EU-12, the estimated coefficient of total private consumption is below 0.3. As an alternative, restricting $\alpha_1 = 1$ and estimating τ the coefficient of the trend becomes negative and fairly large, and the R^2 value decreases considerably. For the projections reported later, choosing between the two formulations of the equation is quite important, as we assume that past trends are phased out over the years.

In summary, because data for the EU-12 are limited, we frequently chose to use aggregated activity variables. The estimation results for the EU-12 are also more uncertain than those for the EU-15. Nevertheless, the assumption of constant waste coefficients is not supported by the data.

European waste policy and management of MSW

Landfill has been the most common waste treatment for decades, despite its numerous negative effects on the environment. One of these effects is the emission of CH_4 from the organic content of the waste, which contributes to global warming. Other negative effects of landfill relate to the loss of raw materials which could have been recycled and used as secondary materials or used to produce energy.

The Sixth EAP sets out the key environmental objectives for 2002–12. The EAP aims at decoupling use of resources and generation of waste from the rate of the economic growth, and at a significant reduction in the volumes of waste generated and waste going for disposal.

The Landfill Directive (1999/31/EC) goes further by setting stringent operational and technical requirements for waste and landfills, to prevent, as far as is possible, their negative environmental effects. Among the provisions of this directive is a set of targets for landfill of BMW: by 2006 to reduce the amount of landfilled BMW to 75 per cent of the BMW generated in 1995; by 2009 to reduce the amount of landfilled BMW to 50 per cent of the BMW generated in 1995, and by 2016 to reduce the amount of landfilled BMW to 35 per cent of the BMW generated in 1995. Countries that have landfilled more than 80 per cent of their BMW can extend these target dates by four years. The main implication of this directive is that an absolute limit is being placed on the quantity of BMW (in tonnes) that can be landfilled, at specific target dates. Thus, if BMW quantities continue to grow, increasing quantities will need to be diverted from landfill.

The Landfill Directive, along with other directives, such as the 1994 Packaging and Packaging Waste Directive (94/62/EC) which sets targets on the recycling and recovery of packaging waste, are expected to have a considerable influence on the management of municipal waste. The effects of the existing European and national waste policies are already visible. Figure 3.1 shows that the landfill of municipal waste in the EU-27 decreased from 62 per cent in 1995 to 41 per cent in 2006. Moreover, the EU is in the process of revising the Waste Framework Directive (75/442/EEC) and one of the outcomes from the process is a target to recycle 50 per cent of glass, paper, metal and plastic waste from households or other origins by 2020. The measures should lead to a further diversion from landfill.

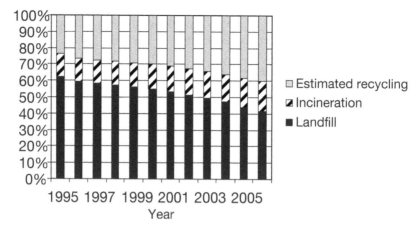

Figure 3.1 Developments in the management of municipal waste: EU-27, 1995–2006

To estimate the future management of municipal waste in our baseline scenario we assessed likely development in each of the 27 countries (EU-15 plus EU-12), based on past developments and to a degree on the targets for BMW in the Landfill Directive. This produces a landfill rate of 26 per cent for the EU-27 in 2020. Of this, 23 per cent will be incinerated and 51 per cent will be recycled. In other words, we assume between 2006 and 2020 an additional 15 per cent of municipal waste will be diverted away from landfill.

The Structural Indicators published by Eurostat include landfill and incineration of municipal waste, but not recycling or recovery. Thus we calculated the quantity of waste that goes for recycling as the residual amount when landfilled and incinerated waste is subtracted from total waste. This may lead to an overestimate of waste recycling, as it includes treatment options not classified as recycling, and options that result in landfill of a substantial proportion of treated waste (e.g. mechanical-biological treatment).

Estimation of GHG emissions from MSW management

The IPCC (2006) provides guidelines on how to estimate GHG emissions from landfill and incineration. The EU member states use these guidelines for their annual reporting to the UN Secretariat for Climate Change as part of their commitment to the UN Framework Convention on Climate Change (UNFCCC) and the Kyoto Protocol.

GHG emissions from the waste sector include carbon dioxide (CO_2), nitrous oxide (N_2O) and CH_4. The results are presented in CO_2 equivalents to enable comparison of the various emissions. The factors used to calculate CO_2 equivalents are: 1 for CO_2, 25 for CH_4 (the global warming potential of one tonne of CH_4 is 25 times higher than for one tonne of CO_2), and 298 for N_2O.

The IPCC guidelines include a series of technical parameters for landfills and incinerators. Countries can choose whether to apply these default values or country-specific values. Generally, we use the data reported by member states for the estimation of GHG from landfill and incineration.

However, for recovery of CH_4 from landfill, rates vary greatly among countries; we use the default value suggested by the IPCC, which implies maximum recovery of 20 per cent. In order to estimate CH_4 emissions from landfill, countries can choose between two methods. The Tier 1 method is time-independent, and CH_4 emissions are assumed to occur in the same year as the waste is landfilled. The Tier 2 method involves the calculation of CH_4 emissions over time and takes into account that fractions of waste decay at different rates (e.g. food waste decays faster than wood waste). The Tier 2 method implies that every tonne of biodegradable waste will continue to emit methane over a period of time after it has been landfilled. According to the IPCC guidelines, the Tier 2 method is considered good practice; thus we use it for our estimations.

Emissions from landfill and incineration of waste are calculated on the basis of a carbon mass balance, that is, they depend on the composition of the waste. In the case of landfilled waste, the higher the biodegradable content the higher will be the CH_4 emissions. Biodegradable waste includes food and garden waste, paper and cardboard, wood and some textiles (cotton). Waste streams such as glass and metal are inert, so their landfill or incineration does not contribute to CH_4 or GHG emissions. The annual reports to the UN Secretariat include the composition of waste.

However, for several countries these reports do not include information on the amount of wood or of some textiles. In these estimates (unlike those in Skovgaard *et al.* 2008), the composition of waste for these countries has been manipulated to include 2 per cent wood and 2 per cent textiles. Also, the recycling of waste fractions is calculated on the basis of the composition of the municipal waste generated, while landfill and incineration are calculated on the composition of the residual waste, that is, after deduction of the fractions going to recycling. Table 3.3 presents the composition of waste in 2005. When reporting to the UNFCCC most countries (but not all) use the same waste composition over time.

To estimate the level of emissions from recycling we used a combination of life-cycle data collected in a study by Villanueva *et al.* (2006) of the environmental impacts of treatment of specific waste streams, and data from Danish and European life-cycle assessment databases. The type of recycling depends on the waste fraction, for example we assumed that 40 per cent of food and garden waste is composted in a closed reactor, 40 per cent is composted in an open reactor and 20 per cent is treated by anaerobic digestion.

Table 3.3 Composition of municipal waste, 2005 (%)

Country	Food waste	Garden waste	Paper waste	Wood waste	Textile waste	Plastics waste	Inert/other waste
Austria	31	0	18	3	8	19	21
Belgium	40	0	18	2	2	4	34
Bulgaria	40	0	10	2	4	12	32
Czech Republic	50	0	8	2	2	4	35
Denmark	33	0	21	13	3	8	22
Estonia	30	0	22	8	6	6	28
Finland	37	7	27	7	1	6	16
France	29	0	25	2	2	11	31
Germany	55	0	18	2	3	5	18
Greece	53	0	17	2	2	10	16
Hungary	34	0	17	2	4	12	31
Ireland	26	0	32	8	6	11	17
Italy	39	0	28	2	5	15	11
Latvia	46	0	16	2	3	15	19
Lithuania	46	0	16	2	3	15	19
Luxembourg	44	0	19	2	2	5	28
Malta	39	0	28	2	5	15	11
Netherlands	38	0	16	10	2	15	19
Poland	46	0	16	2	3	15	19
Portugal	46	0	24	2	3	11	14
Romania	51	0	11	2	5	10	21
Slovakia	37	0	15	2	4	8	35
Slovenia	30	0	12	5	2	5	46
Spain	44	0	21	2	5	11	17
Sweden	53	0	25	1	5	10	7
UK	31	0	30	2	2	13	24

Source: Based on member states' annual reports to UNFCCC (national inventory report or common reporting format), OECD (2001, 2007) and authors' assumptions.

In order to estimate the benefits of recycling and incineration for energy recovery, we included indirect effects. Whereas the direct effects arise from the landfill site, the incineration plant or the recycling facility, indirect effects emerge when recycled materials substitute for raw materials production or when the energy produced at the incineration plant substitutes for fossil fuel energy production. These indirect effects were estimated on the basis of life-cycle data, using the same sources as for recycling.

For a detailed presentation of the assumptions in our estimate of GHG see Skovgaard *et al.* (2008).

A baseline projection for municipal waste

We used the economic and socio-economic variables from a baseline projection developed for DG TREN (European Commission 2006) and the model parameters presented in Tables 3.1 and 3.2, to project the amount of municipal waste generated up to 2020. Key economic and socio-economic assumptions for the baseline scenario are presented in Table 3.4. In 2005–20 the total population of the 27 EU member states is expected to increase by 7 million. This can be broken down into an increase of 11 million persons in the EU-15 and a decrease of 5 million in the EU-12 countries. Combined with a general decrease in household size for both the old and new member states, this will cause the number of households to increase, with the largest increases occurring in the EU-15. Economic growth is expected to continue at almost the same rate as in the period 2000–5. However, the expected annual increase in GDP of around 4 per cent in the EU-12 means that economic growth will be considerably larger for those countries than for the EU-15. That is, per capita income is expected to increase considerably in the new member states.

Figure 3.2 projects the development of municipal waste for the EU-27; figures for 2005 and 2020 are presented in Table 3.5. In these projections the estimated trend (parameter τ in Tables 3.1 and 3.2) is phased out over five years. Over the past 10 years, waste collection systems in many countries have expanded to cover more households and more waste fractions, implying a positive trend coefficient and that more waste has been collected. This is not expected to continue in the long term. For countries where the activity coefficient is restricted to 1.0, the estimated trend coefficient becomes negative, reflecting the fact that in the past municipal waste has increased less than private consumption.

Table 3.4 Key economic and socio–economic assumptions

	EU–15			New EU–12			EU–27		
	2005	*2010*	*2020*	*2005*	*2010*	*2020*	*2005*	*2010*	*2020*
Population (million)	386	391	397	104	102	99	489	493	496
Households (million)	163	175	190	36	39	39	199	214	229
Average household size (persons)	2.4	2.2	2.1	2.9	2.6	2.5	2.5	2.3	2.2

	Annual % change								
	00–05	*05–10*	*10–20*	*00–05*	*05–10*	*10–20*	*00–05*	*05–10*	*10–20*
Gross Domestic Product	2.0	1.9	2.1	4.8	3.8	4.3	2.2	2.0	2.3
Household expenditure	2.0	1.8	2.0	5.0	4.0	4.2	2.1	1.9	2.2

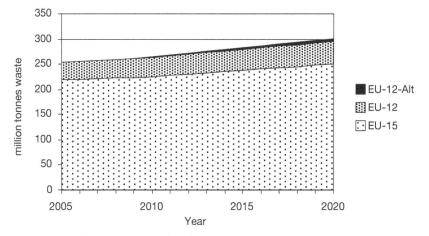

Figure 3.2 Developments in municipal waste: EU-27

From 2005 to 2020 the amount of municipal waste in the EU-27 is projected to increase by around 17 per cent with an increase of 15 per cent in the EU-15 and a much larger increase in the EU-12 of about 29 per cent. In other words, based on the expected economic growth in the new member states, municipal waste will increase more than in the EU-15. Nevertheless, relative to the total amount of municipal waste generated in the EU, the EU-12 accounts for only some 15 per cent of the total.

If we apply the alternative model parameters for Hungary and Poland in Table 3.2 (EU-12-Alt in Figure 3.2) the growth in the amount of waste generated by the new member states is slightly higher, 47 per cent from 2005 to 2020. Although this gives a somewhat different projection for Hungary and Poland, considered in relation to the total amount of municipal waste in EU-27 the change is not very important.

Table 3.5 shows that there are considerable differences in municipal waste per capita between the EU-15 and the EU-12. In 2005 the amount of municipal waste per capita was 562 kg in the EU-15 and 334 kg, or 40 per cent less, in the EU-12. The higher economic growth in the new member states leads to a bigger increase in waste generation per capita compared with the EU-15, but by 2020 waste generation per capita in the EU-12 is still estimated to be lower than in the EU-15 (629 kg per capita in EU-15 and 450 kg per capita in the EU-12). If we compare growth rates for the EU-12 and the EU-15, the change in waste generation per capita in the EU-12 is larger than the growth in the total amount, while the reverse applies to the EU-15. This is due to the decreasing population in the EU-12 and the increased population in the EU-15.

Our results show considerable relative decoupling of waste generation from economic development for both the EU-15 and the EU-12. For the

Table 3.5 Projected changes in municipal waste, population and private consumption, EU−27

	2005	2020	% change 2005−20	% change p.a.
EU−12				
Municipal waste (000 t)	34,596	44,530	29	1.70
Population (000)	103,525	98,951	−4	−0.30
Waste per capita (t)	0.334	0.450	35	2.00
Total final consumption (€ million)	544,193	1,073,719	97	4.63
Waste per total final cons. (t/€ million)	63.6	41.5	−35	−2.81
EU−15				
Municipal waste (000 t)	216,900	250,175	15	0.96
Population (000)	385,686	397,458	3	0.20
Waste per capita (t)	0.562	0.629	12	0.75
Total final consumption (€ million)	4,740,358	6,070,857	28	1.66
Waste per total final cons. (t/€ million)	45.8	41.2	−10	−0.70
EU−27				
Municipal waste (000 t)	251,496	294,705	17	1.06
Population (000)	489,211	496,408	1	0.10
Waste per capita (t)	0.514	0.594	15	0.96
Total final consumption (€ million)	5,284,551	7,144,576	35	2.03
Waste per total final cons. (t/€ million)	47.6	41.2	−13	−0.95

EU-15, the amount of waste per million euros in final consumption decreases by 10 per cent between 2005 and 2020. For the EU-12 the decrease is 35 per cent.

The management of municipal waste is shown in Figure 3.3. Diversion of waste away from landfill is expected to continue up to 2020, when landfill will account for 26 per cent of waste generated. If this projection holds, landfilled waste in the EU will reduce from 62 per cent in 1995 to 26 per cent in 2020. Measured in total amounts, this corresponds to a reduction of 63 million tonnes of waste.

However, it is clear that the pace of waste diversion slows between 2016 and 2020. This is because, first, growth in waste generation makes it relatively more difficult to reduce the amount going to landfill and, second, all the large, clean, homogeneous waste streams will be collected for recycling but it will become increasingly expensive to collect waste fractions separately and achieve high rates of recycling. Countries must then decide whether to invest in waste management systems with very high recycling rates or whether to opt for slightly higher landfill rates or for waste incineration.

For biodegradable municipal waste, it seems likely that the EU will meet the targets set out in the Landfill Directive. In 1995 the EU-27 landfilled 67 per cent of the BMW generated and, based on the assumptions in our model, this will decrease to 45 per cent in 2009 and 36 per cent in 2016 (Figure 3.4).

Our estimates show that between 2016 and 2020 there will be only minor decreases in the landfill of BMW despite the fact that several new member states as well as the UK, Ireland and Greece will be allowed extra time to meet the 2016 targets because these countries landfilled more than 80 per cent of their BMW in 1995. Nevertheless, there are variations among member states in terms of amounts of landfilled BMW, which are due to differences in waste composition, amount of recycled biodegradable waste and growth in the volume of waste. Countries where waste generation is increasing at a faster rate than the rate at which waste is being diverted from landfill will find it difficult to reduce the share of landfilled BMW and will find it even more problematic to meet the maximum amounts of BMW that can be landfilled for 2006, 2009 and 2016. Also, our results are for the entire EU, which means that the largest countries influence the outcomes. For example, the fact that, according to Eurostat, Germany landfilled only 1 per cent of its municipal waste in 2006 is driving a large part of the EU reduction in BMW landfill.

Based on the projection of municipal waste generation and our assumptions about the management of waste, we can estimate GHG emissions. The results

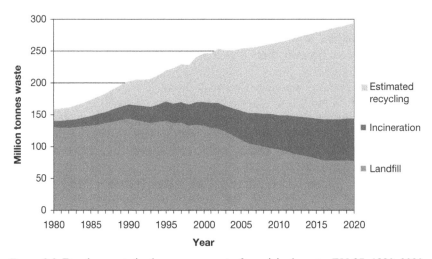

Figure 3.3 Developments in the management of municipal waste: EU-27, 1980–2020

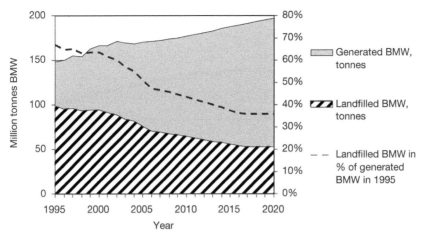

Figure 3.4 Generation and landfill of BMW, and landfilled BMW as a percentage of BMW generated in 1995, 1995–2020

show that net GHG emissions will decrease from around 75 million tonnes CO_2 equivalents in the late 1990s to 18 million tonnes CO_2 equivalents in 2020.

Net GHG emissions are the sum of direct emissions (from landfill sites, incineration plants, recycling operations, waste collection) and indirect emissions. Indirect emissions occur when waste is recycled into secondary materials, thereby replacing raw materials such as plastics, paper, metals, etc., or when waste is incinerated with energy recovery, which substitutes for energy production from fossil fuels. Indirect emissions also include a minor contribution from landfills, namely the CO_2 emissions that are saved when CH_4 is recovered and used as an energy source, substituting for traditional (mostly fossil fuel-based) energy production. In Figure 3.5 indirect emissions are shown below the x axis as *negative* emissions.

Since its environmental effect is global warming, we have taken a global approach to recycling. This means that, even if waste is exported to countries outside the EU for recycling, both the direct and the indirect emissions are ascribed to the EU as the original generator and collector of the waste. In the reports to the UNFCCC these emissions are not included, and emissions from the production of raw materials and energy are accounted for in other economic sectors.

Net GHG emissions depicted in Figure 3.5 are approximately 10 million tonnes CO_2 equivalents, which is higher than the results in Skovgaard *et al.* (2008). This is due to the fact that in a number of countries the composition of waste has changed from inert to biodegradable waste fractions, wood and textiles (maximum 4 per cent of generated waste). Moreover, emissions are calculated on the basis of waste composition after deduction of waste for recycling.

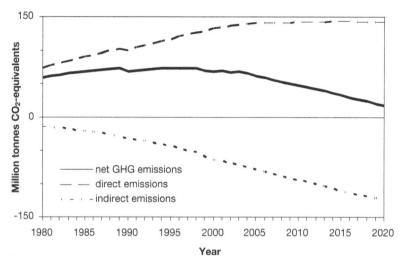

Figure 3.5 Emission of GHG from the management of municipal waste: EU-27, 1980–2020

Conclusion

The analysis in this chapter shows that past developments in the generation of municipal waste can be explained by economic and socio-economic variables. Also, the analysis of past developments shows a decoupling of waste generation from economic development. If we assume that this decoupling will continue, and apply an economic forecast showing an increase in GDP of 2.2 per cent per annum from 2005 to 2020, the generation of municipal waste in the 27 EU member states is projected to increase by 1.1 per cent per annum. This means that it should be possible to achieve the objective of the Sixth EAP, to decouple waste generation from the rate of economic growth. A significant reduction in the volume of waste, however, would seem more difficult to achieve.

The trend towards diversion of waste from landfills is expected to continue to 2020 and even be reinforced as member states introduce measures aimed at achievement of the Landfill Directive's targets for BMW. Based on these developments, it seems that the European Community will meet the 2006, 2009 and 2016 targets and also that landfill of municipal waste will decrease, thereby contributing to the aims of the Sixth EAP.

As a consequence of the generation and management of municipal waste, net GHG emissions should decrease from around 75 million tonnes CO_2 equivalents in the late 1990s to around 18 million tonnes in 2020. The decrease in GHG emissions should occur despite increases in the amount of waste being generated. Net GHG emissions are calculated as the sum of direct emissions and indirect emissions. Since the Tier 2 method of calculating CH_4 emissions implies that biodegradable waste will continue to emit CH_4 for several years after it has been landfilled, there is a delay in the direct emissions from landfill. That is, the direct emissions will continue to increase, or remain at a high level, for several years after amounts of landfilled waste have decreased. The indirect emissions will fall as more waste is recycled and incinerated, thus substituting for the production of raw materials and fossil fuel-based energy.

Note

1   The coefficient is significantly lower than 1.0 if $1 > \alpha_1 + 2 \cdot stdv(\alpha_1)$.

Acknowledgements

The authors would like to thank Alejandro Villanueva and Nanja Hedal for their valuable contributions to the project on GHG emissions estimation. The models for waste amounts and GHG emissions projections were developed for the European Environment Agency (EEA) as part of the European Topic Centre on Resource and Waste Management programme.

References

Andersen, F. M. and Larsen, H. (2006) *En model til fremskrivning af isag data, frida*, Arbejdsrapport fra Miljøstyrelsen 35, Denmark: Danish Environmental Protection Agency (in Danish).

Andersen, F. M., Fenhann, J., Larsen, H. and Schliesner, L. (1998) *A Scenario Model for the Generation of Waste*, Miljøprojekt 434, Copenhagen: Danish Environmental Projection Agency.

Andersen, F. M., Larsen, H., Skovgaard, M., Moll, S. and Isoard, S. (2007) 'A European model for waste and material flows', *Resources, Conservation and Recycling*, 49: 421–35.

Brunvoll, A. and Ibenholt, K. (1997) 'Future waste generation forecasts on the basis of a macroeconomic model', *Resources, Conservation and Recycling*, 19: 137–49.

Council Directive 75/442/EEC of 15 July 1975 on Waste (O.J. L 194, 25 July 1975) amended by Council Directive 91/156/EEC of 18 March 1991 (O.J. L 78, 26 March 1991), Brussels: European Commission.

Council Directive 1999/31/EC of 26 April 1999 on the Landfill of Waste (O.J. L 182, 16 July 1999), Brussels: European Commission.

EEA (2007) *Annual European Community GHG Inventory 1990–2005 and Inventory Report 2007: Submission to the UNFCCC Secretariat*, Technical report 7/2007, Copenhagen: European Environment Agency.

European Commission (2006) *European Energy and Transport: Trends to 2030: Update 2005*, Luxembourg: European Communities.

European Parliament and Council Directive 94/62/EC of 20 December 1994 on Packaging and Packaging Waste (O.J. L 365 31 December 1994), Brussels: European Commission.

Eurostat, Statistical Office of the European Communities. Database, http://epp.eurostat. ec.europa.eu (accessed July 2008).

——Structural Indicators: Municipal waste generated, Municipal waste landfilled, Municipal waste incinerated, http://epp.eurostat.ec.europa.eu (accessed July 2008).

IPCC (various authors) (2006) *IPCC Guidelines for National Greenhouse Gas Inventories*, Vol. V, IPCC National Greenhouse Gas Inventories Programme, Technical Support Unit, Kamiyamaguchi, Hayama, Kanagawa, Japan: Institute for Global Environmental Strategies.

OECD (2001) *Environmental Outlook*, Paris: OECD.

——(2007) *Environmental Data Compendium*, chapter 8, 'Waste', Paris: OECD, April.

Skovgaard, M., Hedal, N., Villanueva, A., Andersen, F. M. and Larsen, H. (2008) 'Municipal Waste Management and GHGs', Working Paper 1/2008, Copenhagen: European Topic Centre on Resource and Waste Management.

Villanueva, V., Vrgoc, M., Dall, O., Vogt, R., Fehrenbach, H. and Giegrich, J. (2006) 'Pilot study: Prioritisation of Waste Materials and their Treatment based on Environmental Impacts', Working Paper 2/2006, Copenhagen: European Topic Centre on Resource and Waste Management.

4 The drivers of MSW generation, disposal and recycling

Examining OECD inter-country differences

Katia Karousakis

The concept of sustainable or integrated waste management, aimed at providing the correct incentives for waste disposal, has been gaining increased attention among the developed nations since the mid-1980s. Recognition of the issues relating to waste has heightened as a result of often monotonically increasing waste levels, scarcity of land for landfill development in certain regions, and increasing public opposition, expressed in terms of the 'not in my back yard' (NIMBY) phenomenon, to landfill and incinerator siting. This has resulted in an increase in the theoretical and empirical literature devoted to efficient waste management and waste policy.

Most studies have focused on theoretical models or empirical analyses at household or community level. There are some extensive surveys of this literature (Kinnamon and Fullerton 1999), thus we do not offer a review in this chapter except to observe that only Beede and Bloome (1995) and Johnstone and Labonne (2004) examine the generation of municipal solid waste (MSW) at the country or macro-economic, level. The aim of this chapter is to add to this strand of the literature by examining the determinants of MSW generation, and its disposal and recycling, at the macro-economic level. Using cross-sectional time series data from the Organisation for Economic Co-operation and Development (OECD) countries for the period 1980–2000, this chapter provides a systematic analysis of the determinants of MSW generation before examining the underlying factors that determine the way MSW is managed. Specifically it examines: (i) the proportion of MSW that is disposed of in landfill; (ii) the proportion of paper and cardboard that is recycled as a percentage of apparent consumption; and (iii) the proportion of glass that is recycled as a percentage of apparent consumption. In addition to economic and demographic variables, two policy variables are included in the analysis, namely a waste legislation and policy index, and the level of landfill taxes that have been introduced in a number of countries. The results provide important insights into the nature of future waste trends and the effect that public policy may have on them.

Waste generation and management: a literature review

Some of the earliest macro-economic studies on waste generation emerged as a result of the debate on the environmental Kuznets curve (EKC), where, in the initial stages of development, as economic activity increases, environmental quality deteriorates.

Eventually, continued development leads to improvements in environmental quality. In these studies, data on per capita income is regressed on MSW generation, revealing that, in contrast to the inverted U of the EKC hypothesis, MSW generation is increasing monotonically (Shafik and Bandyopadhyay 1992; Cole *et al.* 1997; Lim 1997). Very little empirical analysis has been conducted to examine how additional variables may affect MSW generation at the macro-economic level. Demographic and policy factors that may influence MSW per capita generation rates include population density, geographic location, household size, waste legislation, public attitudes, source reduction and recycling initiatives, and the frequency of garbage collection (Reinhart 2006). One exception is the study by Beede and Bloom (1995), who examine the relative importance of growth in real per capita income and population in MSW generation rates. Using data from a cross-section of 36 countries they found income elasticity to be 0.34 and population elasticity to be 1.04. They also conducted time-series analyses for the US (1970–88) and Taiwan (1980–91) and found income elasticity to be 0.86 and 0.59 respectively, and population elasticity to be 0.63 and 1.63 (not statistically significant). The second exception is the study by Johnstone and Labonne (2004), who apply the model based on household utility maximization proposed by Kinnamon and Fullerton (1997). They regressed household solid waste generation on final consumption expenditures per capita, urbanization, population density, and percentage of children in the population. They found that household MSW generation rates are relatively inelastic with respect to household final consumption expenditures; that population density and, more ambiguously, degree of urbanization have a positive effect on MSW generation; and finally that the proportion of children in the population has a significant and negative influence on MSW generation.

The lack of empirical analysis of how MSW is disposed of among landfill, incineration, and recycling is notable. Indeed, in the context of the EKC, it has been argued that the environmental impact of municipal waste is masked by the fact that the volume of municipal waste produced is no indication of how much of it is recycled (Cole *et al.* 1997). Two studies that provide some evidence on the determinants of recycling are Terry (2002) and Berglund *et al.* (2002). Terry (2002) uses time-series data from 1960–90 for the US and regresses the proportion of MSW generated, on income, MSW composition, landfill disposal, and other demographic characteristics. The results indicate that the coefficient of income is positive, but not significant at the five per cent level, while percentage of population aged between 25 and 44, disposal in landfill, durable and packaging waste and time trend are statistically significant. Berglund *et al.* (2002) examine the determinants of paper recycling and regress the recovery rate for paper on GDP per capita, population density, and percentage of the total population living in urban areas. Using cross-sectional data from 89 countries, they find that the coefficients of GDP per capita and population density are statistically significant with a positive sign. The adjusted R-squared value, however, is only 0.24, and they argue that a similar study might benefit from the use of panel data and the inclusion of policy variables.

Description of the data and models

The data set is a combination of cross-sectional and time-series data, suggesting the appropriateness of panel data analysis. Panel data analysis has the advantage of improving the reliability of the estimates and controls for individual heterogeneity and unobservable or missing values (Baltagi 2005). Denoting the cross-section dimension as i, where $i = 1, \ldots, N$ and the time-series dimension as t, where $t = 1, \ldots, T$ the model, is given by:

(1) $y_{it} = \alpha + \beta' x_{it} + \varepsilon_{it}$

(2) $\varepsilon_{it} = \mu_i + v_{it}$

μ_i is the unobservable individual-specific time-invariant effect that takes account of any individual specific effect not in the regression; v_{it} denotes the disturbance. Assume that μ_i represents fixed parameters that need to be estimated and the remaining disturbance is stochastic, with v_{it} independently and identically distributed, iid $(0, \sigma_v^2)$. If the set of regressors x_{it} is assumed to be independent of v_{it} for all i and t, then the fixed effects (FE) regression is the appropriate model specification.

That the FE estimator can be interpreted as a simple OLS regression of means-differenced variables is the reason why this estimator is often referred to as the within-groups estimator. That is, it uses only the variation *within* an individual's set of observations. Random effects (RE) assumes μ_i is not correlated with the regressors and is a (matrix) weighted average of the estimates produced by the between and within estimators. It applies generalized least squares (GLS) to estimate the coefficients (Hsiao 2003; Baltagi 2005).

The data for the 30 OECD countries and their sources are described in Table 4.1.

The waste legislation and policy index (POLDX) assigns scores based on national government policy to implement waste management plans, waste eco-taxes, producer responsibility, waste prevention, and recovery/recycling programmes and whether governments have ratified the Basel Convention on the transboundary movements of hazardous waste.

Table 4.1 Description and sources of the data

MWPC	Waste generated per capita (municipal and household), 1980–2000, five-year intervals. *Source:* OECD Environmental Data Compendium
LDFL	Proportion of MSW disposed of at landfills, 1995–2003, for the EU-25 countries. *Source:* Eurostat (2004)
PAPER	Paper and cardboard recycled, defined as percentage of apparent consumption, 1980–2000. *Source:* OECD Environmental Data Compendium
GLASS	Glass recycled, defined as percentage of apparent consumption, 1980–2000. *Source:* OECD Environmental Data Compendium
GDPPC	Gross domestic product (GDP) per capita, in 1995 prices and purchasing power parities (PPP) in US dollars, 1980–2004. *Source:* World Bank (2004)
POPD	Population density, defined as people per square kilometre, 1980–2004. *Source:* World Bank (2004)
URB	Urban population, defined as percentage of total, 1980–2004. *Source:* World Bank (2004)
LDTX	Landfill taxes, 1980–2004. Source: OECD/EU Environmentally Related Taxes database 2001, updated from several sources
POLDX	Waste legislation and policy index, 1995. *Source:* European Environment Agency (1998).

The indices for each country are listed in Appendix 4.1.[1] The descriptive statistics for all the data are reported in Table 4.2.

The full list of countries and further information on their waste legislation and policy indices are reported in the appendix. Due to some missing observations, the data are an unbalanced panel. Analysis is restricted to the OECD countries because of the better availability of reliable waste data for these countries.

For each of the variables, total variation is decomposed into between and within class variation, and an F test is conducted to test the hypothesis that between class variation is large relative to within class variation, which is shown by the fact that for all of the variables, Prob > F = 0.000 (Table 4.3).

Panel data analysis and discussion

MSW generation

To obtain a better understanding of the underlying factors affecting MSW generation, economic, demographic and policy variables are included in the model. These are GDP per capita (GDPPC), population density (POPD), urbanization (URB) (which serves as a proxy for geographical location), and the waste legislation and policy index (POLDX). The econometric model is thus given by:

$$(5)\ \mathrm{MWPC}_{it} = \alpha + \beta_1 \mathrm{GDPPC}_{it} + \beta_2 \mathrm{POPD}_{it} + \beta_3 \mathrm{URB}_{it} + \beta_4 \mathrm{POLDX}_{it} + \epsilon_{it}$$

All the variables are expressed in log form to allow the coefficients to be interpreted as elasticities. It is expected that waste generation levels will rise with income. The expected sign on POPD is somewhat ambiguous. Some argue that this is because there are significant economies of scale in the provision of waste collection services, thus reducing the cost of service provision (Johnstone and Labonne 2004). Others argue that high population densities imply scarce land resources and, thus, more pressure to preserve land and environmental quality, and improve waste management (Matsunaga and Themelis 2002). The variable URB is expected to be positive, as residents in rural areas, for example, will be more likely to grow and prepare their own food, thus reducing packaging waste. Some evidence to this effect is apparent – at least in the US (US EPA 1994). Finally, the coefficient of POLDX is expected to be negative as higher indices indicate greater national commitment to sustainable management of the generation and disposal of waste.

The argument related to POPD by Matsunaga and Themelis (2002) implies a correlation with POLDX. There is thus likely to be some

Table 4.2 Descriptive statistics

Variable	Obs.	Mean	Std dev.	Min.	Max.
GDPPC	750	17935.898	7374.898	1122.97	55102.73
POPD	750	129.716	122.3737	1.91	488.03
URB	750	72.23851	12.729	29.44	97.23
MWPC	110	448.3636	135.7516	190	760
LDFL	220	0.5524	0.2857	0.0267	1
PAPER	408	39.083	14.6393	1.6	73.09
GLASS	354	41.7259	22.4370	4.96	73.09
LDTX	750	4.8999	14.6602	0	83.61
RLDTX	750	3.9813	12.5752	0	83.61
POLDX	750	7.7	1.7975	5	10

Table 4.3 Analysis of variance for all the variables

Variable	Between	Within	Total	F test
GDPPC	3.074e+10	1.000e+10	4.074e+10	76.32
POPD	11168657	47867.975	11216525	5792.82
URB	114956.95	6401.52	121358.47	445.85
MWPC	1511445	497260	2008705.5	8.79
LDFILL	16.6544	1.2292	17.8836	92.42
PAPER	60548.703	26675.463	87224.117	31.95
GLASS	94217.602	83488.934	177706.54	14.81
POLDX	2420	0	2420	–
LDTX	62646.854	98329.536	160976.39	15.82
RLDTX	40133.496	76412.595	116546.09	12.82

ambiguity in the interpretation of the results as it is not easy to disentangle what the different variables capture. Furthermore, as can be seen from Table 4.3, the within class variation of POPD is very small, indicating that there is not much variation across time. This implies that much of the same information is captured in the FE.

An RE and an FE model are estimated for equation (5) and the results are reported in Table 4.4.

In both the RE and the FE models, GDP per capita and URB are positive and statistically significant, indicating that higher income levels and the more urbanized the country, the higher is the generation of MWPC. In both models, URB is shown to have a stronger influence than GDPPC. POPD is statistically insignificant in both the RE and FE models. It should be noted that the rate of urbanization and population density are not highly corre-lated. In the sample, the correlation coefficient of these two variables is only -0.242, thus it does not seem to be the case that a large part of the variation on POPD can be explained by the variation in URB. POLDX shows the intuitively correct negative sign, and is statistically significant at the 10 per cent level. The Hausman test statistic with $\chi^2(3) = 2.08$, Prob $> \chi^2 = 0.556$,

Table 4.4 Parameter estimates for MSW generation

	Random Effects	Fixed Effects
	Coefficient (Z value)	Coefficient (t value)
GDPPC	0.422 (6.28)***	0.4540 (4.31)***
POPD	−0.036 (−1.43)	0.861 (0.21)
URB	0.477 (2.76)***	0.557 (1.88)*
POLDX	−0.229 (−1.65)*	dropped
Constant	0.5769 (0.82)	−1.08 (−0.80)
No. observations	110	110
No. groups	29	29
R−squared	within = 0.4197 between = 0.5783 overall = 0.5069 Wald $\chi^2(5)$=88.21 Prob>χ^2=0.000	within = 0.5266 between = 0.5587 overall = 0.5262 F(3,78)=18.88 Prob>F= 0.000 F test that all u_i=0: F(28, 78) = 5.44 Prob>F = 0.000

Note: significance at 10%, 5% and 1% is denoted by *, ** and ***, respectively.

suggests that the RE regression is the appropriate model for these data. Diagnostic tests were conducted to test for heteroskedasticity and serial correlation in the data. The Breusch–Pagan/Cook–Weisberg test for heteroskedasticity with $\chi^2(1) = 12.14$, and Prob $> \chi^2(1) = 0.0005$, which is more than the critical $\chi^2(1) = 3.84$. The null hypothesis of homoskedasticity is therefore rejected. The Wooldridge test for autocorrelation, $F(1, 19) = 15.071$, indicates that there is autocorrelation in the data (Prob $> F = 0.0010$). The method of feasible generalized least squares (FGLS) is therefore used to estimate the model in STATA, which allows estimation in the presence of AR(1) autocorrelation within panels, as well as heteroskedasticity across panels. The results are presented in Table 4.5.

Thus, as countries grow richer, the FGLS results suggest, more waste will be generated per capita. Furthermore, the positive and significant sign of URB is not encouraging, as projections show that the share of total population living in urban areas will continue to grow (WRI 1996). Population density is negative and statistically significant, and also the waste legislation and policy index is negative and statistically significant, suggesting that national commitment to sustainable waste management has a significant impact on reducing the amount of MSW generated.[2]

The above analysis provides evidence on the economic and demographic determinants of generation rates in MSW. It represents a first attempt at including an important potential influence on MSW generation, that of public policy, proxied by the waste legislation and policy index. The data indicate that per capita MSW generated is increasing monotonically and that this trend is unlikely to be reversed in the near future.

These data do not provide any information on the way that the volume of waste is managed, however. Waste disposal management is an area that has not received much attention in the literature and could provide additional and important insights. This is the focus of the following sections.

The proportion of waste deposited in landfills

Recently available data on the proportion of MSW generated that is disposed of at landfills (LDFL) are used as the dependent variable. The variable

Table 4.5 FGLS estimates of MSW generation

Variable	Coefficient	Std error	z	P>|z|
GDPPC	0.4356	0.0352	12.36	0.000
POPD	−0.0395	0.0067	−5.92	0.000
URB	0.4718	0.0645	7.31	0.000
POLDX	−0.1884	0.0387	−4.86	0.000
Constant	0.3739	0.3505	1.07	0.286

Note: Wald χ^2 (4) = 458.92. Prob. $> \chi^2$ = 0.0000. Log likelihood = 2.2594.

GDPPC is included to examine how this affects LDFL, and is expected to be negative. Variables for population density (POPD) and urbanization (URB) are also included and are expected to be negative. This is because in densely populated regions and/or where people are clustered in highly urbanized areas, the likelihood is that landfill prices will be high, as will be the cost of landfill disposal. Furthermore, higher population density lowers the cost of recycling, thereby indirectly lowering demand for landfill disposal. The waste policy and legislation index (POLDX) is included to test the assumption that, *ceteris paribus*, the higher the POLDX, the lower will be the LDFL. An additional policy variable is introduced in the regression, namely the real landfill tax (RLDTX) for the various countries,[3] in order to determine whether higher landfill taxes are associated with a smaller proportion of waste disposed of in landfill.

It is important to note that the role of prices and/or taxes has not been fully examined in the literature on waste disposal management. To date, there are only a few EKC studies that include a price variable in the regression analysis. De Bruyn *et al.* (1998), for example, include energy prices in their model to examine carbon dioxide (CO_2), nitrous oxide (NO_x) and sulphur dioxide (SO_2) emissions in four countries (Netherlands, UK, US, West Germany). These are statistically insignificant in two cases. Agras and Chapman (1999) included energy (gasoline) prices in their analysis of CO_2 emissions and found that income was no longer the most relevant indicator of environmental quality. Lindmark (2002) investigated the relationships among CO_2 emissions and proximate explanatory factors, including economic growth, fuel prices, technology and income levels, in Sweden in the nineteenth and twentieth centuries and found that fuel prices were statistically significant. Finally, Culas and Dutta (2002) include an export price index to assess the effect this has on deforestation. Their results indicate that the export price index is significant only for Latin America.

In the case of waste, average national prices for landfill disposal (also known as *tipping fees*) have been rising over time, making it more expensive to dispose of waste in landfills. In the US, for example, average *tipping fees* increased from \$10 in 1983 to \$50 in 1990. For the analysis in this chapter, ideally data on average national tipping prices at landfills along with data on landfill taxes should be used. Panel data on the former, however, are not readily available. However, landfill prices have been increasing across the board, as a result of international waste legislation, and it is assumed that any inter-country differences in the proportion of MSW deposited in landfills will show up most clearly as a result of changes in landfill taxes.[4] Governments' imposition of landfill taxes is intended to divert waste away from landfill disposal, that is, towards incineration and recycling. Also, POPD may serve as a proxy for landfill prices, since population density drives up the price of land.

The equation for the proportion of municipal waste disposed of in landfills is written in log-linear form and formulated as:

$$(6)\ \text{LDFL}_{it} = \alpha + \beta_1 \text{GDPPC}_{it} + \beta_2 \text{POPD}_{it} + \beta_3 \text{URB}_{it}$$
$$+ \beta_4 \text{POLDX}_{it} + \beta_5 \text{RLDTX}_{it} + \varepsilon_{it}$$

As before, equation (6) is estimated using RE and FE models. Diagnostic tests for heteroskedasticity and serial correlation indicate that both are present in the data. The method of FGLS is therefore used and the results are presented in Table 4.6.

In the FGLS model all the variables are significant, with the exception of the RLDTX. The estimated coefficient on GDPPC is −0.352. POPD and URB are both negative, indicating that, as these levels increase, the percentage of waste deposited at landfills declines. A 10 per cent increase in the population in urban areas results in a 7.8 per cent decrease in the proportion of MSW generated disposed of in landfill. The sign on the estimated coefficient on POLDX is negative and statistically significant, implying that a higher POLDX is associated with a lower percentage of waste deposited in landfill. The RLDTX is insignificant in the FGLS model.

The proportions of paper and cardboard and glass recycled

The relationship between recycling and economic growth can provide further useful insights into the dynamics of waste. Ideally, we should examine the proportion of MSW recycled, as for MSW disposed of in landfill (above). Unfortunately, panel data on the percentage of MSW generated that is recycled are not available for all countries. However, the OECD does have annual cross-sectional and time-series data on waste recycling rates for paper and cardboard, and for glass, as a percentage of apparent consumption, for the period 1980–2000. Thus here we adopt a slightly different approach: the recycling equations for each of the two materials are written in log-linear form and formulated as:

$$(7)\ \text{RCYC}_{it} = \alpha + \beta_1 \text{GDPPC}_{it} + \beta_2 \text{POPD}_{it} + \beta_3 \text{URB}_{it}$$
$$+ \beta_4 \text{POLDX}_{it} + \beta_5 \text{RLDTX}_{it} + \varepsilon_{it}$$

For both paper/cardboard and glass, it is anticipated that all the coefficients of the independent variables are positive. As income levels rise, preferences for environmental quality improvements become stronger because the environment is considered to be a normal good. Population density affects the economics of recycling, as the recycling of materials becomes more viable in densely populated and urbanized areas where the costs of collecting and separating waste decrease. Further, it is expected that higher policy indices indicate greater efforts to sustainably manage waste, and that higher real landfill taxes will divert greater portions of the two materials away from landfill disposal to recycling.

Equation (7) above extends the analysis by Berglund *et al.* (2002) by examining paper recovery in a panel data setting, and by including two

Table 4.6 FGLS estimates of percentage landfilled

Variable	Coefficient	Std error	z	$P > |z|$
GDPPC	−0.3524	0.0789	−4.46	0.000
POPD	−0.1913	0.0253	−7.56	0.000
URB	−0.7808	0.2814	−2.77	0.006
POLDX	−0.3844	0.1365	−2.82	0.005
RLDTX	−0.0009	0.0014	−0.66	0.512
Constant	7.7867	1.0473	7.43	0.000

Wald $\chi^2(5)$ = 126.44. Prob. > χ^2 = 0.000.
Log likelihood = 202.9489

Note: Percentage LDFL, data not available for Canada.

waste management policy variables in the regression model, namely the waste legislation and policy index and the real landfill tax. Similar analysis is conducted to investigate the determinants of glass recycling.

As before, due to the presence of both heteroskedasticity and serial correlation in the FE and RE models, only the results of the FGLS are reported here (Table 4.7).

In the FGLS model all the variables except URB are statistically significant. GDPPC and POPD have the strongest impact on paper and cardboard recycling, and the RLDTX has a statistically significant and positive impact. The coefficient on POLDX exhibits a statistically significant but negative relationship with recycling. This is intuitively incorrect and may be explained by the fact that the variable POLDX does not vary over time and hence may not adequately capture the relationship with recycling.

These models provide further evidence of the importance of population density as opposed to urbanization on paper and cardboard recycling rates. There is also some indication that higher landfill taxes are associated with more paper and cardboard recycling.

Diagnostic tests were conducted to examine the existence of heteroskedasticity and autocorrelation in the data. The model is therefore estimated using the FGLS method and the results are reported in Table 4.8.

In the FGLS model the estimated coefficients of GDPPC, POPD and URB are all statistically significant and positive. POLDX is statistically significant, but negative. As before, a possible explanation is as in the case of the percentage of paper recycled. The RLDTX is positive but statistically insignificant.

This leads to the conclusion that higher levels of GDPPC have an unambiguous positive influence on the percentage of glass that is recycled. POPD and URB exhibit the strongest influence on glass recycling in the FGLS model, which accounts for heteroskedasticity and autocorrelation in the data. From a policy perspective this is a promising phenomenon, suggesting that these trends are likely to increase in the future. With regard to the policy variables POLDX and RLDTX that are included in the regression, however,

Table 4.7 FGLS estimates of percentage of paper and cardboard recycled

Variable	Coefficient	Std error	z	$P > |z|$
GDPPC	0.4302	0.0714	6.03	0.000
POPD	0.1461	0.0334	4.37	0.000
URB	−0.0592	0.1506	−0.39	0.694
POLDX	−0.2484	0.1208	−2.06	0.040
RLDTX	0.0015	0.0007	2.24	0.025
Constant	−0.4672	0.7906	−0.59	0.555

Note: Wald $\chi^2(5)$ = 67.20. Prob. > χ^2 = 0.000. Log likelihood = 394.5131.

Table 4.8 FGLS estimates of percentage of glass recycled

Variable	Coefficient	Std error	z	$P > |z|$
GDPPC	1.0743	0.0788	13.63	0.000
POPD	0.1984	0.0418	4.75	0.000
URB	0.4321	0.2460	1.76	0.079
POLDX	−0.3046	0.1506	−2.02	0.043
RLDTX	0.0013	0.0012	1.16	0.247
Constant	−9.0678	1.1810	−7.68	0.000

Note: Wald $\chi^2(5)$ = 342.75. Prob. > χ^2 = 0.000. Log likelihood = 153.6321.

there does not seem to be consistently statistically significant evidence that existing waste management policy has been effective in achieving its objectives. The POLDX variable is used as a proxy for national efforts in sustainable waste management. Perhaps this variable is inadequate as a reflection of national *effort* as opposed to national *commitment* to sustainable waste management.

Conclusion and policy implications

Based on panel data for 30 OECD countries for a time period of more than 20 years, this analysis attempts to identify and analyse the main trends in and determinants of MSW generation and disposal management. Despite recent data indicating a decoupling of economic growth and waste generation in certain OECD countries, the MSW generation model suggests that, aside from GDPPC, urbanization also has a positive impact on the generation of municipal waste. This is discouraging, given that projections show that the share of the total population living in cities will grow at a fast rate in the future (WRI 1996).

With regard to the disposal of MSW, this analysis has provided evidence that higher levels of GDP per capita are associated with a smaller fraction of MSW going to landfill. The results indicate that both urbanization and the real landfill tax introduced by national governments have negative impact.

This implies that though urbanization is associated with higher amounts of waste generated, it is managed in a more environmentally friendly way, either via incineration or via recycling. The negative sign of real landfill tax indicates that the higher the landfill taxes on waste the smaller is the proportion of waste that is deposited in landfill. This is a strict policy variable and should be encouraging for governments wanting to divert additional waste away from landfills.

With regard to the proportion of paper and cardboard, and glass that are recycled, the main determinants of recycling are economic growth and population density. In the case of glass recycled, this is also affected by the real landfill tax. Recycling of glass and paper and cardboard, therefore, is determined more by market forces than by policy forces. Higher population densities are expected to lower the collection and recovery costs of recycling, thus increasing the economic viability of this disposal option.

The waste policy and legislation index shows mixed results. One important caveat is that the index is fixed across time and may not accurately reflect changes in national policy targets over the 20 year time period examined here. Future research efforts should focus, therefore, on obtaining more accurate indices for this purpose.

Appendix

List of countries and the waste legislation and policy index (POLDX)

Country	Waste policy (eleven-point scale)	Country	Waste policy (eleven-point scale)
Australia	8	Korea	7
Austria	10	Luxembourg	7
Belgium	10	Mexico	6.5
Canada	8	Netherlands	10
CzechRepublic	*5*	New Zealand	7
Denmark	10	*Norway*	*10*
Finland	10	Portugal	6
France	10	*Poland*	*5*
Germany	9.5	*SlovakRepublic*	*5*
Greece	9	Spain	6
Hungary	*5*	Sweden	9
Iceland	*6*	*Switzerland*	*6*
Italy	9	Turkey	6
Ireland	8	UK	9
Japan	8	US	6

Source: Adapted from Guerin *et al.* (2001); EEA, Europe's Environment: The Second Assessment (1998).

Notes

1 The waste legislation and policy index is computed by summing each country's scores based on its policy initiatives for different aspects of waste management. The scores are based on national government policy in ten categories: waste management plans, priority to prevent and reduce waste harmfulness, waste eco-taxes, producer responsibility, prevention, recovery/recycling programmes, hazardous waste reduction, ratification of the Basel Convention on the Control of Transborder Movements of Hazardous Wastes, bans on hazardous waste, bans on other waste. Each category is assigned one point, with the exception of the category on waste eco-taxes, which can score one point for one eco-tax or two points for two eco-taxes (landfill tax, packaging tax, and tax on waste generation). The 15 countries in regular font are taken from Guerin *et al.* (2001). Scores in italics are from the EEA (1998). The underlined scores are estimated based on information from the Secretariat of the Basel Convention, UNEP, at www.basel.int/, the OECD Environmental Taxes database, and other sources.
2 One caveat here is that the variable POLDX does not vary over time and the coefficient may therefore not adequately capture all the relationship with MSWPC generation.
3 Converted from nominal landfill taxes using the GDP deflator (World Bank 2004).
4 Similar assumptions were made by Rietveld and van Woudenberg (2005) in their analysis of why fuel prices differ.

Acknowledgement

The author would like to thank Dr Nick Johnstone for useful comments on a draft of this chapter.

References

Agras, J. and Chapman, D. (1999) 'A dynamic approach to the environmental Kuznets curve hypothesis', *Ecological Economics*, 28: 267–77.
Baltagi, B. (2005) *Econometric Analysis of Panel Data*, 3rd edn, New York: John Wiley.
Beede, D. N. and Bloome, D. (1995) 'Economics of the Generation and Management of MSW', NBER Working Paper 5116, Cambridge MA: NBER.
Berglund, C., Söderholm, P. and Nilsson, M. (2002) 'A note on inter-country differences in waste paper recovery and utilization', *Resources, Conservation and Recycling*, 34: 175–91.
Cole, M. A. (2003) 'Development, trade, and the environment: how robust is the environmental Kuznets curve?', *Environment and Development Economics*, 8: 557–80.
Cole, M. A., Rayner, A. J. and Bates, J. M. (1997) 'The environmental Kuznets curve: an empirical analysis', *Environment and Development Economics*, 2 (4): 401–16.
Culas, R. and Dutta, D. (2002) 'Underlying Causes of Deforestation and the EKC: A Cross-country Analysis', Working Paper, Sydney: University of Sydney.
De Bruyn, S. (1997) 'Explaining the environmental Kuznets curve: structural change and international agreements in reducing sulphur emissions', *Environment and Development Economics*, 2: 485–503

De Bruyn, S., Van den Bergh, J. and Opschoor, J. (1998) 'Economic growth and emissions: reconsidering the empirical basis of environmental Kuznet's curves', *Ecological Economics*, 25: 161–75.

EEA (1998) *Europe's Environment: The Second Assessment*, Copenhagen: European Environment Agency.

Eurostat (2004) *Waste Generated and Treated in Europe: Data 1990–2001*, Luxembourg: Eurostat.

Guerin, D., Crete, J. and Mercier, J. (2001) 'Multilevel analysis of determinants of recycling behaviour in the European countries', *Social Science Research*, 30: 195–218.

Hsiao, C. (2003) *Analysis of Panel Data*, 2nd edn, Cambridge MA: Cambridge University Press.

Johnstone, N., and Labonne, J. (2004) 'Generation of household solid waste in OECD countries: an empirical analysis using macroeconomic data', *Land Economics*, 80: 529–38.

Kinnamon, T., and Fullerton, D. (1997) 'Garbage and Recycling in Communities with Curbside Recycling and Unit-based Pricing', NBER Working Paper 6021, Cambridge MA: NBER.

——(1999) 'The Economics of Residential Solid Waste Management', mimeo, www.colby.edu/economics/faculty/thtieten/ec476/Fullerton.pdf (accessed July 2008).

Lim, J. (1997) 'Economic Growth and Environment: Some Empirical Evidence from South Korea', Sydney: School of Economics, University of New South Wales.

Lindmark, M. (2002) 'An EKC pattern in historical perspective: CO_2 emissions, technology, fuel prices and growth in Sweden, 1870–1997', *Ecological Economics*, 42: 333–47.

Matsunaga, K., and Themelis, N. J. (2002) 'Effects of Affluence and Population Density on Waste Generation and Disposal of Municipal Solid Wastes', Earth Engineering Center report, www.columbia.edu/cu/earth (accessed July 2008).

OECD, *Environmental Data Compendium*, Paris: OECD, www.oecd.org/env (accessed July 2008).

OECD/EU, *Environmentally related Taxes Database*, Paris: OECD, www.oecd.org/env (accessed July 2008).

Reinhart, D. (2005) 'Waste Characterization', http://msw.cecs.ucf.edu/wastecharacterization.html (accessed July 2008).

Rietveld, P. and van Woudenberg, S. (2005) 'Why fuel prices differ', *Energy Economics*, 27: 79–92.

Shafik, N. and Bandyopadhyay, S. (1992) 'Economic growth and environmental quality', *Oxford Economic Papers*, 46: 757–73.

STATA (2003) *Cross-sectional Time Series: Reference Manual*, Release 8.0, College Station TX: Stata Corporation.

Terry, N. (2002) 'The determinants of municipal recycling: a time series approach', *South Western Economic Review*, 29: 53–62.

US EPA (1994) *Waste Prevention, Recycling, and Composting Options: Lessons from Thirty US Communities*, Environmental Protection Agency, Solid Waste and Emergency Services, EPA 530-R-92-015, Washington DC: EPA.

World Bank (2004) *World Development Indicators*, Washington DC: World Bank, www.worldbank.org/data/wdi2004/ (accessed July 2008).

WRI (1996) *The Urban Environment*, New York: World Resources Institute, United Nations Environment Programme, United Nations Development Programme and the World Bank.

Waste generation, waste management and landfill diversion: policy-oriented and regionally based analyses from Italy

5 Municipal waste generation, socio-economic drivers and waste management instruments

Regional and provincial panel data evidence from Italy

Massimiliano Mazzanti, Anna Montini and Roberto Zoboli

Based on past experience of economic development, consumption of natural resource inputs, such as energy and materials, increases in line with increases in economic production. Recently, however, economists have observed a delinking of resource consumption from increased production, and indicators of delinking are becoming more and more popular for detecting and measuring improvements in the efficiency of economic activity in terms of environmental/resource consumption. Relative delinking is observed if the elasticity of an environmental impact indicator with respect to an economic driver is positive, but less than unity. The descending part of the bell shaped Kuznets curve instead provides evidence of absolute delinking.

The environmental Kuznets curve (EKC) hypothesis extends the basic delinking reasoning, and models a multivariate analysis of the environment–income relationship.

In this chapter we provide empirical evidence on EKC and delinking trends for municipal solid waste (MSW) by considering two disaggregated panel data sets of Italian provinces (20 regions over nine years and 103 provinces over seven years) which contribute to the existing literature in several ways. First, empirical evidence on delinking and EKC for waste is scarce. Research on delinking for materials and waste is far less developed than research on air pollution and greenhouse gas emissions. Although some recent works (Bringezu *et al.* 2003) have produced extensive evidence on material intensity indicators, the still limited research results for the waste sector could become a problem from a policy perspective. Second, there are far fewer analyses exploiting country-specific, highly disaggregated panel data on waste compared with cross-country investigations. Our data sets cover the period 1996–2004 for 20 Italian regions, and 1999–2005 for 103 Italian provinces; data on waste generation are merged with official data on economic drivers at the same level of disaggregation, allowing us to demonstrate the advantages of country-specific analyses.[1] Third, our analysis includes decentralized policy-related variables, in particular: share of municipalities and population in each province, that have shifted from *waste taxes* to *waste tariffs*, the latter actually closest to environmental economic instruments in spirit; and percentage of waste management costs covered by the tax/tariff.[2]

Given the large gap between the southern and northern areas of Italy in terms of environmental and economic performance, our analysis provides insights from a development gap perspective. National case studies may be the starting point for more extended regional analyses (EU, US) when sufficient data become available. To date, we believe that good nationally based data are more available and offer better reliability and heterogeneity than even official sources, such as Eurostat (2003) or the OECD.

Next section provides a short survey of the studies on waste and delinking and then we describe the data set and the empirical model. The empirical evidence is then presented and a final section concludes with policy implications and suggestions for further research.

Waste indicators and delinking: recent empirical evidence

In the last few years, various critical surveys and a discussion on the theoretical underpinnings of delinking and EKC have been produced. Most analyse air and water emissions, mainly carbon dioxide (CO_2), with limited attention to waste streams. The still scarce evidence on waste delinking and waste management and policy tools evaluation is surveyed here[3] with the aim of highlighting the incremental value of this chapter, and suggesting future, unexplored research directions.

In spite of the significant environmental, policy and economic relevance of waste issues, there is very little empirical evidence on delinking even for major waste streams, such as municipal and packaging and other waste categories. Analyses of waste policy effectiveness are also scarce. Works on waste management optimization or evaluation of externalities have largely prevailed in the literature on the economics of waste management, although there are some recent contributions that bring together environmental impact issues, evaluation of externalities and policy effectiveness (Pearce 2004; OECD 2004).

Macro-level evidence exploiting cross-country regression data analysis from the 1980s was first presented in the international report that gave birth to the EKC literature (World Bank 1992). Recent reports (DEFRA 2003) present positive elasticities in waste generation to income as a primary policy concern. Although some studies have provided evidence of a turning point (TP) in the U-inverted EKC curve, that is, a delinking process, waste generation still seems to be characterized by a direct relationship with economic drivers.

For European countries, Mazzanti and Zoboli (Chapter 1 above) and Mazzanti (2008) find neither absolute nor relative delinking; they find no EKC evidence for municipal waste and packaging waste from European panel data sets for 1995 to 2000 and 1997 to 2000 respectively. Estimated elasticities of waste generation with respect to household consumption are close to unity. Andersen *et al.* (2007) recently estimated waste trends for the EU-15 and the EU-10 new entrants, and found that waste generation is linked with economic activity by a non-constant trend, which is in line with the waste Kuznets curve hypothesis. A somewhat descriptive analysis of delinking in EU countries also provides forecasts in favour of relative delinking, but does not confirm waste Kuznets curve evidence. Projections for 2005–20 for the UK, France and Italy show a growth in MSW of around 15–20 per cent, which, at least at first sight, may be compatible with relative delinking with respect to GDP and consumption growth.

In short, the literature on waste determinants and EKC for waste underlines that waste indicators generally tend to increase with income or other economic drivers, such as population and that, in general, an inverted U-shape curve is not in line with the data. A decreasing trend (negative elasticity) is found only for industrialized countries where waste management and environmental policies are more developed. Thus it would seem that waste Kuznets curve trends (or absolute delinking) are associated with only a few rich countries or areas, and can divide countries in terms of waste production and management performance. The reasons for this evidence may be multiple. Some authors have suggested that in terms of stock pollution externalities, for example waste, the pollution income relationship barely resembles an EKC shaped curve, with pollution stocks rising monotonically with income (Lieb 2004). Another structural reason for the lack of evidence on delinking in relation to waste may be that the change in the sign for the elasticity of the environment/income function could occur at relatively lower income levels only for pollutants whose production and consumption can be easily spatially separated, as a result, for example, of associated pollution being exported or activities being relocated. This is likely to be more difficult for waste flows.

In any case, in-depth investigations of the multiple driving forces, policy effects and case studies on single countries (or a homogeneous policy relevant over a sufficiently long period of time), are lacking in the literature. This study attempts to contribute to fill that gap.

Empirical analysis at regional level and provincial level

The data sets

The two data sets include data on MSW generated (collected) in Italian regions and Italian provinces respectively. We exploit all available yearly editions of the Italian Environment Agency's waste report (APAT 1999, 2000, 2001, 2002, 2003, 2004, 2005, 2006), which present a very rich set of waste data, produced according to Eurostat and the European Environmental Agency guidelines (EEA 2003a, b, c). Our data sets cover the period 1996–2004 for the 20 Italian regions and 1999–2005 for the 103 Italian provinces. We merged the data with official data on economic drivers at regional and provincial level respectively.

Although, in analyses of waste trends, consumption is often indicated and used as the driver (Andersen *et al.* 2007), province-level data on consumption were not available, making value added the only reliable and available economic driver at provincial level. At regional level both gross domestic product (GDP) and household expenditure are considered as a proxy for consumption. Additional socio-economic variables relevant for waste, such as share of separately collected waste and population density, are also tested. The analysis includes decentralized policy-related variables, in particular: (i) the share of provincial municipalities and the provincial population covered by the *new waste tariff regime*, which substitutes for the *old waste tax regime*; and (ii) the percentage of waste management costs covered by the tariff. Finally, we check for tourist-related flows, crucial for waste generation and collection in many Italian areas. Table 5.1 presents the dependent and independent variables and their descriptive statistics.

With respect to the policy-related variables, the waste management *tariff* was introduced by Italian bill No. 22/1997 and substitutes for the old waste management *tax*; the latter, however, still prevails in many Italian municipalities because the provisions of bill 22/1997 allow the transition to be gradual and slow. The old waste management tax was calculated on the size of household living spaces, while the tariff is based on principles of full-cost pricing of waste management services. There is a part covering fixed costs and a part aimed at covering variable management costs. The former correlates with the size of household living space and, a new element, with the number of people in the family. The variable costs portion is associated with the (expected) amount of waste produced, which is calculated on the basis of past trends and location-related features. The variable cost is reduced by 10–20 per cent if households adopt domestic composting and/or join garden waste door-to-door collection systems. Effective implementation of the tariff system, however, remains highly dependent on local policy decisions and practices (Callan and Thomas 2006).

Early implementation of the new tariff-based system, which is partly the choice of the municipality, might be a sign of policy commitment. We note that speed of implementation is heterogeneous even across areas with similar incomes and similar social economic variables. The shift from tax to tariff should also capture the incentive effect of the latter, although the impact on waste generation, if any, is not visible in the short term.

Finally, we note that the number of municipalities applying a tariff system is increasing annually, with those in northern Italy predominating. Municipalities applying tariffs increased from 564 in 2004 to 747 in 2005 and, at regional level, the largest increases were in Veneto (212 municipalities in 2005) and Lombardy (160 municipalities). Veneto is the region with the biggest number of municipalities (36.5 per cent) applying the tariff system.

Table 5.1 Descriptive statistics: dependent and independent variables

	Acronym	Variable description	Mean	Min.	Max.	Research hypothesis
Provincial Level	WASTE	MSW generated (kg/capita)	516.26	251.91	893.24	Dependent variable
	VA	Provincial value added per capita (€2,000)	17,653	9,369	28,796	Positively correlated with income, the objective is assessing whether relative or absolute delinking is present
	DENS	Population/surface (inhabitants/km²)	244.1	36.4	2,640.9	Positive and negative correlations may emerge depending on the role of factors like economies of scale and land opportunity costs occurring in urban and densely inhabited areas
	COLLEC	% share of separated collection	18.40	0.03	67.57	Possibly reducing MSW generation through indirect feedback effects, though the direct effect is at waste management level. Possible endogeneity given the positive correlation with respect to income
	TARIFF	Share of population living in municipalities that introduced a waste tariff replacing the former waste tax (%)	9.00	0	99.72	
	TARIFF2	Share of municipalities that introduced a waste tariff replacing the former waste tax (%)	5.03	0	100.00	

(Continued on next page)

Table 5.1 (continued)

Level	Acronym	Variable description	Mean	Min.	Max.	Research hypothesis
Provincial Level	COST-REC	Cost recovery of waste management services (tax/tariff revenues on variable service costs, only one item of data for 2004) (%)	85.61	53.3	104.2	
	TOURIST	Tourist yearly attendance (per capita)	7.18	0.40	58.83	Positively affecting waste generation per capita
Regional Level	WASTE	MSW generated in tons/capita	491.11	335.60	692.55	Dependent variable
	GDP	GDP per capita (€1,995)	17,141	9,885	24,091	The objective is assessing whether relative or absolute delinking is present
	C	Household expenditure per capita (€1,995)	735.2	412.5	1,030	Positively correlated with income
	DENS	Population/surface (km^2)	175.8	36.42	426.54	See DENS above
	COLLEC	% share of separated collection	12.31	0.6	44	See DENS above

The waste Kuznets curve empirical model

The first methodological issue in our analysis is how to specify the waste Kuznets curve functional relationship, on which there is no consensus,[4] Here we test the hypothesis by specifying a proper reduced form, which is usual in the EKC field (Stern 2004):

$$(1) \quad \ln(\text{MSW generation}) = \beta_{0i} + \alpha_t + \beta_1 \ln(\text{value added})_{it}$$
$$+ \beta_2 \ln(\text{value added})_{it}^2 + \beta_3(X)_{it} + e_{it}$$

where the first two terms are intercept parameters that vary across regions or provinces, and across years.[5]

Different specifications are tested, including either waste per capita or total waste as the dependent variable;[6] accordingly, value added is either per capita or total.

The vector X refers to a set of other drivers, added to the core waste Kuznets curve specification as controls and additional drivers of waste generation.[7] In our model the vector includes the percentage shares of separately collected waste, population density and tourist flows, the recovery capacity of waste service costs, and share of population subject to waste tariffs (rather than waste taxes). The main research hypotheses associated with the explanatory factors examined are discussed below and summarized in Table 5.1.

In line with other studies (Johnstone and Labonne 2004), population density is included in the regression, but its expected sign is ambiguous, since, on the one hand, economies of scale may help reduce average waste collection costs (reducing incentives for waste prevention), while, on the other, population density may imply greater scarcity of land resources and, thus, more pressure to preserve land dedicated to waste disposal.

The inclusion of *policy proxies* may be fruitful for valuing the effect of policies within the waste Kuznets curve and generally assessing *ex post* policy effectiveness. Our two decentralized policy variables show strong geographic heterogeneity; they are: (i) share of municipalities that have already implemented the new regime based on the waste management tariff, (ii) percentage of variable costs covered by the tax/tariff for each province, which is correlated to the actual level of the tax/tariff.[8] They allow us to capture waste policy features and policy commitment at the decentralized level. These policy variables are continuous and time variant, unlike the synthetic indexes or time-invariant dummies used in many studies. They should capture the implementation of an instrument that is more market based: unlike the old waste tax, which was not related to waste generation and household income, the tariff is correlated to socio-economic indicators and household behavior. At the same time, they should capture cost recovery, for both public and private waste management companies, as a proxy for the degree of subsidization (the higher the cost of recovery, the lower the subsidy). We would expect that both policy proxies should be (significantly) negatively related to waste generation: the more market-based the system the more waste generation will be discouraged. Nevertheless, we would also expect that their influence, in the short term, will not be significant, provided that changes in production and consumption behaviour take time, and waste generation is less dependent, compared with waste disposal/recovery/recycling, on price-based instruments and management approaches. Furthermore, policy instruments may also present endogeneity with respect to income levels. This is a new issue addressed in *ex post* environmental policy evaluations (Cole *et al.* 2006). Consistent with EKC reasoning, policies may be endogenous with economic development, and may be correlated with income factors (Cagatay and Mihci 2006).

Finally, in order to correct for *tourist hotspots*, such as Florence, Rimini, Rome, Venice among others, we check whether the introduction of tourist flows at provincial level affects the estimates.

For each combination of the dependent and independent variables, we estimate different specifications, including linear regressors only (baseline case), or linear and squared terms (EKC usual case).[9] We observe that our data set is a typical panel that captures more cross-sectional heterogeneity than time-series dynamics, though we would stress that, compared with other current evidence, seven years is a long series for waste indicators. Baseline panel specifications are tested against first-order serial correlation and heteroskedasticity. In the case that null hypotheses were rejected, corrected estimates are presented.

Empirical evidence

Provincial level

This section describes the results across different specifications. Preliminary tests on serial correlation and heteroskedasticity signal that only the latter is problematic in this data context. Thus, all specifications are estimated using the Prais–Winsten correction technique.[10]

The results of the econometric estimates of logarithmic[11] forms are summarized in Table 5.2. In linear form the elasticity of waste generation to value added is around 0.35. Contrary to non-corrected specifications, a (very high) TP arises, at around €36,000, outside the range of observed values.

When separately collected waste and population density are included as additional variables, the estimated elasticity increases to 0.43 in linear forms, while the TP decreases to €31,600, which is close to the maximum observed value (e.g. the province of Milan). Population density is positively impacting on waste generation: economies of scale in waste management do not seem to outweigh scale effects on the waste generation side. More densely populated urban areas produce relatively more waste. This result has implications for the forecasting of future waste trends driven by population changes. The share of separated collection presents a negative expected coefficient. Stronger

Table 5.2 Provincial level: base estimations and additional specifications

Variable					Model				
	1	2	3	4	5	6	7	8	9
Constant	***	*	***	***	***	***	***	***	***
ln VA	0.349***	4.555**	0.431***	6.685***	6.313***	8.777***	7.366***	9.441***	7.827***
(ln VA)²	...	-0.216**	...	-0.323***	-0.312***	-0.436***	-0.367***	-0.464***	-0.387***
ln DENS	...	...	0.035***	0.041***	0.061***	0.038***	0.059***	0.045***	0.062***
COLLEC	...	...	-0.003***	-0.003***	-0.002**	...	...	-0.004***	-0.002***
TARIFF	...	...	...	...	...	0.001***	0.001**	0.002***	0.001***
COST-REC	...	...	...	...	...	-0.002***	-0.003***	-0.002***	-0.003***
ln TOURIST	...	...	...	...	0.075***	...	0.075***	...	0.072***
Turning point	/	36,518	/	31,611	25,227	23,515	22,586	26,246	24,494
Panel-level heteroskedasticity LR test	544.910***	544.860***	571.600***	563.690***	546.910***	614.130***	591.210***	622.790***	587.200***
χ^2 prob.	0.0000	0.0000	0.0000	0.0000	0.0000	0.0000	0.0000	0.0000	0.0000
N	721	721	721	721	721	721	721	721	721

Note: Coefficients are shown in cells; significance at 10%, 5% and 1% is denoted by * , ** and ***, respectively.

commitment to waste flow separation and recycling seems to have an impact on the amount of waste generated. Possible endogeneity (the higher the amount of waste the higher the volume of separated collection) is not found here, though it would be worth checking. Waste management performance impacts backwards on waste generation along the waste productive chain/filiere.

The inclusion of geographic dummies (south, north-east, north-west, centre) slightly reduces the elasticity (0.333), and a waste Kuznets curve emerges. Results for central, south and north-west Italy are the most significant, with positive, negative and negative coefficients respectively (geographic dummies are not shown in Table 5.2). The negative coefficients for the northern region dummies confirm the insights on north–south structural differences, and also on the southern region dummies, at least with respect to the islands (Sardinia and Sicily).

Finally, the introduction of a tourist flow factor, aimed at further correcting estimates for the omitted variables bias, shows that, as expected, total provincial tourist presence positively influences per capita waste generation and is highly significant. It is not highly correlated with value added. The TP is further decreasing with respect to the above regressions: €25,227, which is within the range of observed value added. The elasticity of waste generation to tourist attendance is 0.0758.[12]

As an additional exercise we tested a model for total (rather than per capita) waste generated, where the dependent variable is waste generation, and the explanatory variables are value added, population and share of separated collection (estimates not shown). Value added and population are positively and significantly linked with waste generation, and separated collection is negatively and significantly linked with waste generation. Elasticities of waste generation to value added and population are estimated to be within the ranges 0.43–0.93 and 0.56–0.59 respectively. These elasticities confirm the results in the literature (Johnstone and Labonne 2004).

To sum up, the results of our analysis show some evidence of a waste Kuznets curve, although they need further confirmation given the very high TP, which nevertheless is within the observed income range in the most comprehensive specifications, including tourist flows. Graphical plots support (weak) waste Kuznets curve evidence. We could argue that, instead of a real first sign of absolute delinking, we are observing a stabilization of waste generation for some of the richer areas.[13] Neither share of separated collection nor population density, though significant, affects the evidence for an EKC relationship between waste and income. This evidence may be the first sign, emerging from a very detailed and heterogeneous provincial data set, of a process in which the structural feature are reversing, from a positive to a negative elasticity of waste generation with respect to income/value added drivers. Further empirical evidence is needed to confirm these results. Overall, there is strong evidence of a relative delinking, with elasticities that are much lower than those estimated in previous studies on the EU (Mazzanti 2008), and more in line with new estimates (Chapter 2 of this book).[14] If there is no clear evidence of an EKC, at least a levelling off of MSW generation with respect to socio-economic drivers is emerging. Here, we would stress the value of provincial data, which allow a more in-depth investigation of income–environment trends by exploiting more (latent) heterogeneity.

We tested two proxies for a policy shift towards more market-oriented waste management approaches: (i) share of total population living in municipalities that had introduced the waste tariff in place of the old waste tax (TARIFF); (ii) the percentage of total waste management cost recovered by waste management utilities (COST-REC, this variable should capture the way that the approach to waste management is moving towards an enterprise approach, even within the sphere of public ownership/management).[15] We use only 2004 data (which are reliable) because, in this case, the time trend is less relevant than cross-section heterogeneity. The two variables, as expected, are positively correlated. However, since they capture different economic and institutional trends, this correlation is not high (0.18).[16]

When including the above-mentioned variables, waste Kuznets curve evidence persists, with TP estimated in the range €23,500–€26,000. Thus the inclusion of policy variables further reduces the estimated TP level; it persists at the high income level, but some provinces exceed it.[17]

TARIFF is positively and significantly correlated with waste generation, perhaps signalling endogeneity of policy cycles with regard to income: richer areas show a stronger environmental policy commitment. This is of critical importance in decentralized policy environments.

As far as COST-REC is concerned, we found a negative effect.[18] Table 5.2 shows that including COST-REC and TARIFF jointly does not change the result. The more waste utilities adopt market behaviour by covering at least the variable cost of the service through tariffs the higher the local performance in terms of less waste generated, regardless of the private/public/ mixed kind of ownership. This information is useful for policy: although the transition from the tax to the tariff system is slow (and endogenously driven), the full-cost pricing mechanism impacts negatively on waste generation trends even in the early implementation phase.

Our work quantitatively assesses that at least the initial phase of policy implementation may be associated with endogeneity and, consequently, it will increase the differences between the richer and poorer areas of a country. Nevertheless, our results seem to suggest that instruments implemented at the level of waste management (recycling, collection, disposal) can generate feedback effects on waste prevention by reducing the amount of generated waste to an extent. Evaluating policy processes during their initial phases can be useful for reshaping tools and processes.[19]

Regional level

The results of the analysis at regional level are summarized in Table 5.3. We use two alternative economic drivers: GDP and household expenditure. The

Table 5.3 Regional level: base estimations and additional specifications

Variable				Model				
	1	2	3	4	5	6	7	8
Constant	–	–	–	–	–	–	***	–
GDP	0.037***	0.054***	–	–	–	–	–	–
GDP²	–	–0.0000009	–	–	–	–	–	–
ln GDP	–	–	1.154***	0.881***	0.871***	–	–	–
ln C	–	–	–	–	–	0.133***	0.352***	0.106**
DENS	–	–0.61	–	–	–0.0011	–0.009***	–	–2.380***
COLLEC	–	1.850***	–	0.003***	0.032**	0.008***	–	0.009***
Turning point	–	€31,034	–	–	–	–	–	–
FEM/REM	FEM	FEM (AR(1))	FEM	FEM	FEM (AR(1))	FEM	REM	FEM
Adj. R²	0.9088	0.832	0.906	0.919	0.91	0.91	0.845	0.927
F test and χ² prob.	0.000	0.000	0.000	0.000	0.000	0.000	0.000	0.000
N	180	180	180	180	180	160	160	160

Note: Significance at 10%, 5% and 1% is denoted by * , ** and ***, respectively.

latter (not available at provincial level) could emerge as being a more accurate driver of waste generation. A fixed effects model (FEM) is here preferred as estimation framework.

When using regional GDP (non-logarithmic specifications), the base specification with income terms only does not show evidence of an EKC. An autocorrelation (AR) corrected model leads to some (weak)[20] EKC evidence (and the TP is outside the income range), with and without the variable COLLECT (share of separated collection) and population density.

In the linear form estimates the two significant covariates, both with a positive sign, are added value (GDP) and COLLECT; their inclusion does not affect the significance of added value. We find positive coefficients for some dummies associated with southern regions, and negative signs for northern ones, confirming the above comments. In terms of GDP, estimated elasticities in linear specifications are in the range 0.36–1.31, showing high variability, depending on the specification. Elasticities are 1.31, 1.15 and 0.71 in the linear models, corrected and not corrected for serial correlation[21] and heteroskedasticity. In the uncorrected model the value of the elasticity is reduced. The inclusion of separated collection reduces the elasticity from 1.31 to 1.01 in the uncorrected model, from 1.15 to 0.79 in the corrected model and from 0.41 to 0.36 in a least squares dummy variable (LSDV) with time period effects.

The logarithmic specification confirms the higher plausibility of the linear specification: the elasticity in this case is estimated across different specifications (only GDP, with separated collection, with correlation correction; specifications 4–6) in the range 0.87–1.15 (lower when additional factors are estimated). Those values are higher than at provincial level, and also higher than the evidence from international studies.

The squared model generates not significant terms when COLLECT is added, and when the correlation corrected model is applied. In the uncorrected model the coefficients are significant, but the signs are reversed. This confirms that, as noted in the literature, EKC evidence is dependent on the specification used.

To sum up, elasticity to GDP ranges between 0.41–1.31 across different log and non-log specifications. When using household expenditure as an economic driver (we lose one year due to data availability), the non-logarithmic specifications do not provide robust regression results and the economic drivers, in linear and squared terms, do not emerge as significant. The logarithmic specification, however, confirms the significance of the linear term and separated waste collection: nevertheless, the estimated elasticity is lower, estimated in the range (across specifications) 0.10–0.35.[22]

We test a model that includes variables in absolute (not per capita) terms, but add population level as an explanatory factor. Here, population emerges as a driving force at regional level only when the variable related to separated collection, which is again found to be positively significant, is omitted.[23] Confirming the evidence from international studies, population elasticity, at both regional and provincial levels, is higher than income elasticity. Our regional data set, which exploits GDP data rather than added value, provides higher elasticities for both driving factors.[24]

Thus the regional data set seems to provide relatively less robust empirical evidence compared with the province-level analysis. We argue that the main cause is the higher heterogeneity that enriches the provincial data set.

Conclusions and policy implications

This chapter provides empirical evidence on the relationship between economic drivers (income and socio-economic and policy factors) and municipal waste generation by analysing two sets of panel data for Italy: 20 regions for the period 1996–2004 and 103 provinces for the period 1999–2005. The results provide evidence in favour of an EKC for waste, with rather high TPs, but within the observed income range, at least for most specifications. This evidence emerges mainly from province-level data. The TP is estimated to be in the range €22,586–€31,611 of value added per capita. Baseline specifications show a TP at €36,518, while specifications that include socio-economic drivers and policy factors have a TP around €23,000–€26,000. These values are higher than the median and mean values for value added in the period considered, and quite close to the maximum value added observed across Italian provinces. Only a few of the 103 Italian provinces either exceed or come close to this threshold.

All other drivers, such as population density, separated waste collection, tourist flows and policy factors, are statistically significant, with the expected signs. Policy factors, particularly the transition from the tax to the tariff system, highlight the possible effectiveness of full-cost pricing. However, only the richest provinces in northern Italy tend to be more innovative in terms of new institutional/policy approaches (market-oriented management, market-based instruments, better enforcement of waste policies), but they produce more waste per capita. Although the innovative approaches to waste policy adopted by the richer Italian provinces are aimed mainly at recovering waste management costs, and rather less at reducing waste generation at source, they could have a favourable impact on local waste generation performance. The two policy variables do not affect the core waste Kuznets curve evidence.

To our knowledge, these results are the first evidence in support of EKC for waste generation. However, identification of an EKC for waste largely depends on the availability for analysis of in-country highly disaggregated data. When exploiting within-country heterogeneity, different relationships between environmental pressures and economic drivers may arise, calling for different policy interventions.

If national/local situations differ with respect to abatement costs and with respect to the point along the waste Kuznets curve at which the country/region lies, this would call for more heterogeneity in national/local waste policies (Pearce 2004). Our investigation is specific to Italy, a country where the role of decentralized waste policies is structurally and increasingly relevant, and allows some consideration of north–south differences. Nevertheless, the results for Italy should be of interest to other EU countries that have decentralized policy implementation and where within country heterogeneity is crucial; this would apply especially to important countries such as Germany and Spain. The US is a country that, along with some differences, shares some similarities in this respect.

Finally, although our results may suggest a somewhat weak reversal of the waste–income relationship, they show that we cannot rely only on the expected endogenous effects of economic growth for achieving lower levels of waste generation. More effective waste prevention policies are needed, which decouple waste generation from its income-related drivers. Similar to what is emerging at European level, the results for Italy seem to confirm that waste policies are more successful in developing waste recovery/recycling and new disposal routes than in promoting waste prevention. The problem of lack of incentives to prevention is common to other environmental policies but seems to be particularly acute in the case of waste policies.

Notes

1 Value added is the (incremental) component of produced wealth that is attributable to the geographical area. Value added is the only economic driver available at province level. Other potential drivers are GDP and its components, consumption and investments.
2 We are unable to use policy variables related to landfill taxation, since in Italy landfill taxes are implemented at a decentralized level and tax values are available only for the main northern regions. We exploit available information on waste management instruments.
3 A general and updated survey can be found in Chapter 2, to which we refer to avoid duplication. Moreover, Table 2.1 in chapter 2 shows a brief summary of the recent waste Kuznets curve literature.
4 Some authors adopt second-order polynomials, others estimate third and even fourth-order polynomials, comparing different specifications for relative robustness. It is worth noting that neither the quadratic nor the cubic function can be considered a fully realistic representation of the income–environment relationship: the cubic specification implies that environmental degradation will tend towards a plus or minus infinity as income increases; the quadratic specification implies that environmental degradation could eventually tend towards zero. Third or fourth-level polynomials could also lead to N rather than U-shaped curves. The N shape would be justified by a non-linear effect of the scale of economic activity on the environment.
5 In the OECD countries, MSW accounts for around 14 per cent of total waste generated and includes household and similar waste. It includes bulky waste, garden waste, and waste from small businesses and institutions.
6 We should stress that, according to Italian classifications, municipal waste generation includes a variety of waste sources in addition to household waste, such as commercial and public administration waste generated at the municipal level.
7 As stated by Fonkych and Lempert (2005: 29), 'different EKCs are likely to exist for different countries and pollutants, and explanatory variables other than per capita income may be better determinants of emission trajectories'.

8 The exact tax/tariff level is information that is not readily available, since it is determined by the individual (private or public) utility company managing the waste flows at municipal or provincial level.

9 As expected, cubic specifications are not significant.

10 Diagnostic tests indicate the presence of heteroskedasticity, but not serial correlation. Thus the models are estimated using Prais–Winsten feasible generalized least squares, assuming panel heteroskedasticity but not serial correlation. This yields parameter estimates along with panel-corrected variance estimates. Johnstone and Labonne (2004) recognize the necessity of testing both correlation and heteroskedasticity but note problems in coping with both, given missing values in their OECD data.

11 Logarithmic transformations are preferred because from a theoretical standpoint it is more correct to implement significance tests on logarithm data. The assumptions of the most common significance tests (z tests, t tests and F tests) is that variables are normally distributed. We note that per capita waste values are right-skewed, and the log transformation generates a more symmetrical distribution.

12 If we split tourist flows into national and foreign (0.73 correlation) the aforementioned regression is still significant. National tourist flows are associated with a relatively higher positive elasticity.

13 A similar picture emerges for Europe, for the EU-15 and for the EU-25 samples. Some richer countries are showing a stabilizing or reversing trend.

14 In other words, a diminishing, but not a negative, marginal effect.

15 For both waste and water management, Italy is currently undergoing a long-run shift towards an institutional setting in which, even when they remain the owner and the manager of the service, the local public agents take on a variety of utility configurations. These can include private entities, and, in any case, the service must be put out to tender in the market. Therefore the trend is towards increasing full-cost recovery, based on the shift from tax to tariff, at least for the variable part of costs.

16 It is true that the outcomes of policy analysis may be flawed owing to the short-term nature of the data. Nevertheless, unlike most studies, we exploit time variant indexes. Then – and this is a core point in our study – environmental and waste policies, especially in the initial phase, are characterized by endogeneity with regard to other features. Policies are not exogenous, as the theory might prescribe, but are often related to income and institutional features.

17 To sum up, TPs across specifications are quite close to the maximum value observed. Only a few of the 103 provinces exceed the estimated lower bound of the range of estimated TPs across regressions, i.e. Rome, Mantua, Florence, Bologna, Modena, Milan, Bolzano, Parma. Taking the highest level in the range, only Milan and Bolzano are strictly higher than the estimated TP.

18 As an alternative to TARIFF, we confirmed whether the share of municipalities in a province (rather than the population) that introduced the tariff (TARIFF2) produced different evidence. This variable is independent from effects deriving from huge urban areas opting for tariffs, since each municipality within a province has the same weight. It is nevertheless not significant, with a negative coefficient.

19 If waste management and waste policies are income-driven, early implementation may affect the dynamic. Poorer regions with poor policy performance may undermine the future possibilities of reversing the relationship. Though the optimal dynamic of environmental investments for a region over dynamic development is difficult to assess, the recent EKC literature shows that, if the defined thresholds are exceeded at an early stage, irreversible or very high costs may emerge, making environmental management more difficult and more costly at the (income) stage where society values the environment.

20 The squared term is very close to a 10 per cent significance level.

21 The test (not shown) confirms this hypothesis, both in the base LSDV model and in the LSDV with time effects.
22 AR correction reduces the significance of the consumption term. Overall, the regional dataset seems to produce a less robust result and, unexpectedly, the model with consumption rather than GDP does not perform better. Provincial heterogeneity may be indicated as the main statistical added value.
23 When separated collection is included added value is significant, with an associated elasticity of 0.37. When separated collection is excluded the elasticity increases to 0.60, while the elasticity of waste generation with respect to population is 1.22.
24 For provinces, we also tested a two-stage model, estimating first the predicted values for waste generation, in order to include this element as an explanatory factor of separated waste collection: the results are the same.

References

Andersen, F., Larsen, H., Skovgaard, M., Moll, S. and Isoard, S. (2007) 'A European model for waste and material flows', *Resources, Conservation and Recycling*, 49: 421–35.
Andreoni, J. and Levinson, A. (2001) 'The simple analytics of the environmental Kuznets curve', *Journal of Public Economics*, 80: 269–86.
APAT (2006) *Rapporto rifiuti 2006*, Rome: Ministry of the Environment, Rome: APAT.
——(2005) *Rapporto rifiuti* [Waste Report] *2005*, Rome: Ministry of the Environment.
——(2004) *Rapporto rifiuti 2004*, Rome: Ministry of the Environment.
——(2003) *Rapporto rifiuti 2003*, Rome: Ministry of the Environment.
——(2003) *Rapporto rifiuti 2002*, Rome: Ministry of the Environment.
——(2001) *Rapporto rifiuti 2001*, Rome: Ministry of the Environment.
——(2000) *Rapporto rifiuti 2000*, Rome: Ministry of the Environment.
——(1999) *Rapporto rifiuti 1999*, Rome: Ministry of the Environment.
Beede, D. and Bloom, D. (1995) 'Economics of the Generation and Management of MSW', NBER Working Papers 5116, Cambridge MA: NBER.
Berrens, R., Bohara, A., Gawande, K. and Wang, P. (1998) 'Testing the inverted U hypothesis for US hazardous waste: an application of the generalized gamma model', *Economic Letters*, 55: 435–40.
Bringezu, S., Schültz, H. and Moll, S. (2003) 'Rationale for and interpretation of economy-wide material flow analysis and derived indicators', *Journal of Industrial Ecology*, 7: 43–64.
Brock, W. and Taylor, S. (2003) 'The Kindergarten Rule of Sustainable Growth', NBER Working Papers 9597, Cambridge MA: NBER.
——(2004) 'The Green Solow Model', NBER Working Papers 10557, Cambridge MA: NBER.
Cagatay, S. and Mihci, H. (2006) 'Degree of environmental stringency and the impact on trade patterns', *Journal of Economic Studies*, 33: 30–51.
Callan, S. and Thomas, J. (2006) 'Analyzing demand for disposal and recycling services', *Eastern Economic Journal*, 32: 221–40.
Cole, M., Elliott, R. and Fredrikkson, P. (2006) 'Endogenous pollution haves: does FDI influence environmental regulations?' *Scandinavian Journal of Economics*, 108: 157–78.
Cole, M., Rayner, A. and Bates, J. (1997) 'The EKC: an empirical analysis', *Environment and Development Economics*, 2: 401–16.

Concu, N. (2000) 'La tirannia del trade-off sconfitta? Turismo, ambiente naturale e rifiuti solidi urbani: la ricerca di una EKC', CRENOS working paper, Cagliari: CRENOS.

Copeland, B. R. and Taylor, M. S. (2004) 'Trade, growth and the environment', *Journal of Economic Literature*, 42: 7–71.

DEFRA/DTI (2003) *Sustainable Consumption and Production Indicators*, London: DEFRA.

Dinda, S. (2004) 'Environmental Kuznets curve hypothesis: a survey', *Ecological Economics*, 49: 431–55.

EEA (2003a) *Evaluation Analysis of the Implementation of the Packaging Directive*, Copenhagen: European Environment Agency.

—— (2003b) *Assessment of Information related to Waste and Material Flows*, Copenhagen: European Environment Agency.

—— (2003c) *Europe's Environment: The Third Assessment*, Copenhagen: European Environment Agency.

European Commission (2003a) *Towards a Thematic Strategy for Waste Prevention and Recycling*, COM (2003) 301, Brussels: European Commission.

—— (2003b) *Towards a Thematic Strategy on Sustainable Use of Natural Resources*, COM (2003) 572, Brussels: European Commission.

Eurostat (2003) *Waste Generated and Treated in Europe: Data 1990–2001*, Luxembourg: Office for Official Publications of the European Communities.

Fischer-Kowalski, M. and Amann, C. (2001) 'Beyond IPAT and Kuznets curves: globalization as a vital factor in analyzing the environmental impact of socio-economic metabolism', *Population and the Environment*, 23: 7–47.

Fonkych, K. and Lempert, R. (2005) 'Assessment of environmental Kuznets curves and socio-economic drivers in IPCC's SRES scenarios', *Journal of Environment and Development*, 14: 27–47.

Jacobsen, H., Mazzanti, M., Moll, S., Simeone, M. G., Pontoglio, S. and Zoboli, R. (2004) *Methodology and Indicators to measure Decoupling, Resource Efficiency, and Waste Prevention*, ETC/WMF, P6.2-2004, Copenhagen: European Topic Centre on Waste and Material Flows and European Environment Agency.

Johnstone, N. and Labonne, J. (2004) 'Generation of household solid waste in OECD countries: an empirical analysis using macroeconomic data', *Land Economics*, 80: 529–38.

Karousakis, K. (2006) 'MSW Generation, Disposal and Recycling: a Note on OECD Inter-country Differences', paper presented at ENVECON 2006: Applied Environmental Economics Conference, London: Royal Society, 24 March.

Leigh, R. (2004) 'Economic growth as environmental policy? Reconsidering the environmental Kuznets curve', *Journal of Public Policy*, 24: 327–48.

Lieb, C. M. (2004) 'The environmental Kuznets curve and flow versus stock pollution: the neglect of future damages', *Environmental and Resource Economics*, 29: 483–506.

Lim, J. (1997) 'The effects of economic growth on environmental quality: some empirical investigation for the case of South Korea', *Seoul Journal of Economics*, 10: 272–93.

Mazzanti, M. (2008) 'Is waste generation delinking from economic growth?' *Applied Economics Letters*, 15: 287–91.

OECD (2004) *Addressing the Economics of Waste*, Paris: OECD.

——(2003) *Response Indicators for Waste Prevention within the OECD Area*, Paris: OECD.

——(2002) *Indicators to measure Decoupling of Environmental Pressure from Economic Growth*, Paris: OECD.

Pearce, D. W. (2004) 'Does European Union waste policy pass a cost–benefit test?' *World Economics*, 5: 115–37.

Seppala, T., Haukioja, T. and Kaivo-oja, J. (2001) 'The EKC hypothesis does not hold for direct material flows: environmental Kuznets curve hypothesis tests for direct material flows in five industrial countries', *Population and Environment*, 23: 217–38.

Stern, D. (1998) 'Progress on the environmental Kuznets curve?' *Environment and Development Economics*, 3: 173–96.

——(2004) 'The rise and fall of the environmental Kuznets curve', *World Development*, 32: 1419–38.

Wang, P., Bohara, A., Berrens, R. and Gawande, K. (1998) 'A risk-based environmental Kuznets curve for US hazardous waste sites', *Applied Economics Letters*, 5: 761–3.

World Bank (1992) *Development and the Environment*, World Bank report, Oxford: Oxford University Press.

6 Embedding landfill diversion in economic, geographical and policy settings

Regional and provincial evidence from Italy

Massimiliano Mazzanti, Anna Montini and Francesco Nicolli

Reducing the amounts of waste going to landfill is a primary aim of European environmental policies related to climate change. The effectiveness of European policies will be based on sound implementation at the levels where waste is being generated and disposed of.

European efforts at reducing landfill are a priority in the waste hierarchy, and one of the pillars of EU waste strategy is the 1999 Landfill Directive (EEA 2007), which is being implemented at member state level in association with national efforts regarding waste management, such as separate collection, recycling, incineration, and disposal and use of waste. These actions are devoted to diverting waste from landfill and reducing waste generated at source, to achieve a decoupling of different stages of the waste production chain.

The EEA (2007: 3) has assessed that:

> countries can be categorised under three waste management *groupings*, according to the strategies for diversion of municipal waste away from landfill, and the relative shares of landfill, materials recovery (mainly recycling and composting) and incineration. The first grouping comprises countries that have high levels of materials recovery and incineration, and relatively low levels of landfill. The second grouping includes countries with high materials recovery rates and medium levels of incineration, and medium dependence on landfill. The third grouping comprises countries where levels of both materials recovery and incineration are low, and dependence on landfill is relatively high.

Though northern Italy has some rapidly evolving strategies for high levels of recycling, composting and incineration, on average, disposal of waste is still dominated by landfill, as the dramatic news from southern areas, such as Campania, confirms. However, some northern regions of Italy are encountering landfill criticalities based on the increasing scarcity of land in physical and economic terms (opportunity costs) and the non-decreasing or stabilized, trend in waste generation.

This chapter analyses the process of delinking of landfill trends, within a framework in which economic, institutional, geographic and policy variables play a role. On the basis of recent decreases in amounts of landfilled waste at EU level we investigate what are the main drivers of this phenomenon, and whether there are differences if the focus is on decentralised, provincial settings. We exploit a rich panel data set from official sources (APAT, the Italian environmental agency) which is merged with provincial and regional based information, covering the 103 Italian provinces, in the period 1999 to 2005. This extended, decentralized and recent source of data is of major interest for an investigation of waste processes and for policy evaluation, where evidence is typically scattered, of poor quality and rather scarce. This evidence will complement EU level analyses (Mazzanti and Zoboli, Chapter 1; Andersen *et al.* 2007; Chapter 3)[1] on the driving forces of past and future waste trends, and is a consequence of recent studies on the drivers of waste generation in Italy; it demonstrates that environmental Kuznets curve (EKC) evidence is far from being a fact for many regions, and that waste strategies may play a role that is complementary to exogenous drivers, such as income (see previous chapter).

The value added of this chapter is multiple. First, it offers unique evidence on landfill diversion trends. This is highly relevant, as existing waste analyses suffering from a lack of robust econometric panel-based evidence. Second, it exploits a wide array of drivers related to economic, geographical and policy factors and suggests outcomes useful for *ex post* policy evaluation of landfill and assessment of Kuznets delinking trends for landfill. Policy levers are investigated at the levels of waste management (collection) and final disposal (landfill tax, incineration regional strategies), in order to check direct and indirect effects along the waste management–disposal chain. Third, it relies on a very decentralized data set; at this level Kuznets shapes can be assessed more robustly, since they exploit richer heterogeneity. In the case of Italy this is of especial importance, as that country presents high structural diversification between the northern and southern areas, differences that are extremely relevant to waste management and disposal. Fourth, the analysis complements EU-level panel-based investigations of delinking and policy evaluation for waste generation, recycling and landfill, and analyses of waste generation delinking trends for Italy conducted in recent years. The complete set of evidence will be an important source of information for policy makers and researchers on the set of dynamics operating in the waste sector.

A case study of Italy is considered valuable, as Italy is an important member of the EU, thus it can provide useful information on the evaluation of policies such as the 1999 Landfill Directive. Also, its heterogeneous and problematic economic, institutional and environmental performance provides the basis for an interesting analysis of how economic and policy levers impact on the dynamics of landfill in such settings. Finally, as waste management and landfill policies are implemented at a very decentralized level, this case study analysis provides food for other policy making processes in place or being planned along similar lines.

The chapter is structured as follows. Next section presents a short survey of the studies of waste and delinking, which highlights the lack of comprehensive empirical analyses of landfill, compared with waste generation and other environmental issues, and other analyses of landfill, including the evaluation of costs and benefits. Then we present the empirical model and describe the panel data source. Some comments on the empirical evidence at both regional and provincial levels follow. The final section concludes with policy implications and suggestions for further research.

Waste generation and disposal: the state of the art

A general and updated survey can be found in Chapter 2, to which we refer to avoid duplication. In this section we provide a brief survey and some comments of the still scarce evidence on waste delinking, waste management, and waste disposal, with the focus on the evaluation of policy tools.

In spite of the significant environmental, policy and economic relevance of waste issues, there is very little empirical evidence on delinking, even for major waste streams, such as municipal and packaging. Analyses of policy effectiveness are similarly scarce. Existing work is largely oriented towards the optimization of waste management or evaluation of externalities, regarding landfill and other waste disposal strategies, with a few purely theoretical analyses on waste management and landfill management (Calcott and Walls 2005; Daskalopoulos *et al.* 1998; Andre and Cerda 2004; Ozawa 2005). The focus on cost–benefit analyses and landfill siting decisions is in part due to the lack of reliable country-level and within-country data (Pearce 2004).[2] The EU (Eurostat data) and a few individual countries have produced detailed and reliable (panel) data that give robust empirical insights into diverse waste issues. Analysis of endogenous and exogenous drivers, including policies, is an important area, to which this chapter aims to contribute, that brings together environmental Kuznets curve analyses (waste Kuznets curve, WKC, for waste)[3] and *ex post* studies of policy effectiveness.

As already mentioned, the economic analyses of landfill have predominantly focused on cost–benefit assessments of relative externalities. A rare case is the IVM report (IVM 2005) on landfill tax effectiveness in the EU. Some specific studies have been done on the evaluation of the EU Landfill Directive and the well established (since 1996) UK landfill tax. (Turner *et al.* 1998 provide a rare evaluation based specifically on externalities.) Among more recent works we would refer the reader to Davies and Doble (2004), who monitored the UK landfill tax from its introduction and offer insights on future evolution, criticalities and externality evaluation. Such works are by definition qualitative, given the lack of data and the aims of these analyses.

Phillips *et al.* (2007) provide one of the most recent UK-specific regional assessments of waste strategies. However, regionally based analyses are still very rare.

This survey of the literature, which is still developing slowly even within the waste framework, lacks any in-depth investigation of driving forces and policy effects, and does not contain any single-country case studies or investigations of homogeneous policies in force over sufficiently long periods of time. Also, landfill-oriented analyses are in the minority even within the area of waste. In our study we have tried to bring together different strands of research and analyse exogenous and endogenous landfill diversion drivers by exploiting the intrinsically higher heterogeneity of decentralized regional data. We provide a specific focus on waste management and policy levers. It should be noted that some waste management strategies are to an extent endogenous, being driven by income and geographical differentiation (something that we comment on in a subsequent section). The different commitment and performance of the northern and southern regions in Italy, is a clear example here.

Overall, it can be said that landfill is still the predominant option for the treatment of the EU's municipal waste, and that Italy's performance in terms of waste disposal is being constantly monitored and evaluated. In 2004 about 45 per cent of total municipal waste in Italy was landfilled while 18 per cent was incinerated. However, there are significant differences in how dependent different countries are on landfill. Figure 2.2 showed that several countries – the Netherlands, Denmark, Sweden and Belgium – have already achieved very low rates of landfill. These countries not only have substantial levels of incineration, they also have high levels of materials recovery. In general, there seem to be two strategies for diverting municipal waste from landfill: high materials recovery combined with incineration, or materials recovery that includes recycling, composting and mechanical biological treatment (EEA 2007).

The empirical framework

Data sources and research hypotheses

The analysis uses two data sets, a regional one and a provincial one, that exploit the statistical information in the available yearly editions of the Italian Environment Agency's waste report (APAT 2001, 2002, 2003, 2004, 2005, 2006). These reports provide a very rich set of waste data, produced according to Eurostat and EEA guidelines (EEA 2003a, b, c).

The provincial data set includes data on MSW generated (collected) and landfilled (Figure 6.1) in all the 103 Italian provinces and covers the period 1999–2005. We merge these data with official data on provincial level economic drivers. Although consumption is often used as coherent driver in analyses of waste trends (Andersen *et al.* 2007), we do not have provincial-level data on consumption; thus value added is the only reliable economic driver available. Additional socio-economic variables relevant to waste, such as MSW generated and incinerated (Figure 6.2), share of separately collected waste (Figure 6.3) and population density, are tested. We also check for tourist-related flows, a crucial factor in waste generation and collection for many Italian provinces.

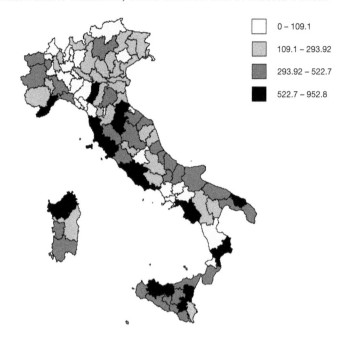

Figure 6.1 Per capita landfilled waste in Italian provinces (kg, 2005)

Finally, we include decentralized policy-related variables, especially: (i) the share of provincial municipalities and the provincial population covered by the *new waste tariff regime*, which substitutes for the *old waste tax regime*; and (ii) the percentage of waste management costs covered by the tariff. With respect to the policy-related variables, the waste management *tariff* was introduced by Italian law No. 22/1997, and substitutes for the former waste management *tax*. The tax, however, is still in force in many Italian municipalities because law 22/1997 provides for a transition phase that is quite gradual and slow. The tax was calculated on the size of household living spaces, while the tariff is based on principles of full cost pricing for waste management services.[4] Effective implementation of the tariff system remains highly dependent on local policy decisions and practices and is partly based on the choices made by the municipalities. Early implementation of the new tariff-based system, therefore, may be a sign of policy commitment. We note that implementation is heterogeneous even across areas with similar incomes and similar social economic variables. The shift from tax to tariff should also capture the incentive effect of the latter, although the impact on waste generation, if any, is not visible in the short term.

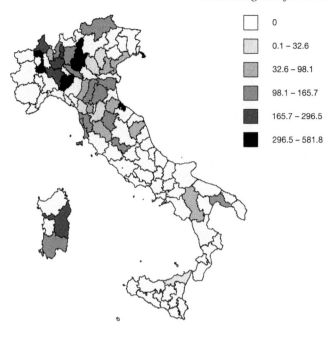

☐	0
▨	0.1 – 32.6
▨	32.6 – 98.1
▨	98.1 – 165.7
▨	165.7 – 296.5
■	296.5 – 581.8

Figure 6.2 Per capita incinerated waste in Italian provinces (kg, 2005)

The regional data set includes all the information in the provincial data set plus data on annual household consumption expenditure per component, and landfill tax (both variables are available only at regional level). Tables 6.1 and 6.2 present the dependent and independent variables, the descriptive statistics and the research hypotheses related to the provincial and regional data sets respectively.

The model

We estimate the model by specifying our research hypothesis with the following general panel-based reduced form (Dijkgraaf and Gradus 2004; Stern 2004):

$$(1) \quad \ln(\text{landfilled MSW per capita}) = \beta_{0i} + \alpha_t + \beta_1 \ln(\text{economic driver})_{it}$$
$$+ \beta_2 \ln(\text{socio} - \text{economic factors})_{it}$$
$$+ \beta_3 (\text{environmental policy})_{it} + \varepsilon_{it}$$

where the first two terms are intercept parameters that vary across regions or provinces, and years.

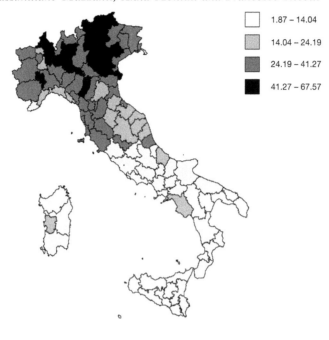

☐	1.87 – 14.04
▨	14.04 – 24.19
▩	24.19 – 41.27
■	41.27 – 67.57

Figure 6.3 Separately collected waste share in Italian provinces (%, 2005)

Different specifications are tested by including as the dependent variable either landfilled waste per capita (or per area) or landfilled waste in total terms; accordingly, value added is either per capita or total.

Other socio-economic factors are added to the core specification as controls, and possible additional significant drivers of waste generation. In our model they include population density, percentage share of separately collected waste, incinerated waste per capita, tourist numbers and, related to environmental policy, recovery capacity of waste services costs, and share of population (or municipalities) subject to waste tariffs (rather than waste taxes).

Using provincial data only, we estimate a semi-logarithmic model to deal with the zero values that correspond to the absence of a landfill site.[5] Spatial econometric analyses are a definite future extension of this work that would investigate the role of flows between provinces by analysing contiguity and distance.

Empirical evidence

Regional analysis

Analysis of the regional data set involves a panel of 140 observations (20 regions observed over seven years: 1999–2005). Most variables are time-variant, thus

Table 6.1 Descriptive statistics and research hypothesis (*provincial* data set): dependent and independent variables

Acronym	Variable description	Mean	Min.	Max.	Research hypothesis
LAND-WASTE	MSW yearly generated and landfilled (kg/capita)	326.38	0	1133.78	Dependent variable
VA	Provincial yearly value added per capita (€2,000)	17,653.6	9,369.12	28,796.07	Positively correlated with income, the objective is assessing whether relative or absolute delinking is present
DENS	Population/surface (inhabitants/km^2)	244.10	36.43	2,640.92	Positive and negative correlations may emerge depending on factors such as economies of scale and land opportunity costs in urban and densely inhabited areas
COLLEC	Share of separated collection (%)	18.40	0.03	67.57	Negatively affecting landfilled waste per capita
INC-WASTE	MSW generated yearly and incinerated (kg/capita)	49.93	0	581.81	Negatively affecting landfilled waste per capita
TAR POP	Share of population living in municipalities that introduced a waste tariff substituting the former waste tax (%)	9.00	0	99.72	Possibly reducing MSW generation through indirect feed back effects, though the direct effect is at waste management level. Possible endogeneity, given the positive correlation with respect to income
TAR MUN	Share of municipalities that introduced a waste tariff substituting the former waste tax (%)	5.03	0	100.00	
COST-REC	Cost recovery of waste management services (tax/tariff revenues on variable service costs, 2004 data only) (%)	85.61	53.3	104.2	
TOURIST	Annual tourist numbers (per capita)	7.18	0.40	58.83	Positively affecting landfilled waste per capita

Table 6.2 Descriptive statistics and research hypothesis (*regional* data set): dependent and independent variables

Acronym	Variable description	Mean	Min.	Max.	Research hypothesis
LAND-WASTE	MSW generated and landfilled (kg/capita)	358.07	80.00	620.00	Dependent variable
GDP	Gross domestic product per capita (€2,000)	20,331	12,741	27,905	Positively correlated with income, the objective is to assess whether there is relative or absolute delinking
CONS	Household consumption expenditure (per component)	9,716.8	6,504.5	13,423.6	Positively correlated with income
DENS	Population/surface (inhabitants/km²)	176.12	36.43	426.11	Positive and negative correlations may emerge, depending on factors such as economies of scale and land opportunity costs in urban and densely inhabited areas
COLLEC	Share of separated collection (%)	15.85	0.70	47.76	Negatively affecting landfilled waste per capita
INC-WASTE	MSW generated and incinerated (kg/capita)	36.00	0	170.00	Negatively affecting landfilled waste per capita
LAND-TAX	Landfill tax (€/kg, 2004-05 data only)	0.015	0.005	0.023	Negatively affecting landfilled waste per capita
TAR POP	Share of population living in municipalities that introduced a waste tariff substituting the former waste tax (%)	8.91	0	65.68	Possibly reducing MSW generation through indirect feedback effects, though the direct effect is at waste management level. Possible endogeneity, given the positive correlation with respect to income
TAR MUN	Share of municipalities that introduced a waste tariff substituting the former waste tax (%)	4.19	0	36.49	
COST-REC	Cost recovery of waste management services (tax/tariff revenues on variable service costs, only one data for 2004) (%)	63.40	47.05	72.03	
TOURIST	Annual tourist number (per capita)	8.44	1.72	41.26	Positively affecting landfilled waste per capita

we can compare the REM (random effects models) and the FEM (fixed effects models) through the usual Hausman test. We subdivide the empirical investigation and comments into three separate but consequential steps: analyses of baseline specifications, assessment of additional structural and socio-economic factors and the effects of policy elements. Regarding the latter, some policy aspects capture both cross regions and time heterogeneity/dynamics, others (landfill tax) do not vary over time, due to data availability. However, landfill tax is not usually adjusted on an annual basis, so this lack of variance is a minor problem compared with the value of having fully decentralized information on landfill tax for all regions of a country such as Italy. This analysis is in line with the assessment of landfill tax implementation, given that the levy is managed by regional authorities.

The model of reference for the regional analysis is:

(2) $\ln(\text{landfilled MSW per capita}) = \beta_{0i} + \alpha_t$
$$+ \beta_1 \ln(\text{gross domestic product})_{it}$$
$$+ \beta_2 \ln(\text{socio} - \text{economic factors})_{it}$$
$$+ \beta_3 (\text{environmental policy})_{it} + \varepsilon_{it}$$

where the first two terms are intercept parameters that vary across regions, and years.

All variables are in logarithmic form unless they present 0 values. In contrast to the provincial-level analysis (see later), this is not the case for the dependent variable. At regional level, landfilling is not and probably never will be zero for some regions, even if faced with decreasing landfilled waste.

First, we comment on the baseline specifications. Linear forms are not significant, though the coefficient associated with GDP shows the expected negative sign (Tables 6.3 and 6.4). This negative relationship becomes significant if we introduce the squared term: the U shape shows a potential upturn of the relationship. Nevertheless, this is currently only a potential threat: in fact the observed TP is around €19,000 per capita, and the average is around €20,000. This signals that, without corrections, becoming richer may induce an increase in the amount of landfilled waste per capita.[6]

This baseline model may also be deficient in explaining landfill trends. If we include the most relevant control structural factor, population density, this becomes highly significant, while GDP loses its explanatory power (Table 6.5). It seems, then, that structural factors matter more than pure economic drivers. This result does not signal that waste is not economically/driven: the significance for density, as expected, shows that where opportunity costs are higher (in urban areas, in densely populated areas) and disamenity effects are affecting more people, landfill diversion is stronger.

Table 6.3 Landfilled waste per capita: regional data, 1999–2005

Variables	Specification			
	1	*2*	*3*	*4*
Constant	–	2.225	–	148.78
		(0.420)		(0.188)
GDP/POP	−0.2819	−0.3350	−85.93	−30.11
	(0.737)	(0.229)	(0.006)***	(0.189)
(GDP/POP)^2	...	...	4.35	1.512
			(0.006)***	(0.194)
N	140	140	140	140
Model^a	FEM	REM	FEM	REM

Note: ^{a}Coefficients and significance are shown (10%*; 5%**; 1%***); std. err. in brackets.

Table 6.4 Landfilled waste per area: regional data, 1999–2005

Variables	Specification			
	1	*2*	*3*	*4*
Constant	–	2.084	–	345.61
		(0.661)		(0.010)**
GDP/POP	−0.2781	−0.2826	−84.30	−70.14
	(0.732)	(0.557)	(0.005)***	(0.010)**
(GDP/POP)^2	...	...	4.276	3.549
			(0.005)***	(0.010)**
N	140	140	140	140
Model	FEM	REM	FEM	REM

Note: Coefficients and significance are shown (10%*; 5%**; 1%***); std. err. in brackets.

As well as GDP-based explanations of waste generation there are other factors that impact on the final stage, of waste disposal. GDP does not have a coherent, direct impact. It may act as an indirect lever, as we show below. Also, and rather counter-intuitively in relation to Italy, the geographical dummies are not significant (this is confirmed at the provincial level), and tourist flows do not affect landfill trends, although they have an impact on waste generation (see previous chapter).

Second, returning to our discussion, we observe that there are other socio-economic levers that are relevant. One factor, that is a combination of policy, institutional and local cultural aspects, is the share of separated waste collected. As expected, it is significant. In the regression that includes GDP, and also the regression that includes only density, both variables are highly significant. Overall, it seems to outweigh the previously mentioned economic

Table 6.5 Other specifications with landfilled waste per capita, 1999–2005 (20 regions)

Variables	Specification									
	1	2	3	4	5	6	7	8	9	10
Costant	–	2.278	–	3.133	2.29	–	2.924	1.929	–	–
GDP	–0.6829	–0.348	2.362**	–0.4361	–0.255	–.04208	–0.3151	0.4106	–0.7430	–0.5296
DENS	–7.34***				–0.166*	–6.93**	–0.2277	–0.2397	–7.74***	–5.89***
North–west		0.126								
North–east		–0.104								
Centre		0.290								
Islands		0.225								
COLLEC			–0.22***							
TOURIST				0.0516						
No. incinerators/surface					–25314.2					
No. landfills/surface						3449***				
LAND–TAX							–.0554			
COST–REC								–1.430		
TARPOP									0.0007	
TARMUN										–0.006*
N	140	140	140	140	140	140	140	100	140	140
Model	FEM	REM	FEM	REM	REM	FEM	REM	REM	FEM	FEM

Note: Coefficients and significance are shown (10%*; 5%**; 1%***). Empty cells mean the variable is not included in the regression.

effect, being linked more directly with the chances of landfill diversion. The coefficients signal that 1 per cent more of separated waste reduces landfill by 0.08–0.2 per cent. This may indicate problems in transforming collection performance in landfill diversion. An increased level of separated collection could not (in the short term) automatically generate more innovative waste management; it is unlikely that the entire filiere would be structured on landfill diversion options and technologies.

It should be noted that adding in the relevant socio-economic factors generates regressions where the FEM is plausibly chosen as the preferred specification, given that we are reasoning based on the entire population, not a sample of regions.

Other waste-related structural factors, which we deem to be exogenous (driven by institutional, policy and geographical factors in the short run), are the ratio of incinerators and landfill sites in both per capita and per area terms. We see that the first factor (incinerators) is not significant, while the number of landfill sites per area drives up the amount of waste that is landfilled. This result seems somewhat tautological; nonetheless, it signals and proves the existence of lock-in effects due to past investments in disposal sites. Lock-in effects may characterize technology, even recycling and incineration. The decision to invest in a landfill strategy locks the region in, for the time during which the investment is being made, and typically is not a short-term, fully reversible phenomenon.

Finally, we test the relevance of: (i) waste management related factors and (ii) regional landfill taxes. The latter turns out not to be effective. It seems that it is not the direct cost of landfill taxes that drives landfill diversion, but that it is other opportunity costs (density), and to some extent waste management innovation, that increase the financing and performance of collection, and separated collection. The non-significant impact of landfill tax may be due to its quite recent implementation, and even more to its relatively low level, compared with other countries. However, we noted above that even in leading countries, such as the UK, some authors have cast doubt on the effectiveness of this instrument. Waste management may matter more, given its centrality in the waste chain. Landfill pricing is the last option at the end of the waste production filiere. Diversion is driven more by actions taken before the landfill stage.

As far as waste management dynamics are concerned, we looked at the evolution of the waste tariff system from the tax-based one, and the share of variable costs covered by the tax. Both elements proxy the dynamics of system privatization, seen as the move towards tariffs linked to volume of waste produced, and based on the ultimate goal of full cost recovery, i.e. the move from the provision of a pure public good to a user-oriented approach. Within this approach, even public utilities may 'go private' by changing their objectives and behaviour. Most utilities in Italy are still publicly owned, or under shared participation: it is the management of these utilities that will change rather than ownership of the assets.

Though all the signs are negative, as expected, we observe a significant coefficient only for the variable that captures the share of municipalities, within a region, linked with a tariff. This share is steadily increasing. It shows that, more than the share of population – driven by the introduction of the tariff in large municipalities – it is the number of local authorities that matters. In other words, it seems that the *joint* transition of several municipalities matters more than a transition by some of the big cities. Given the high relevance of governance interconnections among local authorities for waste management in local/regional areas, this is not unexpected.

We compare these results with the provincial-level analysis that exploits original data aggregated to enable the regional investigation.

Provincial analysis

The provincial data set offers a higher possibility of investigating the determinants of landfill diversion by exploiting a much more heterogeneous and larger collection of data than are available at the regional level. Thus it constitutes a robustness test for the regional analysis, and offers the possibility of new insights. Though the two are complementary investigations, we can state that, with one exception (landfill tax assessment), the provincial analysis is stronger overall. However, it will be seen that the differences are small and the two levels of analysis are coherent with one another.

The main methodological problem is the nature of the dependent variable, the landfilled MSW per capita, which, at province level, presents *zero values*: some (five, as previously noted) of the 103 provinces observed over 1999–2005 did not have a landfill sites for MSW, and thus did not landfill. Others, such as Milan, closed their landfill sites during the period, thus they show zero values after that particular year.

We present and compare the outcomes for three specifications of the dependent variable: a semi-log model where only the dependent variable is in non-logarithmic form, an unbalanced panel where zero values are omitted, reducing the number of units to 658 from 721, and, as a third best way of coping with the problem, a fully logarithmic specification where previously we had substituted very low values tending to zero in place of zero. This is plausible if we assume that in reality the statistical zeroes are very low values of landfill.

Further investigations could examine autocorrelation and heteroskedasticity and, more important, the eventual specifications of a two-stage Heckman model, which poses higher complexity but addresses the eventual selection associated with the five provinces that did not have a landfill site over the study period, for perhaps political or idiosyncratic motivations.

The models of reference for the semi-log (balanced panel) and the log-log (unbalanced panel) specifications respectively are:

(3) landfilled MSW per capita $= \beta_{0i} + \alpha_t$
$$+ \beta_1 \ln(\text{value added per capita})_{it}$$
$$+ \beta_2 \ln(\text{value added per capita})_{it}^2$$
$$+ \beta_3 \ln(\text{socio} - \text{economic factors})_{it}$$
$$+ \beta_4(\text{environmental policy})_{it} + e_{it}$$

(4) $\ln(\text{landfilled MSW per capita}) = \beta_{0i} + \alpha_t$
$$+ \beta_1 \ln(\text{value added per capita})_{it}$$
$$+ \beta_2 \ln(\text{value added per capita})_{it}^2$$
$$+ \beta_3(\text{socio} - \text{economic factors})_{it}$$
$$+ \beta_4(\text{environmental policy})_{it} + e_{it}$$

where the first two terms are intercept parameters that vary across provinces and years.

We added to the core specification, as controls and additional drivers of landfilled waste, a set of other socio-economic and policy related factors. Next, we comment on the main findings.

Semi-logarithmic balanced specifications

Semi-log specifications attached to model (3) show the following results. We include, in addition to the baseline speciation with value added (VA) and density, one factor at a time, to avoid collinearity problems. Thus in our specifications there are three variables, two of which, VA and density, are always present as pillars of the model.

First, for the baseline specification (VA as the economic driver, and density as the structural control factor) in the FEM (strongly preferred by the Hausman test here and in all other regressions, which is a plausible result), both show a negative sign, with respectively 10 per cent and 1 per cent significance (Table 6.6).[7] This evidence confirms that delinking relative to income growth is relevant, but it is mostly structural factors that have an impact, and should be included to account for the drivers of landfill diversion. This confirms the regionally based analysis.

If we include tourist flows per capita, we observe that the significance of VA decreases to below 10 per cent: the only impact factor is that population density, related to the aforementioned (see the regional analysis) opportunity costs and environmental impacts, is higher and more critical in densely populated areas. Also confirming the regional analysis, the macro geographic dummies linked with the north, south and centre regions do not seem to explain landfill diversion, which is rather counter-intuitive.

On the other hand, the variable related to the strong differences between north and south in terms of performance and share of separated collection plays a key role in explaining this phenomenon. If we look at regression

Table 6.6 Specifications for landfilled waste per capita (semi−log model, balanced panel), province analysis, 1999–2005

Variable	Specification								
	1	2	3	4	5	6	7	8	9
Constant	-0.191*	-0.169	-0.011	-0.200*		2.780***	2.920***	-0.142	-0.139
VA	-1.403***	-1.423***	-1.269***	-1.410***	-1.590***	-0.210***	-0.164**	-0.809**	-0.726**
DENS					-0.030***	-0.034	-0.037		
TOURIST		-0.036							
COLLEC			-0.026***						
No. incinerators/surface[a]				-1492.00					
No. landfills/surface[a]					197.40				
LAND–TAX						0.043			
COST–REC							-0.179		
TARPOP[a]								-0.001***	
TARMUN[a]									-0.003***
F test (prob)	0.0000	0.0000	0.0000	0.0000	0.0000	0.0000	0.0000	0.0000	0.0000
Model	FEM	FEM	FEM	FEM	FEM	REM	REM	FEM	FEM
Hausman test (p value)[b]	0.000001	0.000001	0.000048	0.00000	0.00000	–	–	0.0227	0.0143

Note: Coefficients and significance are shown (10%*; 5%**; 1%***). Empty cells mean the variable is not included in the regression. Covariates are added separately to the baseline model in order to mitigate collinearity. [a]Not logarithmic covariates; N = 721, 103 provinces.

three in Table 6.6 we can see that VA loses its statistical power completely. The other two are highly significant. If we consider the quite high correlation between VA and share of separated collection, motivated by the different performance in waste management of north and south, the share-related variables, as expected, retain very high significance. If instead we specify a two-stage model (not shown) to address *policy endogeneity*,[8] where in the first step we get the predicted values of separated collection regressed over density and VA, and in the second step we test density (which must be present in both steps) and predictions such as the drivers of landfill diversion, the significance of separated collection is just 10 per cent (1 per cent in pooled ordinary least squares (OLS) and REM). Overall, separated collection is a significant driver of landfill diversion. On the other hand, it might signify that waste management strategies are not so effective: if recovery options are not well implemented, part of the separated collection may still be going to landfill. Even waste management systems that perform well at the collection level may ultimately prove ineffective if disposal options and disposal markets are not sufficiently developed. Landfill remains the easy last resort and the solution to failures occurring in earlier stages of waste management system.

Thus, we decided to test the effect of: (i) the number of incinerators per capita and per area; (ii) the number of landfill sites per capita and per area. Recall that the former variables are not in log forms, given that they present zero values. Also note that although the coefficient linked with incineration is negative, as expected, it is not significant and, similarly, the positive sign for landfill sites per head and per area is positive and not significant. Lock-in effects are not relevant here. We offer some alternative insights when we address the unbalanced model.

At the final level of waste management instruments and landfill tax assessment some new insights emerge. If the non-significance of landfill taxation is confirmed, the tariff-based variables capturing features of the transition to a full cost recovery and privately managed (but not necessarily privately owned) waste managements system offer some different views.

COST–REC, not available for all years, is tested for 2004 values. Heterogeneity is high across provinces; the coefficient is negative as expected, but not sufficiently high in terms of significance.[9] Future analyses could exploit full panel data even for this variable.[10]

On the other hand, and providing some additional relative robustness to the provincial analysis, we find that both share of population and municipalities that have adopted a waste tariff in preference to the tax impact negatively on landfill diversion. The coefficient is not large, but its significance is at the 1 per cent level. This trend emerges more coherently at the decentralized provincial level and indicates that waste management instruments may have some indirect impact on landfill, bearing in mind what was discussed above in relation to separated collection.

Unbalanced panel analyses

Unbalanced panel estimations related to model (4) show the following results (Table 6.7). The first difference is the significance in the log models at regional level of the quadratic term. The related TP is estimated at €19,440, which is a similar value to that for regions. This logarithmic specification originates the U shape that would suggest, based on the TP, that richer areas could (re-)experience a positive relationship between economic growth and landfilled waste.

Population density is confirmed as a main driver of landfill diversion: the sign of the coefficient even in the quadratic specification is negative and highly significant.

Tourist flows in this case are a significant factor: the negative sign indicates that landfill activities are mitigated by the presence of high numbers of tourists. The opportunity cost of land exploitation, and negative externalities, are elements that may undermine the profitability of tourism. Venice and Rimini are examples of two highly tourist-dense provinces which have waste management strategies biased towards recycling and incineration and away from landfill. The business of tourism crowds out the business of landfill. This is a new and interesting result based on our unbalanced panel estimations.

For separated collection we see that, as above, the variable is significant. It should be noted that the fitted values have increased (5 per cent) significance, which is more evident in the unbalanced specification.

Incinerator sites per capita and per area are significant, which is different from the above results: the latter is significant only in the non-quadratic model, at 5 per cent, while the former is significant at 1 per cent in both the linear and non-linear specifications. Also, the variable incinerated waste per capita is strongly significant at 1 per cent.

This result gives robustness to our comments on the relevance of lock-in effects in local waste management strategies. The (increasing) weight of incineration drives down landfilling. Methodologically speaking, it imposes the necessity of further investigating selection models that accommodate *zero* values in the data.

The density of landfill sites in provincial areas, on the other hand, is not significant, though with a positive coefficient: lock-in effects related to landfill site investments are weak at the provincial level (recall the significant effect at regional level), while incinerators investments can be seen to be drivers of landfill diversion, at least in the unbalanced version of the model.

If we focus on the waste management policy covariates, landfill taxes and cost coverage are shown to be meaningless for explaining landfill diversion.[11] Finally, in terms of evolution towards a waste tariff system, both factors (population coverage and municipality coverage) present 1 per cent and 5 per cent statistical significance, respectively.

Table 6.7 Specifications for landfilled waste per capita (log–log model, unbalanced panel) provincial analysis, 1999–2005

Variable					Specificaton						
	1	2	3	4	5	6	7	8	9	10	11
Constant							145.830	144.810			
VA	-51.090**	-52.970**	-24.947	-49.650**	-63.750***	-45.076*	-29.040	-28.460	-60.810**	-66.000***	-78.890***
VA²	2.587**	2.713**	1.282	2.511**	3.263***	2.284*	1.448	1.439	3.101**	3.374***	4.080****
DENS	-6.280***	-6.960***	-5.200***	-6.530***	-6.321***	-6.030***	-0.036	-0.072	-4.152**	-3.789**	-4.341**
TOURIST		-0.880***									-0.607***
COLLEC			-0.128**								
No. incinerators/surface[a]				-18696.2							
INC–WASTE					-5.777***						-5.409***
No. landfills/surface						0.058					
LAND–TAX							0.393				
COST–REC								-1.157			
TARPOP[a]									-0.005**		
TARMUN[a]										-0.011***	-0.011***
F test (prob.)	0.0000	0.0000	0.0000	0.0000	0.0000	0.0000	0.0000	0.0000	0.0000	0.0000	0.0000
Model	FEM	FEM	FEM	FEM	FEM	FEM	REM	REM	FEM	FEM	FEM

Note: Coefficients and significance are shown (10%*; 5%**; 1%***). Empty cells mean the variable is not included in the regression. Covariates are separately added to the baseline model in order to mitigate collinearity. [a]Not logarithmic covariates. [b]p value < 0.10 favours FEM. N = 658, 98 provinces.

Overall, the fully logarithmic unbalanced model confirms the previous outcomes.[12] Statistical significance varies widely, depending on the log form of the quadratic specifications, which perhaps should be taken as a warning that there may be links between income and landfill above a certain threshold. Evidence related to the role of tourist flows shows that there is a negative impact on landfill diversion trends and incineration investments. This variable increases the robustness of the model. The significance of policy and waste management factors is the same as in the semi-log specifications.

To sum up, landfill diversion is stronger when the economic costs deriving from high population density, which is a structural factor, are higher, and when waste management collection systems and economic instruments are associated with higher performance. The main economic driver of landfill diversion has only a weak impact, but this is plausible because of the distance between landfill and waste generation.[13]

The decoupling is driven by a mix of structural factors, density – linked with economic issues – and management actions. We can confirm that just relying on the endogenous path characterized by landfill and economic growth (the baseline EKC scenario) will not assure delinking. Some policy action is needed to shape the delinking. Future analyses may provide more insights on the effectiveness of landfill tax, which has been the subject of debate even in countries with high taxes, such as the UK.

Verifying the relevance of sample bias in landfill siting and diversion

As already noted, there is a methodological issue that needs to be addressed, given the nature of our data, and the zero values for some provinces in some or all of the observed years, and that is the possibility of sample bias. In the foregoing we dealt with it either by specifying a semi log model that allowed the inclusion of all observations, or by specifying an unbalanced logarithmic model that drops zero values (68 cells out of 721). We also employ a two-stage Heckman-like estimator that explicitly takes into account this sample bias as an additional robustness check. Table 6.8 presents the results, which show no striking differences, thus confirming that the previous evidence is robust to sample bias based on some provinces having no landfill sites or on provinces that closed their sites down at a particular point.

The preliminary probit regression shows that the three covariates – VA, DENS, TOURIST – are significant in explaining the dichotomous decision to have or not to have a landfill site in the province. We note only the positive sign of the tourist-related variable: while tourist flows negatively impact on the amount of landfilled waste, presumably to reduce disamenity, landfill siting is necessary where tourist flows are high, with some exceptions to this regularity, such as Rimini. Fit measures (Estrella and McFadden) show good performance and, more important, correct prediction performance is high, with 90.7 per cent of actual 1s and 0s correctly predicted.

Table 6.8 Heckman two–stage regressions (probit + unbalanced panel)

Variables			Specification				
	1	2	3	4	5	6	7
Constant	13.980***			184.097*	190.049**		
VA	-1.039***	-2.607**	-2.847**	-38.609**	-38.969***	-4.406***	-4.282***
VA^2				1.981**	2.023**		
DENS	-0.495***	-7.641***	-7.322***	0.424*	0.421*	-6.565***	-6.199***
TOURIST	0.125*	-0.658**					
COLLEC			-0.116**				
LAND–TAX				0.335			
COST–REC					-1.238*		
TARPOP[a]						-0.004**	
TARMUN[a]							-0.010***
IMR	/	8.642	12.894***	-3.177***	-3.397***	16.777***	16.349***
N	721	653	653	653	653	653	653
F test (prob.)	0.0000	0.0000	0.0000	0.0000	0.0000	0.0000	0.0000
Model	Probit	FEM	FEM	REM	REM	REM	REM

Note: Coefficients and significance are shown (10%*; 5%**; 1%***). Empty cells mean the variable is not included in the regression. Covariates are separately added to the baseline model in order to mitigate collinearity. [a]Not logarithmic covariates. Specification 1 specifies as dependent variable the dummy equal to 1 if the province has a positive amount of landfilled waste. Results are not affected by the linear or quadratic specifications on VA; the quadratic specifications on VA on average provide more robust outcomes in the REM, and the linear ones in the FEM.

The basic unbalanced specification, which now includes the inverse Mills ratio (IMR), confirms the results for the unbalanced model, and the IMR is significant at 10 per cent, highlighting the relevance of introducing the two-stage procedure.

The statistical significance of the IMR increases to 1 per cent in all other regressions, which present significant effects for COLLEC, TAR-MUN, TAR-POP and COST-REC. Landfill tax is nevertheless not significant. Overall, the two-stage Heckman procedure does not alter our evidence, but demonstrates the relevance of investigating the 1/0 binary decision, which seems to depend on socio-economic and structural factors, with some signs that are possibly reversed (TOURIST) compared with the analysis of landfill diversion strategies.

Conclusion

This chapter has analysed the process of delinking in relation to landfill trends by embedding the dynamics in a framework that simultaneously includes economic, institutional, and geographical and policy variables. On the basis of the decreasing trend in landfill which is observed at EU level, the aim was to investigate in depth what drivers may be responsible for such a phenomenon, and whether differences may be observed focusing the lens on a very decentralised provincially based setting.

We exploit a rich panel data set stemming from official sources (Italian environmental agency) merged with other provincial and regional based information. Such an extended, decentralized and recent source of data is of major interest for investigations dealing with waste processes and policy valuation, where evidence is typically scattered and rare, given the paucity of high-quality data.

The case study of Italy merits consideration, given that Italy is a major country of the EU, hence it offers important pieces on information on the evaluation of policies like the 1999 Landfill Directive. Its problematic economic, institutional and environmental performance heterogeneity allows an interesting analysis of how economic and policy levers impact on the dynamics of landfill in such settings. Finally, with waste management and landfill policies implemented at a highly decentralized level, it provides food for thought for policy-making processes that have operated or will operate along similar directions.

Econometric investigations have focused on both regional and provincial disaggregation. The two sets of results are consistent with each other, with some minor differences. Overall, we observe a significant delinking of economic growth and landfill of waste. Nevertheless, the case study shows how the baseline EKC relationship between income and environmental pressure may be not sufficient to explain landfill diversion. Other factors impact on environmental performance. We cannot rely merely on economic growth to reverse the income–environment relationship. In fact, if it is confirmed that the sign of the income–landfill diversion trend is negative, since we already observe a descending path in terms of waste landfill, this link turns out to be not the key one. Structural factors, like population density, matter greatly.[14] This means that, other things being equal, the geographical embedding and the economic (market and non-market) costs of landfill investments are drivers of landfill diversion. Moreover, some specifications also highlight the role of tourism: local systems relying on tourism tend to avoid landfill as a waste management strategy, as additional opportunity costs may arise and negative externalities could affect the business.

But not only structural factors are relevant. If on the one hand landfill taxation is not arising as a significant driver of the phenomenon, even at the more coherent regional level, where the tax is implemented, waste management instruments, when we exploit the provincial data set, are associated with high significant negative effect on landfilled waste. A good performance on managing waste according to economic rationales helps reducing the amount that is landfilled. In association with the features of the tariff system, we also underline the key role played by the share of separated collection where it is higher.

Both the evolution of collection and tariff system are joint factors that may drive a wedge between the comparative waste performance of northern and southern regions.

We note the importance of having panel data for management variables that capture both the time evolution and the cross-sectional heterogeneity of the waste management evolution towards market-based management systems, based on tariffs rather than taxes, and full cost recovery principles.

We finally note that lock-in effects linked to the intensity of incinerator sites in the area are relevant for landfill: though quite obvious, past investments in incineration lock the region into this technological path, which may be associated with less opportunity cost and lower external effects. The lock-in effect driven by the number of landfill sites in the areas is instead significant – a bit counter-intuitively, perhaps – only when analysing regional data.

Summing up, landfill diversion is stronger where the economic costs deriving from high population density, a structural factor, are higher, and waste management collection systems and economic instruments are associated with higher performance. The main economic driver is only weakly impacting, but this is plausible, since is more distant from landfill with respect to waste generation, and landfill.

The decoupling is then driven by a mix of structural factors, density, but linked with economic issues, and management actions. We may affirm that just relying on the endogenous path characterized by landfill and economic growth (the baseline EKC scenario) does not assure delinking. Some policy actions are needed to affect the shape of delinking. Future analyses may provide more insights into landfill tax effectiveness, which nevertheless has been a matter for debate even in countries with high landfill taxes.

Notes

1 See also EEA (2007: 7, figure 1), which shows historical and projected (to 2020) waste generation and landfill trends: the former is not expected to be associated to delinking, while landfill will show weak delinking country heterogeneity is a problem – and there are some critical regional hotspots.

2 We may cite among others Powell and Brisson (1995), Miranda *et al.* (2000), Eshet *et al.* (2004), Brisson and Pearce (1995), Dijkgraaf and Vollebergh (2004) and Seok Lim and Missios (2007). Caplan *et al.* (2007) offer an example of how economic evaluation techniques may inform landfill siting processes.

3 We refer to Cole *et al.* (1997), Dinda (2004), Stern (2004, 1998) for major critical surveys and a discussion on the theoretical underpinnings of delinking and EKC.

4 Part covers fixed costs and part refers to the variable management costs. The former correlate with the size of household living space and, as a new element, with the number of people in the family. The variable part is associated with the (expected) amount of waste produced, which is calculated on the basis of past trends and location-related features. The variable part is abated by around 10–20 per cent if households adopt domestic composting and/or join garden-waste door-to-door collection schemes.

5 In the observed period, five provinces did not have a landfill site at all. A few other observations present zero values owing to the closure of landfill sites during the period.

6 Table 6.4 presents estimates using landfilled waste per regional area, rather than per capita, as the dependent variable. Estimates do not substantially differ, so we do not comment further other than to note that, according to landfill external and market costs, per capita measures better capture the intensity of the problem in a given area.

7 Quadratic specifications are not significant when other controls such as density are included.

8 Recent studies have focused on analysing the drivers of environmental regulation, by defining endogenous factors (Cole *et al.* 2006; Alpay *et al.* 2006). Efforts aimed at establishing environmental policy indexes for climate change, waste and other areas show that developed countries' environmental regulations are more stringent. Consistent with EKC reasoning, policies may be endogenous especially if correlated with income factors at both the supply and demand levels (Cagatay and Mihci 2006). Regarding (paper) waste, the evidence supports higher demand for waste management and environmental policies in more developed, richer countries (Berglund and Soderholm 2003). At more micro level Callan and Thomas (1999, 2006), who studied the drivers of unit price adoption at municipal level, provide evidence of policy (economic instrument) endogeneity with regard to demographics, fiscal capacity and socio-economic determinants. Those analyses are in reality constrained by the cross-section and local nature of the (rich) datasets. Generalisation of results is more difficult.

9 Also, the interaction term between cost coverage and landfill tax, a variable that captures economic instrument impacts for different levels of waste management, is not significant.

10 If we run the analysis just for 2002–4, the period for which panel data related to the coverage of variable cost of waste management are available, the variable is still not significant even in the FEM. We note that the signs and significance of the coefficients for VA and density change, highlighting the VA of having a fairly long time series compared with the more usual short-term panel. This proves the value and robustness of our dataset, which exploits a sufficiently long time series and in-depth regional heterogeneity.

11 Quadratic models show how these time-invariant variables reduce model performance.

150   *Massimiliano Mazzanti, Anna Montini and Francesco Nicolli*

12 In terms of model robustness, the higher R^2 (within) performance is the quadratic form with density, tourist flows, population, tariff coverage and incinerated waste per capita (column 11 in Table 6.6).
13 If we include the amount of waste generation per capita as an explanatory variable, the variable is not significant in a simple model, and significant at 10 per cent when using a two-stage procedure with VA as the driver of waste generation in the first step. Counter-intuitively, the sign is also negative, but this may be due to the correlation between VA and waste generated. The irrelevance of waste generation is plausible if we reason that there is a direct link between economic drivers and waste generation, which indirectly induces effects downstream, at landfill level. Given that separated collection and other waste recovery options drive a wedge between waste generation and landfill, this result is coherent with a waste system associated with fairly good performance, although heterogeneous across regions.
14 A logarithmic model that estimates the impact of population on landfill diversion also shows a negative and significant effect. Both higher density and higher population drive landfilling down.

References

Alpay, S., Caliskan, A. and Mahmud, S. (2006) 'Environmental Policy Performance, Economic Growth and Trade Liberalization: a Cross-country Empirical Analysis', Ankara: Department of Economics, Bilkent University, mimeo.
Andersen, F., Larsen, H., Skovgaard, M., Moll, S., and Isoard, S. (2007) 'A European model for waste and material flows', *Resources, Conservation and Recycling*, 49: 421–35.
Andre, F. and Cerda, E. (2004) 'Landfill construction and capacity expansion', *Environmental and Resource Economics*, 28: 409–34.
APAT (2006) *Rapporto rifiuti* [Waste report] *2006*, Rome: Ministry of the Environment.
——(2005) *Rapporto rifiuti 2005*, Rome: Ministry of the Environment.
——(2004) *Rapporto rifiuti 2004*, Rome: Ministry of the Environment.
——(2003) *Rapporto rifiuti 2003*, Rome: Ministry of the Environment.
——(2002) *Rapporto rifiuti 2002*, Rome: Ministry of the Environment.
——(2001) *Rapporto rifiuti 2001*, Rome: Ministry of the Environment.
Berglund, C. and Soderholm, P. (2003) 'An econometric analysis of global waste paper recovery and utilization', *Environmental and Resource Economics*, 26: 429–56.
Berrens, R., Bohara, A., Gawande, K. and Wang, P. (1998) 'Testing the inverted U hypothesis for US hazardous waste: an application of the generalized gamma model', *Economic Letters*, 55: 435–40.
Bringezu, S., Schütz, H. and Moll, S. (2003) 'Rationale for and interpretation of economy-wide material flow analysis and derived indicators', *Journal of Industrial Ecology*, 7: 43–64.
Brisson, I. and Pearce, D. (1995) 'Benefit Transfer for Disamenity from Waste Disposal', CSERGE Working Paper 6, London: University College London.
Brock, W. and Taylor, S. (2004) 'The Green Solow Model', NBER Working Papers 10557, Cambridge MA: NBER.
Burnley, S. (2001) 'The impact of the European Landfill Directive on waste management in the United Kingdom', *Resources, Conservation and Recycling*, 31: 349–58.
Cagatay, S. and Mihci, H. (2006) 'Degree of environmental stringency and the impact on trade patterns', *Journal of Economic Studies*, 33: 30–51.

——(2003) 'Industrial pollution, environmental suffering and policy measures: an index of environmental sensitivity performance', *Journal of Environmental Assessment Policy and Management*, 5: 205–45.

Calcott, P. and Walls, M. (2005) 'Waste, recycling and "design for the environment": roles for market and policy instruments', *Resource and Energy Economics*, 27: 287–305.

Callan, S. and Thomas, J. (2006) 'Analyzing demand for disposal and recycling services', *Eastern Economic Journal*, 32: 221–40.

——(1999) 'Adopting a unit pricing system for MSW: policy and socio-economic determinants', *Environmental and Resource Economics*, 14: 503–18.

Caplan, A., Grijalva, T. and Jackson-Smith, D. (2007) 'Using choice question formats to determine compensable values: the case of a landfill-siting process', *Ecological Economics*, 60: 834–46.

Cole, M., Elliott, R. and Fredrikkson, P. (2006) 'Endogenous pollution haves: does FDI influence environmental regulations?', *Scandinavian Journal of Economics*, 108: 157–78.

Cole, M., Rayner, A. and Bates, J. (1997) 'The EKC: an empirical analysis', *Environment and Development Economics*, 2: 401–16.

Daskalopoulos, E., Badr, O. and Probert, D. (1998) 'An integrated approach to municipal solid waste management', *Resources, Recycling and Conservation*, 24: 33–50.

Davies, B. and Doble, M. (2004) 'The development and implementation of a landfill tax in the UK', in OECD, *Addressing the Economics of Waste*, Paris: OECD.

DEFRA (2005) *A Study to Estimate the Disamenity Costs of Landfill in Great Britain*, London: DEFRA.

DEFRA/DTI (2003), *Sustainable Consumption and Production Indicators*, London: DEFRA.

Dijkgraaf, E. and Gradus, P. (2004) 'Cost savings in unit-based pricing of household waste: the case of the Netherlands', *Resource and Energy Economics*, 26: 353–71.

Dijkgraaf, E. and Vollebergh, H. (2004) 'Burn or bury? A social cost comparison of final waste disposal methods', *Ecological Economics*, 50: 233–47.

Dinda, S. (2004) 'Environmental Kuznets curve hypothesis: a survey', *Ecological Economics*, 49: 431–55.

EEA (2007) *The Road from Landfill to Recycling: Common Destination, Different Routes*, Copenhagen: European Environment Agency.

——(2003a) *Evaluation Analysis of the Implementation of the Packaging Directive*, Copenhagen: European Environment Agency.

——(2003b) *Assessment of Information related to Waste and Material Flows*, Copenhagen: European Environment Agency.

——(2003c) *Europe's Environment: The Third Assessment*, Copenhagen: European Environment Agency.

Eshet, T., Ayalon, O. and Shechter, M. (2004) 'A Meta-analysis of Waste Management Externalities: A Comparative Study of Economic and Non-economic Valuation Methods', Haifa: Haifa University, mimeo.

European Commission (2003a) *Towards a Thematic Strategy for Waste Prevention and Recycling*, COM (2003) 301, Brussels: European Commission.

——(2003b) *Towards a Thematic Strategy on Sustainable Use of Natural Resources*, COM (2003) 572, Brussels: European Commission.

Eurostat (2003) *Waste Generated and Treated in Europe: Data 1990–2001*, Luxembourg: Office for Official Publications of the European Communities.

Fischer Kowalski, M. and Amann, C. (2001) 'Beyond IPAT and Kuznets curves: globalization as a vital factor in analyzing the environmental impact of socio-economic metabolism', *Population and the Environment*, 23: 7–47.

IVM (2005) *Effectiveness of Landfill Taxation*, Amsterdam: IVM Institute for Environmental Studies, Vrije Universiteit.

Jacobsen, H., Mazzanti, M., Moll, S., Simeone, M. G., Pontoglio, S. and Zoboli, R. (2004) *Methodology and Indicators to measure Decoupling, Resource Efficiency, and Waste Prevention*, ETC/WMF, P6.2-2004, Copenhagen: European Topic Centre on Waste and Material Flows and European Environment Agency.

Jenkins, R., Maguire, K. and Morgan, C. (2004) 'Host community compensation and municipal solid waste landfills', *Land Economics*, 80: 513–28.

Kaurosakis, K. (2006) 'MSW Generation, Disposal and Recycling: a Note on OECD Inter-country Differences', paper presented at ENVECON 2006: Applied Environmental Economics Conference, London: Royal Society, 24 March.

Lang, J. C. (2005) 'Zero landfill zero waste: the greening of industry in Singapore', *International Journal of Environment and Sustainable Development*, 4: 331–51.

Martin, A. and Scott, I. (2003) 'The effectiveness of the UK landfill tax', *Journal of Environmental Planning and Management*, 46: 673–89.

Mazzanti, M. (2008) 'Is waste generation delinking from economic growth?', *Applied Economics Letters*, 15: 287–91.

Mazzanti, M., Montini, A. and Zoboli, R. (forthcoming) 'Waste generation, economic drivers, and the EKC hypothesis', *Applied Economics Letters*.

Miranda, M. L., Miller, J. and Jacobs, T. (2000) 'Talking trash about landfills: using quantitative scoring schemes in landfill siting processes', *Journal of Policy Analysis and Management*, 19: 3–22.

Morris, J. and Read, A. (2001) 'The UK landfill tax and the landfill tax credit scheme: operational weaknesses', *Resources, Conservation and Recycling*, 32: 375–87.

Morris, J., Phillips, P. and Read, A. (1998) 'The UK landfill tax: an analysis of its contribution to sustainable waste management', *Resources, Conservation and Recycling*, 23: 259–70.

OECD (2003) *Response Indicators for Waste Prevention within the OECD Area*, Paris: OECD.

——(2002) *Indicators to measure Decoupling of Environmental Pressure from Economic Growth*, Paris: OECD.

Ozawa, T. (2005) 'Hotelling rule and the landfill exhaustion problem: the case of Tokyo city', *Studies in Regional Science*, 35: 215–30.

Pearce, D. W. (2004) 'Does European Union waste policy pass a cost–benefit test?', *World Economics*, 5: 115–37.

Phillips, P. S., Adams, K. T., Read, A. D. and Green, A. E. (2007) 'Regional variations in waste minimizations in England: challenges and issues for policy development', *Regional Studies*, 34: 297–302.

Powell, J. and Brisson, I. (1995) 'Benefit Transfer for Disamenity from Waste Disposal', CSERGE working paper, London: University College London.

Seok, Lim J. and Missios, P. (2007) 'Does size really matter? Landfill scale impacts on property values', *Applied Economics Letters*, 14: 719–23.

Seppala, T., Haukioja, T. and Kaivooja, J. (2001) 'The EKC hypothesis does not hold for direct material flows: environmental Kuznets curve hypothesis tests for direct material flows in five industrial countries', *Population and Environment*, 23: 217–38.

Stern, D. (2004) 'The rise and fall of the environmental Kuznets curve', *World Development*, 32: 1419–38.

——(1998) 'Progress on the environmental Kuznets curve?', *Environment and Development Economics*, 3: 173–96.

Taseli, B. (2007) 'The impact of the European Landfill Directive on waste management strategy and current legislation in Turkey's specially protected areas', *Resources, Conservation and Recycling*, 52: 119–35.

Turner, K., Salmons, R., Powell, J. and Craighill, A. (1998) 'Green taxes, waste management and political economy', *Journal of Environmental Management*, 53: 121–36.

World Bank (1992) *Development and the Environment*, World Bank report, Oxford: Oxford University Press.

7 Reducing uncertainty in the monetary assessment of environmental liabilities from waste landfilling

Tiziana Cianflone and Kris Wernstedt

Natural Resource Damage (NRD) resulting from production activities represents a market failure for two reasons: first, the environment is a public good that may not be appropriated and, therefore, has no market clearing factor or output price; second, damage to the environment is considered a negative externality, a social cost not fully internalized within the accounts of the parties causing it (Cropper and Oates 1992) that is imposed on the whole community (Monti 2003).[1] Following Pigou (1918), a socially optimal allocation of resources in the presence of such market failure requires the producer to bear the cost that the externality imposes on society. This provides an economic rationale for regulation (Alberton 2003; Germani 2004).

In most developed countries two main regulatory approaches have evolved to address these market failure problems: an *ex ante* system (command and control regulation)[2] and an *ex post* system (a liability regime). A control is *ex ante* if it is applied before, or, at least, independently of, the occurrence of harm, while *ex post* controls are applied after the damage has occurred and been detected. There is a substantial body of work that investigates the optimal use of these two systems, and a general consensus that some combination of these systems is generally desirable. The common ground in these works is that these regulatory systems are not mutually exclusive (Germani 2004; Shavell 1987).[3]

Liability regimes aim at deterring the generation of externalities, but, since NRD can still occur under a deterrence regime, liability policy also should provide compensation mechanisms that promote cost internalization and thus (*ex ante*) incentives to avoid activities that would result in NRD (in other words, environmentally undesirable behaviour, or EUB). An effective liability regime, therefore, should incorporate the objectives of Pigouvian efficiency and deterrence. This does not always happen. The European Environmental Liability Directive,[4] for example, establishes a framework for environmental liability based on the 'polluter pays' principle, with a view to both preventing and remedying environmental damage. Its emphasis on compensation to restore the damaged environment to its previous condition effectively constitutes an efficiency objective and does not necessarily assure deterrence.

In Italy, one of the major causes of NRD is Environmentally Undesirable Waste Management (EUWM), which entails a variety of illegal or improper waste management activities, particularly those involving waste disposal in landfills. This specific EUB comes under a fault-based liability regime, since it includes those waste management activities that are illegal and that result in NRD. It also could incur remediation costs under a strict liability regime, since environmentally undesirable waste management activities result in what is defined in law as a contaminated site.[5] Both regimes comprise some uncertainties in terms of the effective implementation of the 'polluter pays' principle and the prevention and remediation of environmental damage. These uncertainties bedevil other environmental policy goals Italy is required to pursue to accord with European legislation directives, such as the prevention or reduction of waste generation and a decrease in the volume of waste for disposal through recovery by reuse, recycling and other operations (EEA 2007).[6]

Increasing the effectiveness of environmental liability regimes could mitigate the problems that Italy and other countries face in achieving effective waste management practices. In particular, if environmental externalities are characterized as being the product of EUWM (activities that cause NRD), an effective liability regime could reduce inefficient producer behaviour by reducing the uncertainties that rational agents face in valuing the cost–benefit trade-offs from EUWM.

This chapter extends work in this area by treating legal and institutional uncertainties as exogenous and focusing on economic assessment uncertainties, emphasizing the need to standardize economic NRD assessment methods for use in liability regimes. It considers three related issues: scope of NRD valuation; characterization of natural recoverability and human-directed restorability of resource damage; and partial standardization of NRD valuation methods. We provide an example to show that the implementation of standardized approaches to the reduction of landfill waste disposal can result in a reduction in the assessment uncertainties, thereby increasing both the predictability of the costs of NRD that need to be internalized and their efficacy in deterring EUB.

The chapter is structured as follows. Our next section provides the theoretical background to deterrence in environmental liability regimes. A discussion about standardization of NRD assessment, which focuses on technical approaches and an integrative framework for NRD assessment, then follows. Next we examine possible means to measure and reduce the externalities deriving from EUWM in the context of landfilled waste, highlighting the features of an integrated NRD assessment. Summary comments and suggestions for future research conclude the chapter.

Background

The literature on deterrence in an *ex post* regulatory system owes a large intellectual debt to the economic theory of crime and punishment developed by Becker (1968). This pioneering work, which focuses on factors that determine antisocial behaviours,[7] centres on a simple economic principle: assuming that an agent is a profit maximizer that rationally weighs the benefits and the costs when deciding whether to behave antisocially, then antisocial behaviour will not be chosen unless its expected benefits exceed expected costs.

Both EUB and EUWM can be considered to be antisocial. A potential polluter is a rational agent in terms of choosing whether to act in an undesirable way, adopting EUB if the gains from doing so are expected to exceed the monetary value of the enforcement requirements that the regulatory system imposes on the polluter for EUB. These requirements, which we will call sanctions in this chapter, compel the polluter to restore damaged resources to their pre-injury condition and provide compensation for losses.[8]

EUB gains may arise if the polluter can avoid the investment and/or operation costs necessary to prevent NRD, or if EUB allows an increase in revenues. If the regulatory system is the only legal instrument available to force a potential polluter to forgo EUB, the system must ensure that the potential polluter's expected sanction – the imposed sanction multiplied by the probability of detection and conviction – exceeds the additional gains from such behaviour. Hence, if there is a credible *ex post* liability system for EUB, the expected utility (EU) of a rational potential polluter is:

$$(1)\ EU = pU(G - S) + (1 - p)U(G)$$

where upper-case letters indicate arguments expressed in monetary terms; G represents EUB gains (i.e., the difference between the revenues (R) from and costs (C) of the behaviour); p represents the enforcement probability of the regulatory system (the authority's ability to catch and convict the polluter);[9] and S represents the sanction that the polluter must pay for EUB or if the regulator detects a violation which causes a NRD and takes action.

The potential polluter thus will balance the expected sanction (pS) against G gains in deciding whether to undertake EUB. Consequently, the effectiveness of a regulatory system's deterrence would be enhanced by an increase either in the cost of the EUB to the polluter, S, or in the ability to catch and convict the polluter, p. Most of the theoretical economics literature on crime and punishment argues that increasing the sanction is preferable to increasing the enforcement probability – defined as the use of public agents to detect and to sanction violators of legal rules[10] – because it inflicts less cost on society (Adams and Steven 1990; Polinsky and Shavell 1991; Posner 1992).

In practice, the barriers to increasing p and/or S in a liability regime are strong. Budget constraints curtail the ability to increase enforcement probabilities, while a very high level of sanctions is problematic because courts generally require the magnitude of S to be proportional to the harm caused.

In addition, many polluters may enjoy a de facto limited liability shield if their organization as a corporate entity or a subsidiary of a shielded parent company allows them to employ insolvency as an effective backstop (Cortenraad 1999; Hausmann and Wraakman 1991). Consequently, expected sanctions often are too low to make a liability regime credible and increase its deterrence effect, especially in relation to EUWM.

The literature considers many of the institutional and legal uncertainties that complicate the application of sanctions, and identifies tools to address these uncertainties, such as insurance mechanisms, dedicated funds, lender liability schemes and financial assurance requirements. Germani (2004), for instance, notes that the economic analysis of law literature has analysed environmental liability regimes with respect both to their capacity to provide (*ex ante*) incentives to avoid environmental damage (*deterrence* objective) and to their capacity to guarantee (*ex post*) the proper compensation of victims (*compensation* objective). Work in these two areas has focused mainly on the role of legal institutions and common law rules in achieving efficiency and distributive goals (Calabresi 1970; Landes and Posner 1987; Shavell 1987), particularly in the area of environmental policy (Kornhauser and Revesz 1994; Landes and Posner 1984; Polinsky 1980; Tietenberg 1989). Institutional and legal uncertainties constitute the principal theme in much of this work. Also, many studies have examined the enforcement of specific liability regimes (Hawkins 1984; McKean 1980; Richardson *et al.* 1982; Russell *et al.* 1986; Shavell 1987; Russell 1990), while others have concentrated on deterrents to NRD, particularly with respect to emissions associated with inefficient economic behaviour, and the legal instruments to accomplish deterrence. Optimal penalty structures and the use of criminal sanctions have also attracted attention (Faure and Visser 2004; Segerson and Tietenberg 1992).

The bulk of this substantial body of literature treats NRD as an exogenous variable. As a consequence, it generally neglects assessment uncertainties in both the physical and the monetary dimensions of NRD quantification, and their related roles in liability regimes, which can be significant. Focusing on the institutional and legal uncertainties is not always enough to achieve optimal deterrence and efficiency rates in a given environmental liability regime: it may also be necessary to look at reducing uncertainties in the process of assessing NRD damage. More specifically, we argue that standardization within a liability regime of the economic aspects of NRD could achieve more optimal deterrence and compensation rates by reducing the unpredictability of the potential polluter's NRD costs.

In liability regimes, uncertainties can occur in the methods and procedures used to assess NRD caused by EUB. The S in equation (1) in reality is not known until it is formally assessed *ex post* and, thus, the expected sanction can be highly uncertain if assessment techniques are variable or implemented unevenly. At the extremes, it could range from 0 to S^* for any given EUB, depending on the liability regime and precedence.[11] Assuming that S^*

represents the maximum monetary cost of the sanction, we can represent the uncertainty associated with the implementation of different NRDA practices as an unknown fraction of S^*. If we call this uncertainty q, the actual assessed *ex post* sanction ($\hat{S}$) depends on the NRD assessment techniques used;[12] that is, $\hat{S} = qS^*$, where $0 \leq \hat{S} \leq S^*$, and $0 \leq q \leq 1$.

Under an environmental liability regime, the expected utility estimated by the potential polluter in considering whether to undertake EUB therefore becomes:

$$(2)\ EU = p[U(G - \hat{S})] + (1 - p)U(G)$$

Thus, if q represents the unknown proportion of the maximum sanction that the variable NRD practices yield, the expected sanction becomes $pqS^* = p\hat{S}$ making it more uncertain than the standard pS when S is posited to be *ex ante* identifiable in equation (1).[13]

This formulation highlights that the uncertain nature of assessment exacerbates the difficulties that the potential polluter faces in contemplating EUB. With good information the economic agent can make decisions within a risk framework even where assessment practices vary. In this context a risk framework would require the combination of a well characterized probability distribution of the occurrence of an event (the probability of generating NRD and being sanctioned, p), and knowledge about the scale of the event were it to occur (the sanction the polluter would incur, qS^*). If both are sufficiently known, the potential polluter can incorporate them into its decision making.

However, uncertainty arises when the probability distribution is not known or the scale of the event, were it to occur, is known inaccurately or only imperfectly. In the context of EUB generating NRD, in Italy and other countries, liability regimes are characterized by high uncertainty, particularly in relation to the NRD assessment method used to yield the sanction we have defined as $\hat{S}$. This means that the potential polluter lacks a good characterization of the likely costs of EUB. The objective of the approach described below is to decrease this uncertainty through standardization of NRD assessment methods, which would provide a potential polluter with more information on which to characterize the probability distribution of the sanction.

Within this framework, regulatory authorities could increase the deterrent effect by increasing q, thus driving $\hat{S}$ closer to S^*; that is, by increasing the expected sanction through the application of assessment practices that suggest to the potential polluter both a better specified probability distribution of q and a higher expected q. This would yield a more costly sanction in the event that the polluter engages in EUB and causes NRD. Establishing standard assessment rules for categories of NRD can be effective for reducing some of the assessment uncertainties *ex ante*, thereby increasing the predictability of

NRD and the potential polluter's ability to efficiently internalize expected NRD costs.

In particular, the aim of standardization at minimum should be to increase the predictability of the $\hat{S}$ that would apply if NRD occurs. It may not be possible *ex ante* to completely specify the sanction, but it is feasible to specify financial assessment techniques *ex ante* that yield a minimum expected sanction for pqS^*. Thus we can separate the estimated sanction into two parts based on the ability to signal its value *ex ante*:

(3) $\hat{S} = \underline{S} + \tilde{S}$

where $\underline{S}$ is determinable *ex ante* since it depends on well -specified financial assessment techniques that provide partial estimates of NRD, and $\tilde{S}$ represents the monetary value of the NRD that remains after application of financial assessment techniques. Estimation of $\tilde{S}$ requires the application of economic valuation techniques and, thus, is more difficult to standardize *ex ante*. However, since $\underline{S}$ can be estimated *ex ante*, the predictability of the actual *ex post* assessed sanction ($\hat{S}$) will increase.

Currently, the *efficiency* objective of the European liability regime effectively imposes a sanction that involves *restoration to the status quo*, compelling the polluter to provide resource compensation to pre-injury conditions. However, reparation of the NRD is not the only action that may be required. This is because failure to comply with an environmental regulation may entail not only an undesirable loss to some other party (the community as a whole), which warrants restoration, but also an undesirable gain to the polluter.[14] Increasing internalization of the NRD, therefore, might attain one of objectives of the sanction (*efficiency*) but does not assure the other objective of *deterrence*, that is, the monetary compensation for the NRD within a liability regime is not necessarily related to the polluter's gain in undertaking the EUB that caused NRD. Hence the potential polluter could still choose to exercise EUB if the gains from EUB are greater than $p\hat{S}$.

If full deterrence (along with the objective of compensation) is the primary objective of a liability regime this could be ensured by imposition on those polluters gaining from their EUB the requirement to forgo all or a portion of their G, as well as to provide NRD compensation.[15] In such a regime, the adjusted expected utility estimated by the polluter is:

(4) $EU = p[U(\tilde{G} - \hat{S})] + (1 - p)U(G)$

where $\tilde{G}$ is the portion of G retained by the polluter after the regulator's requirement for the polluter to forgo the marginal revenues deriving from EUB. In practice, effective implementation of the charges to G would require a broad understanding of numerous institutional and legal perspectives.

To assure deterrence the minimum sanction, $\underline{S}$ should include charges that erase EUB gains. We largely ignore this aspect in our discussion, but reducing assessment uncertainties is highly relevant in this context of EUB-driven revenue gains. As noted earlier, the implementation of a standard NRD economic assessment approach, *ceteris paribus*, would promote more efficient internalization of potential NRD claims. The *ex post*-determined $\hat{S}$ becomes more narrowly bounded, allowing a more efficient balancing of $\hat{S}$ against possible EUB gains and, thereby, deterring EUB among those polluters who are over-discounting possible sanctions. In addition, standardization would facilitate the categorization of NRD, which would increase the predictability of the possible sanction in the potential polluter's decision calculus, and help to spotlight the EUB activities that generate revenue gains at the expense of causing NRD.[16]

Standardizing NRD assessments

To reduce the uncertainties in an NRD assessment (NRDA) and, by doing so, to increase the predictability of expected sanctions and send signals to the potential polluter to deter EUB, it is necessary to understand how they operate. Most immediately, the uncertainties depend on the specifics of the liability regime that identifies the objects to value, an identification process that is general and incomplete. In addition, uncertainties derive from the lack of an adequate multidisciplinary approach to support NRDA.

The lack of clarity about the object of valuation drives the problem of large uncertainties in NRD assessments. Definition of the object to be valued monetarily in an NRDA may appear tautological, in so far as it is NRD itself that is at stake. However, in practice there are inconsistencies between (i) the monetary value of NRD, from a conventional economic perspective, and (ii) the monetary value of NRD that needs to be estimated for the purposes of compensation.

From an economic perspective, damage to the environment is a case of negative externality, an external cost (typically expressed in non-monetary terms) that is not fully internalized into the accounts of the parties that cause it by undertaking their production activities (Cropper and Oates 1992). As much of the natural environment is a public good, this externality imposes a social cost on the community as a whole (Monti 2003). In this context, traditional economic valuation techniques aim at estimating monetarily the entire set of negative changes to total economic value (TEV)[17] in the whole community caused by the EUB.

Within a liability regime approach, in which NRD represents the conditions that define the polluter's liability, the technical aspects of the damage need to be assessed, in terms of their physical and temporal extents. Often it is not necessary to denominate these in monetary terms; liability requirements usually enforce the restoration of damaged environmental resources and service to the identified original condition (baseline), as well as compensation for temporary and permanent losses of resources and services (Stellin and Candido 2005).

Differences between the valuation of NRD from an economic perspective, and the valuation made for compensation claims, create uncertainty for the polluter and diminish the credibility of the liability regime. An inadequate multidisciplinary appreciation exacerbates this difficulty. In particular, a problem arises in the application of economic techniques in a legal forum. The legal system requires evidence to reach a minimum level of certainty and concreteness, a level that some economic assessment techniques may not achieve. This is particularly the case when non-market estimation techniques are employed in NRD evaluations. Courts frequently have to grapple with the validity of economic evidence in NRD cases, sometimes rejecting it even when theoretically sound.

Identifying standard rules for NRDA within the confines of the current liability regime could mitigate the evidentiary problem that contributes to the mixed and incomplete signals of sanctions that potential polluters must sift through. Such standardization needs to start by identifying the minimum components necessary for making the process and outcomes of NRDA more predictable.

Clarifying the technical approach to NRDA

An integrated economic perspective for NRDA fundamentally requires that the selection and application of the best available economic assessment technique for any given NRD depend on the context of the valuation. The characteristics that are important here include: how liability is defined as an obligation to provide resource compensation; the willingness of the identified polluter to actually provide the resource compensation deemed necessary; the presence of residual NRD; and finally the level of certainty and concreteness required for valuation in the judicial context. The last characteristic is particularly relevant when the (preferred) market-based valuation is not applicable. As noted earlier, non-market valuation techniques[18] are open to more challenges in judicial proceedings.[19]

Neither previous and existing Italian rules on liability nor the European Liability Directive establish clear economic techniques to apply to estimate the monetary value of NRD. However, we can infer some useful assessment rules. The European Liability Directive states that NRD compensation has to be achieved through primary remediation. This aims at restoring the damaged natural resources and services to their baseline condition (*primary remediation*); when it does not result in restoration to baseline, then *complementary remediation*[20] must be undertaken. In addition, *compensatory remediation*[21] must be undertaken to compensate for interim losses.[22]

In Italy the legal basis of the liability regime for NRD was established before the publication of European Directive 2004/35/CE. Prior to 2006, Article 18 of law No. 349 of 8 July 1986[23] guided the general legal basis of fault liability for environmental damage.[24] According to this law, any private or public party whose illegal behaviour caused NRD, defined as the alteration, deterioration, or partial or total destruction of the environment, had to pay monetary compensation to the state. Judicial authorities also could impose obligations to restore NRD to the conditions that existed before the illegal behaviour occurred, if such restoration were possible. If exact quantification of NRD for the purposes of establishing monetary compensation was impossible, the courts could establish a value on the basis of restoration costs, the polluter's illegally generated gains, or degree of fault. Decree No. 152 of 30 April 2006 establishes that, if the Italian Ministry of the Environment launches a judicial proceeding, it can claim resource compensation or equivalent monetary compensation based principally on the costs of restoration of the NRD.

The liability regimes instituted under the 2006 decree in Italy and the European Liability Directive support similar assessment rules, since they both follow the *equivalence resource and service principle*. This principle imposes a sanction that in monetary terms represents the sum of the remediation costs (as a maximum).[25] Thus the sanction that could be imposed on the polluter by the liability regime would be:[26]

$$(5) \ S^* = \text{primary remediation costs} + (\text{compensatory remediation costs} \\ + \text{complementary remediation costs})$$

If primary remediation fully repairs the injured resource, the component of S^* in the parentheses typically will comprise only those measures undertaken to compensate for *interim losses* from NRD. However, when remediation does not result in full repair of the NRD it may be necessary also to recover compensation for *permanent losses* by providing other complementary eco-system resources and services at the same or alternative sites.[27] Hence the liability regime effectively defines the value of NRD as the sum of the monetary value of losses, both interim and permanent, and the costs required to restore them as closely as possible to pre-injury conditions. Because interim and permanent losses represent the residual NRD after remediation, in monetary terms *the monetary value of residual NRD* under this liability regime equals:

$$(6) \ \text{compensatory remediation costs} + \text{complementary remediation costs}$$

Complementary remediation costs are zero in the case of full repair of the injured resource. Therefore, except in the case of instantaneous natural recoverability of NRD – where interim losses also equal zero – the economic value of residual NRD equals or exceeds the economic value of interim losses (compensatory remediation costs).

NRD economic valuation techniques measure the negative utility flow coming from the reduction in available natural resources and services (APAT 2002, 2006; Stellin and Candido 2005). The sum in equation (5) should equal or exceed the utility loss represented in a financial assessment of NRD. This is based on the underlying premise in the assessment rules that society values a natural resource and its ecosystem services at least as much as it would spend to restore the resource to its initial quantity and quality were it damaged. This motivates the *remediation cost method* as the appropriate approach for NRDA.

The literature generally does not consider the remediation cost method as a fully defensible economic valuation technique owing to the absence of a formal theoretical relationship between remediation costs and TEV. However, because, in practice, liability regimes have established the priority of resource compensation, and since the remediation cost method entails a more straightforward approach to value damage, some economic studies identify remediation cost as an appropriate revealed preference technique. The European Commission (2001), for example, argues that in a liability regime that imposes remediation cost as a measure of compensation the *remediation cost method* can be used to estimate TEV; at the extreme, it represents a minimum estimate of TEV. Moreover, although this method is challengeable on theoretical grounds, it is consistent with sanctions imposed for liability compensation purposes. It also achieves the level of certainty and concreteness required in the judicial context.

More broadly, remediation costs can be considered to be part of a larger group of cost-based valuation approaches. These include (Table 7.1): defensive (or mitigation) cost method, or DCM; remediation cost method, or RCM; surrogate (or replacement) cost method, or SCM; avoided cost method, or ACM.

The defensive and remediation cost methods together measure primary remediation interventions. Under the liability regime, surrogate and avoided costs represent the portion of complementary and compensatory costs that is based on use values, and can be a proxy measure for the monetary value of the residual NRD (interim and permanent losses).[28] As implied in our remediation cost discussion, none of the cost-based approaches yields strict measures of economic value, since all are based only on people's willingness to pay for a product or service. They do not include non-use values, which constitute the $\tilde{S}$ not known *ex ante*. Rather, they bound the economic value under the assumption that natural resources and services must be worth at least as much as people are willing to pay or do to prevent, defend, substitute or remediate them.

Resource recoverability and restorability

It is not always straightforward to estimate even primary remediation costs. Negative utility flows from NRD emerge at different times and are dynamic

Table 7.1 Cost-based valuation approaches

Defensive (or mitigation) cost method (DCM)

Represents the first actions to fully repair an injured resource. It is a component of primary remediation costs. The aim is not restore lost utility, but to limit the loss. In the US, defensive costs include assessment costs (Ofiara 2002). Defensive costs may be equivalent to primary remediation costs if damage is not restorable through human intervention and is irreversible through natural recovery processes (attenuation).

Remediation cost method (RCM)

Represents the costs necessary to eliminate the loss of utility from environmental damage by restoring injured natural resources to their baseline condition. Requires the identification of a best remediation technology (National Oceanic and Atmospheric Administration 2000; Ofiara 2002; Touaty and Giè 2004; World Bank 1998).

Surrogate cost method (SCM)

Method to estimate NRD that are only partially restorable (Di Cocco 1960; Garrod and Willis 1999; Michieli and Michieli 2002; National Oceanic and Atmospheric Administration 2000). The approach depicts the costs necessary to substitute non-restorable injured natural resources with other goods that provide the same services and utility. Because the method applies to services not traded in the market, but for which private goods can substitute, the applicability of the method depends on the degree of replaceability of the damaged natural resource.

Avoided cost method (ACM)

Represents costs involved in preventing the NRD. The assumption is that the cost of conserving natural resources and services is a reasonable estimate of their value. Typically, averting expenditures are utilized. These measure how much people are willing to pay to avoid or protect themselves from a decrease in environmental quality.

Source: Adapted from APAT (2006) and European Commission (2001).

(Boyd 2003; Howe 1990; Ofiara 2002). Moreover, the relevant time horizon for measurement depends on the *natural recoverability* of NRD, which relies on natural recovery involving chemical, physical and biological processes; the *feasibility of restoration* through human intervention, which depends on technical and financial limitations of the human interventions; and the possibility of reproducing naturally resources to yield ecosystem services. At the extremes, the appropriate time horizon is finite and determinate if NRD are fully naturally recoverable and restorable, and indefinite if NRD entail interim and permanent losses (APAT 2006).

The intersection of our broader group of cost-based methods with the concepts of natural recoverability and restorability defines four categories of NRD for valuation within a cost-based approach. Table 7.2 shows the possible application of different methods of monetary assessment to determine $\underline{S}$ depending on the degree of natural recoverability and human-directed restorability of the damaged resources.

These four categories simplify NRD but nonetheless are useful for examining assessment from the perspective of the type of damaged resource and service.[29] Table 7.2 shows that, for any damage caused, a cost-based method

Table 7.2 Natural recoverability of NRD and human-directed restorability of natural resources and services

| NRD | Human-directed restoration of natural resource and services | |
	Possible	*Impossible*
Naturally recoverable	A Defensive costs Remediation costs Surrogate costs of interim losses Avoided costs of non-replaceable interim losses	B Defensive costs Surrogate costs of interim losses Avoided costs of non-replaceable interim losses
Not naturally recoverable	C Defensive costs Remediation costs Surrogate costs of interim losses Avoided costs of non-replaceable interim losses	D Defensive costs Surrogate costs of interim and permanent losses Avoided costs of non-replaceable interim and permanent losses

Note: Defensive costs are temporary in cases A–C and permanent in case D; defensive costs and restoration costs are two components of primary remediation.

always requires consideration of defensive and surrogate measures (as well as avoided cost measures if non-replaceable losses exist and they are identified in NRDA). Restoration costs warrant consideration if natural resources and services are restorable through specific interventions (cases A and C). Of these two, case C entails the higher cost, since it represents a situation where NRD can be addressed only by human-directed restoration, without the possibility of natural recovery. Defensive permanent actions, permanent substitution and non-replaceable utilities must be considered if NRD are not naturally recoverable and natural resources and services are not restorable (case D).

This categorization provides a structure that can be operationalized in a standardized approach able to accommodate the specifics of different situations. However, in practice, technical difficulties would affect implementation of the structure. In particular, the order of the components of the monetary value of the sanction (one to two to three, and then to four) in all the cells in Table 7.2 reflects the greater difficulties involved in the assessment. This derives from the increasing technical uncertainties in assessing the higher levels of the structure. For example, while remediation actions refer only to liability NRD, surrogate and lost utility relate to residual NRD, which must cope with the same technical assessment complexities as liability NRD but has additional economic uncertainties. As the number of NRD components increases, assessment of the monetary value of NRD becomes more complicated.

Similar relationships hold for economic valuation uncertainties, with the greatest uncertainty occurring in the valuation of non-replaceable losses and lost utilities. Under a conventional assessment, these often entail significant non-use values, suggesting the need for non-market-based approaches. However, in practice, stated preference techniques often are not employed, since they fail to provide the level of certainty and concreteness demanded by courts and may require too large investments in money, time and staff resources for the regulatory agencies to undertake. Because of these practical limitations we argue that an avoided cost approach should be used to infer the value of non-replaceable losses. Moreover, while this is not wholly consistent with conventional economic approaches to valuing resource losses – it does not fully capture the values that communities might attribute to lost natural resources – it does relate to the deterrence rate, and is often linked with EUB gains.

The routinized application of cost-based methods can substantially reduce the technical difficulties in NRDA. This would facilitate more accurate *ex ante* estimation of the minimum sanction that would apply to EUB. Specifically, the minimum sanction in any given situation would equal the sum of: *defensive costs* (at least temporary ones) and *surrogate costs* of interim and permanent losses that are replaceable (at least those losses identified in the span between the occurrence of the damage and NRD claims in judicial proceedings that can be substituted for).

In addition, it may be possible to estimate the *avoided costs* of interim and permanent losses that are non-replaceable, and lost utilities (at least those identified in the span between the occurrence of the damage and NRD claims in judicial proceedings). The sum of *defensive, surrogate* and *avoided* costs in such a cost-based approach is represented by $\underline{S}$ in equation (3). Defensive costs are part of primary remediation, while surrogate and avoided costs represent an underestimated proxy for interim and permanent losses. In cases A and C preliminary technical data should allow identification of the best technology for remediation and the range of related costs that should constitute the minimum estimate of the sanction. This minimum, $\underline{S}$ can be estimated *ex ante* and lends more certainty to the total sanction.

The signals sent by a clarification of the cost-based approaches do not necessarily eliminate uncertainty in practice. *Ex ante* estimation of $\underline{S}$ also would benefit from the collection and publication in a readily accessible database of the costs of previous NRD. These would improve transparency and predictability for potential polluters and constitute firmer ground and precedents for judicial proceedings. Increasing accessibility to past NRD costs also would help to reduce the variability of monetary benchmarks applied by different assessors in different NRDAs. At the same time it could reduce uncertainties in assessing *ex post* sanction ($\tilde{S}$) after technical assessments are completed, because the assessors could reference database costs.

Notwithstanding our emphasis on financial assessments, conventional economic valuation techniques remain relevant to the valuation of NRD.

Not only do they help regulators to develop a more sophisticated approach to deterring specific types of EUB, they also provide direction for setting new guidance, directives and regulations.[30] Assessment experts given the task of estimating NRD at a site could use the categorization of NRD displayed in Table 7.2 to better define the links between NRD and the economic activities that caused damage at the site. A multidisciplinary group including economists, biologists and chemical and environmental engineers could use the categorization to identify EUB gains, which could then be evaluated by conventional economic valuation. EUB gains would require market investigation into proper prices and the costs of harmful production activities, while the economic valuation of NRD would require one or more of several available economic valuation techniques (listed in order of preference):

1 *Benefit transfer*, the process used to adapt a measure or a value function estimated in a previous site-specific study to another context;[31]
2 *Revealed preference approaches*, including hedonic price and travel cost methods that capture the use values of goods and services not directly traded in the market;
3 *Stated preference approaches*, such as contingent valuation and choice experiments, which could be employed if lost non-use values are relevant, the previous approaches are not realistic, and NRD claims are large.

The development and application of these three approaches is strengthened if experts carry out valuation in a transparent, publicly funded process (such as through a national environmental agency or a European Commission working group). This may help to mitigate some of the criticism that frequently follows valuation.

Deterring illegal waste disposal by liability regimes

Externalities from the improper disposal of waste, or its disposal in poorly designed, inadequate landfills (illegal disposal), constitute some of the most vexing environmental problems in Europe. In Italy, for example, EUWM activities are one of the major contributors to NRD, constituting in some regions the main cause of contaminated sites and illegal behaviours judged in proceedings.[32]

Appropriate and legal waste management should internalize all the known costs and externalities in the landfill gate price (tipping fee). To ensure that the gate price reflects these, it is necessary that all landfills are regulated to an agreed set of minimum environmental standards, the effect of which will be to raise the costs of landfill disposal above current levels. In addition, landfill gate fees could include remaining unpriced externalities (those effects that cannot be eliminated by enforcing landfill operating standards, such as the cost of resource depletion, emissions during virgin material extraction and other life cycle externalities associated with a product).

Although the legal disposal of waste in landfills is often an inexpensive option because externalities of waste generation and disposal are unpriced, illegal behaviour continues to be widespread. Poor detection and enforcement of violations, combined with unclear NRDA practices, fail to create adequate disincentives to deter environmentally harmful practices. A liability regime that would address this situation effectively is highly desirable. If the regime were well designed and implemented, it could simultaneously achieve the two related goals discussed earlier, namely the compensation of victims for NRD that does occur (*efficiency objective*) and deterrence of EUWM activities that generate NRD (*deterrence objective*). The current difficulties in Italy over reducing improper and illegal disposal of waste in landfills make this latter objective and the design of a liability regime to achieve it particularly important.

The technical uncertainties faced in NRDAs for EUWM are similar to those relating to other types of EUB. They include lack of data about the baseline status of pre-injured resources, variability in how to ascertain the mechanisms through which EUB-caused damage, and lack of information on the time period required to meet restoration or surrogate targets. Uncertainties over monetary assessment and low deterrence rates also characterize NRD caused by EUWM. In addition, at least in Italy, data collection focuses on measuring NRD liability in the case of contaminated sites or identifying prosecutable offences in the case of illegal waste disposal. Thus authorities often neglect to collect basic data about the source of the NRD, including: quantity and type of waste; the time period over which the waste was improperly or illegally disposed of; the land area affected by EUWM; and the authorized land uses in areas at or near waste disposal locations. Such information is essential for clarifying and reducing the technical uncertainties that suffuse NRDA, and, where it is lacking, the financial assessment and economic valuation techniques discussed earlier for estimating $\hat{S}$ may be problematic.

Estimating components of $\underline{S}$

Table 7.3 highlights different approaches for estimating $\underline{S}$ the determinable *ex ante* sanction for EUWM that depends on well specified financial assessment techniques using concepts and the categorization developed earlier.

Case A: naturally recoverable NRD and restorable natural resources and services

NRD from disposal of biodegradable waste is often naturally recoverable, and when the injured resource is contained, natural resource restoration is usually possible. For example, an aquifer contaminated with a leachate of organic sewage that is contained within the aquifer could be restored to an initial condition that satisfies human consumption demands. Natural processes

Table 7.3 Improper or illegal waste disposal that causes NRD

	Human-directed restoration of natural resource and services	
NRD	*Possible*	*Impossible*
Naturally recoverable	A Disposal of *biodegradable* waste in *contained* natural resource	B Disposal of *biodegradable* waste in *non-contained* natural resource
Not naturally recoverable	C Disposal of *non-biodegradable* waste in *contained* natural resource	D Disposal of *non-biodegradable* waste in *non-contained* natural resource

may be able to attenuate the NRD, but the recovery could be enhanced by restorative measures. In this case the monetary NRD assessment at a minimum must consider any actions that need to be undertaken to limit harmful effects (*defensive costs*), such as barriers to prevent the dispersion of contamination; restore damaged natural resources and services as much as possible (minimum of the *remediation cost range*), such as pump and treat techniques to clean up the damaged groundwater; provide surrogates (*surrogate costs*) for interim losses until the baseline is achieved, if the damaged natural resource and services are replaceable, such as temporary provision of water from alternative sources in situations where drinking water supplies have been contaminated.

In addition to these, if non-replaceable interim losses exist and are identified, *avoided costs* should be accounted for, such as the costs of properly managed biodegradable waste.

Case B: naturally recoverable NRD but non-restorable natural resources and services

NRD resulting from the improper or illegal disposal of biodegradable waste may be naturally recoverable, but for non-contained natural resources adequate restoration interventions are often technically or economically impossible. For example, contaminants in a discharge of biodegradable waste into a river will disperse quickly, making remediation technically and economically infeasible.[33] In such a case the NRD assessment at minimum must consider action that needs to be taken to limit harmful effects (*defensive costs*), such as action to avoid the dispersion of contamination or provide surrogates (*surrogate costs*) for interim lost or damaged natural resources and services that are replaceable, such as the temporary relocation of recreational activities.

In addition to these, if non-replaceable interim losses exist and they are identified, *avoided costs* should be accounted for, such as the costs of properly managed biodegradable waste.

Case C: not naturally recoverable NRD but restorable natural resources and services

NRD resulting from the improper or illegal disposal of non-biodegradable waste may not be naturally recoverable, but, in situations where a natural resource is contained, adequate remediation interventions are usually technically or economically possible. For example, an aquifer with NRD resulting from a leachate of non-biodegradable waste in groundwater that is contained within the aquifer may be restorable by cleaning groundwater of the pollutant compounds. In this case the NRD assessment at a minimum has to consider action that needs to be taken to limit harmful effects (*defensive costs*), such as barriers to prevent the dispersion of contamination; restore damaged natural resource and services as much as possible (*minimum of the remediation cost range*), such as pump-treat techniques to clean up damaged groundwater (if appropriate for the magnitude of the NRD and the type of waste); and provide surrogates (*surrogate costs*) for interim losses until the baseline is achieved, if the damaged natural resource and services are replaceable, such as temporary provision of water from alternative sources in situations where drinking water supplies have been contaminated. In addition, if non-replaceable interim losses exist, and they are identified, *avoided costs* should be accounted for, such as the costs of properly managed biodegradable waste.

Case D: not naturally recoverable NRD and non-restorable natural resources and services

NRD resulting from the improper or illegal disposal of non-biodegradable waste may not be naturally recoverable, and in non-contained natural resources adequate remediation interventions are often technically or economically unavailable. For example, contaminants in a discharge of non-biodegradable waste in a river can readily disperse, making restoration technically and economically impossible. In this case the NRD assessment at a minimum has to consider actions that need to be undertaken to limit harmful effects (*defensive costs*), such as barriers to prevent the dispersion of contamination; provide surrogates (*surrogate costs*) for interim losses until the baseline is achieved, if the damaged natural resource and services are replaceable, such as the temporary relocation of recreational activities; and provide surrogates (*surrogate costs*) for permanently lost damaged natural resource and services that are replaceable. In addition, if non-replaceable interim and permanent losses exist, and they are identified, *avoided costs* should be accounted for, such as the costs of properly managed biodegradable waste.

Other considerations

The range of techniques available for developing monetary estimates of $\hat{S}$ can be unduly circumscribed, or sanctions can be underestimated, if data on the quantity and type of waste that caused the NRD are insufficiently robust. These failings would result in a reduced deterrence effect, because lack of data also affects the estimation of $\underline{S}$. For example, data on the quantity of waste are necessary for computing the avoided costs of foregoing proper waste management, while data on the quality of the waste are necessary to allow technical analysis of the likely damage to ecological and human services. In addition, information on the time span between pollutant discharge and regulatory attention would allow preliminary estimation of defensive and remediation costs.

The categorization of NRD from EUWM pertains to both water, as developed above, and soil damage. However, in the latter case, the illegal disposal of waste in an inadequate landfill or the discharge of waste directly onto the land (unlawful landfill) represents an additional loss of environmental services that is often ignored. Land provides the essential service in waste management, namely the physical medium in which the waste is deposited. Land suitable for modern landfills is scarce in many areas and is non-replaceable. Yet, once used for illegal or improper disposal, natural recovery will not occur unless all negative externalities from the landfill fall to zero, which is unlikely. Thus NRD caused by illegal disposal of waste in an inadequate landfill, or the discharge of waste on to soil, falls into categories C or D in Table 7.3, depending on the possibility of restoration. Landfill service loss will be *interim* if remediation is possible and *permanent* if it is impossible.

In this context the economic value of a loss in landfill services equals the sum of private costs and external costs. Private costs correspond to the cost of waste disposal in a landfill, while external costs represent the negative externalities not already internalized in the private costs. These have been well explored in the literature. For example, a European Commission study (COWI 2000) enumerates a variety of external costs of waste disposal in landfills, including costs related to the generation of greenhouse gases, conventional air pollutants and airborne toxics that cause negative health effects, leachate to soil and water, and disamenity effects such a noise, odour and visual aesthetics.[34] Such costs can be either *fixed* or *variable*, depending on whether their scale varies according to waste volumes. Fixed externalities result from the existence of the landfill site, and include the loss of property value, visual pollution, reduction in amenity values, psychological concern over potential health impacts and other negatives. Variable externalities relate to the volume of waste being treated, and include such impacts as higher traffic volumes and emissions, increased greenhouse gas emissions from the landfill, and contamination of groundwater (Brisson and Pearce 1995; COWI 2000).

In principle, estimates of the costs of both these private and external costs could be included in NRDA in cases where waste is illegally dumped or improperly managed in landfills. Clarifying the methods by which these costs could be estimated, and incorporated into sanctions, would add to the deterrence objective of a regulatory system by imbuing the assessment with more certainty. These methods depend on the nature of the externality. Private costs are already well specified and represent the market price of disposal in a legal landfill. These costs can easily be collected and disseminated. External costs present more challenges, but numerous published studies have developed estimates, and a commitment to meta-analysis[35] of some of these studies and/or the application of benefit transfer methods would provide a strong signal to economic actors of the NRDA techniques likely to be applied if their EUWM damages natural resources. In addition, to the degree that they signal higher costs for disposal, these methods also would contribute to the European Landfill Directive's goal of decreasing the volume of waste disposal.

Conclusion

Our aim in this chapter was to apply theoretical concepts developed in the economics literature, and a simple analytical model to address the exigencies of NRD assessments, as a means of improving valuation of NRD claims and recovery. Implicitly this involved manipulating the theoretical niceties of economic assessment to conform to the practical limitations of regulatory and judicial practices, while at the same time extending current NRDA practice to yield outcomes that are more economically rational.

The principal building block of our approach is the recognition that liability regimes should have the twin objectives of deterrence and compensation. While intuitively appealing, in practice this dual objective is difficult to achieve. In part, this reflects policy shortcomings that have yielded incompletely designed liability regimes, but the difficulty also derives from a methodological failure to consistently define the appropriate framework for NRD valuation. In particular, techniques favoured by economic theory aim to define the total economic value of the loss to a community from NRD. In contrast, valuation methods more favoured in liability regimes focus on compensation for NRD and, thus, often use remediation costs as a proxy for value. Neither approach on its own is fully satisfactory from a policy perspective. The first may be impractical given the budgetary and time limitations. It also may suffer from limited acceptance by the courts, particularly if non-market approaches are used, since they often entail a level of uncertainty that defendants can easily exploit. The second, besides being objectionable on theoretical grounds, often fails to deliver appropriate signals to deter EUB.

The problem of competing valuation frameworks compounds the uncertainty that potential polluters face when they contemplate undertaking EUB. A lack of standardization of NRDA practice, coupled with unavoidable uncertainties in the technical aspects of NRD – for example, establishing the baseline conditions for the measurement of NRD, determining the time frame necessary for restoration, and defining appropriate resource substitutes if damage is not restorable – mean that potential polluters often lack enough information to efficiently internalize NRD costs. Thus the uncertainty endemic to assessments under most liability regimes means that, in practice, the regimes frequently fall short of their potential in terms of both compensation and deterrence objectives.

NRDA standardization is essential for increasing certainty, for both potential polluters and the experts conducting the NRDA. The first requires more careful articulation and transparent application of the types of restoration and costs that may be encountered in a given NRD claim. At the simplest level, only *primary remediation* may be necessary to return an injured ecosystem resource or service to its pre-injury condition. If primary remediation leaves residual contamination, then *complementary remediation* may be necessary on or off site to compensate for the resources that were not fully restored. In addition, if there are interim losses while remediation is taking place, *compensatory remediation* may be necessary to address the interim loss in resource values from the onset of the loss until primary and complementary remediation have been completed.

The appropriate sanction to impose for NRD, which if clearly signalled *ex ante* also defines the expected sanction that potential polluters should internalize, is the sum of the costs for primary, complementary and compensatory remediation. In some situations the full extent of these may be impossible to estimate *ex ante*, but it is possible to estimate a large proportion of them. However, the abundance of technical uncertainties can complicate the estimation of even primary remediation costs. These complexities also pose challenges for assessing complementary and compensatory remediation costs, which, typically, also involve greater financial assessment challenges.

We argue that, on practical grounds, cost-based approaches that yield financial values are the most appropriate methods for estimating remediation costs. Depending on the degree of natural recoverability and human-directed restorability of the damaged resource, avoided cost, defensive cost, remediation cost or surrogate cost methods can provide estimates that are defensible from a theoretical viewpoint, as well as practical and applicable in regulatory or adjudicated settings. They also can be related to the economic concepts of utility, and, by relying on engineering approaches, they avoid some of the more knotty uncertainties associated with economic assessment techniques.

To improve the application of these methods, standardization of NRDA techniques could adopt two straightforward protocols that would not require legal changes to the liability regime in many cases. First, a simple, transparent, prioritized list of cost-based approaches would reduce the range of choices available to NRD assessors when undertaking assessments. This could reduce the uncertainty that potential polluters face *ex ante* about the costs that the liability regime may impose if the polluters undertake EUB that results in NRD. It also would benefit the assessors. Second, for the portion of NRD that represents non-use values that are not amenable to cost-based methods, the development and application of standardized monetary estimates that could be applied through benefits transfer could decrease the range of the monetary values applicable to NRDA in a liability regime. This would send signals to potential polluters and could increase the acceptability of NRD estimates in the courts.

NRD from EUWM activities may be a particularly attractive target for a liability regime. These activities have resulted in significant environmental damage in Italy, where EUWM remain ubiquitous. We argue that, even in the absence of legal or regulatory changes, the existing liability regime could achieve substantial EUWM reductions by sending clearer signals about potential sanctions. In particular, the cost-based valuation methods that we advocate are well suited to deterring EUWM because these methods (i) can be clearly specified *ex ante* and (ii) provide clear signals that the remediation costs for NRD will almost inevitably exceed the potential benefits from non-compliance that potential polluters consider when deciding whether to engage in EUWM activities.

In addition to standardization along the lines outlined in this chapter, a number of other opportunities offer potential for greater deterrence of environmentally undesirable behaviour and better compensation processes. First, since elements of an NRD claim will be spread over different time periods, a discrete time horizon should be identified to discount the cost components of NRDA. This would allow comparison of alternative options on a common basis. Thus the choice of discount rate in NRDA warrants further scrutiny and discussion.

Second, more attention needs to be paid to the problem of double counting resource damage when multiple impacts are in play. This requires deliberate separation of the various resources and their damage, and careful delineation of the costs and damage to each individual natural resource and service. The ecosystem and human services provided by one or more natural resources need to be differentiated and separately estimated – especially as they will likely involve different challenges. For instance, when a resource, such as a stream, is polluted, estimating a surrogate cost for lost recreation due to damage to the stream is likely to be more straightforward than estimating a surrogate cost for a lost ecosystem service that the stream provided. Such an exercise could help to define the minimum NRDA data required to enable public agents to identify improper or illegal production activities that cause NRD.

Third, collection and publication in a readily accessible database of past NRD costs should be promoted to provide greater transparency and predictability to potential polluters, as well as to establish more concrete grounds and precedents for judicial proceedings. Increasing the accessibility of past NRD costs would also reduce the variability in the monetary benchmarks that different assessors use in NRDAs.

Finally, standardization of the sentences and judicial protocols concerning NRD claims could elevate current discourse in judicial proceedings and improve interactions among judges, technical experts, economists and other experts. This might help to reduce the often large gap between the monetary

NRD estimates developed in compensation claims, and the actual amounts established in court decisions.

The concepts that we have outlined, and changes in practice that are consistent with these concepts, could significantly reduce the uncertainties associated with NRD and shift a potential polluter's expectations about sanctions, resulting in a reduction in EUB. Thus conventional economic assessment techniques have a critical role to play in operationalizing liability regimes, by forcing the definition of the EUB that should be included in an effective regime, namely those activities that generate negative economic values from environmental externalities. An effective liability regime is one that both deters natural resource damages and compensates victims when they occur.

Acknowledgements

We would like to thank our respective institutions and colleagues for their support for our work; all the views expressed in this chapter, and all errors and omissions are our own. We especially want to acknowledge Cindy Anderson and Paola Di Toppa for their valuable comments which shaped our understanding and thinking.

The views expressed in this chapter are those of the authors and do not necessarily represent the positions of their institutions.

Notes

1 We adopt the definition of externality used by ExternE, a European Commission research project (http://externe.jrc.es/All-EU+Summary.htm). It defines externalities as the costs and benefits which arise when the social or economic activities of one group of people have an impact on another, and when the first group fails to fully account for their impact.

2 'Command and control' regulations refer to an approach that establishes specific environmental standards, administrative obligations, prohibitions and technologies that the regulator imposes on the economic actors and that the actors are obliged to meet or use. This approach contrasts with market-based regulatory approaches, which use price signals through taxes, marketable pollution rights and other mechanisms, which give economic actors flexibility to choose potentially lower-cost means to meet their environmental requirements.

3 Shavell (1987) argues that a complete solution to the problem of the control of risk evidently should involve the joint use of liability and regulation, with the balance between them reflecting the importance of the determinants. Between an *ex post* regulatory system that works by attributing liability and an *ex ante* regulatory system that imposes standards there is a complementary rather than a substitutive relationship (Kolstad *et al.* 1990).

4 Directive 2004/35/EC of the European Parliament and of the Council of 21 April 2004.

5 In this context, fault-based liability refers to holding a polluter responsible for actions for which the polluter is at fault or negligent. Strict liability refers to holding the polluter responsible for activities that cause damage or harm regardless of whether the polluter was at fault or negligent. The economics and law literature is not clear whether strict liability regimes, which do not need to establish

fault, yield better environmental performance than fault liability regimes (Germani 2004). In fact, there is empirical evidence that in some situations strict liability may increase the frequency of accidental releases of contaminants into the environment (Alberini and Austin 1999).

6 At the European level the environmental waste hierarchy and the Landfill Directive prioritize the reduction of landfill. The directive is aimed at preventing or reducing the adverse effects of landfill waste on the environment, especially surface water, groundwater, soil, air and human health. Hence any activity that operates counter to waste reduction should be discouraged. Although European countries have adopted different strategies for diverting waste from landfill and with differing results (EEA 2007) excess waste generation and illegal diversion of waste from landfills remain ubiquitous. Both impose significant externalities on communities. In Italy, landfill still dominates as a waste management option and significant reductions in waste volumes have not been realized.

7 In his Nobel lecture in 1992 Becker (1993: 386) noted: 'The economic analysis of crime incorporates into rational behaviour illegal and other antisocial actions.' Thus his approach is not limited to crime *per se* but includes any behaviour unacceptable to the community.

8 We borrow the term 'sanction' from the crime and punishment literature and use it in our discussion to represent the monetary value of the requirements that the liability regime imposes on a polluter. Although 'sanction' typically comprises punitive action in a formal legal context, we employ the term to refer to remedial and compensatory costs expressed in monetary terms that support a remedy for environmental damage and compensation for lost resources and services.

9 If $p = 0$ the specific EUB is not included in any *ex post* regulatory system. Therefore, expected utility would follow the traditional micro-economic model of the producer's choice.

10 See Polinsky and Shavell (2005) for details.

11 The maximum sanction, S^*, that any given economic actor must contemplate will depend also, of course, on the economic activity involved (type of activity, scale of operation, materials used, etc.), since that will influence the resulting NRD. This is implicitly included in S^* in equation (2) and the subsequent equations and discussion.

12 The difficulties encountered in technical and economic assessments are numerous and well known. Although often treated separately, economic assessments fundamentally depend on having sufficiently robust technical information, so the two parts of the NRD assessment need to kept within a similar framework. The ability of the assessment to capture the full NRD (q) represents these difficulties.

13 S^* is expressed in monetary terms, as before, but in a liability regime it can involve both monetary and non-monetary characteristics. This implies that the potential polluter's predictability under a liability regime is lower than in a regulatory system where S is identified *ex ante*.

14 In estimating the economic benefits from illegal activities a panel of the US Environmental Protection Agency's (EPA) Science Advisory Board made a similar point, remarking, 'It should be noted, however, that removing the economic benefit is not the only action that might be required in order to restore the status quo. This is because the failure to comply with a federal regulation may entail not only an unwarranted gain to the violator but also an unwarranted loss to some other party' (US Environmental Protection Agency 2005: 1).

15 The question of gains to the producer from EUB introduces an aspect of the deterrence problem that is often ignored. Even if, for a potential polluter contemplating EUB, the probability of detection and the imposed sanctions are relatively low, it must consider the potential loss of revenue resulting from a reputation loss due to a conviction for EUB that would brand it as a polluter. Loss of

reputation can entail considerable costs for firms (through loss of business), and thus the threat of it provides an additional *ex ante* deterrent. Furthermore, depending on the legal system, fighting a conviction could incur substantial legal costs to the firm and risk a negative reputation in the business and regulatory domains. For example, the firm may find it more difficult in the future to obtain licences, find it is excluded from new contracts and/or work, face barriers to establishing a new legal entity, encounter more and tougher inspections and be forced to pay higher insurance premiums (Faure and Visser 2004). Motivations for good behaviour that go beyond the impact on production costs closely parallel themes in the extensive literature on voluntary environmental behaviour (Lyon and Maxwell 2004), which identifies factors that encourage improved environmental performance, such as regulatory (Khanna and Anton 2002; Segerson and Miceli 1998), market (Arora and Gangopadhyay 1995) and social (Blackman and Bannister 1998) pressures.

16 The first form of environmental (fault) liability regime in Italy was enacted in 1986 (Article 18 of Law No. 349 of 8 July 1986). This established that a court could consider any illegally generated gains in imposing a compensation claim when NRD values were irresolvable. The current liability regime, established in 2006, does not specify this possibility.

17 The total economic value (TEV) of a change is the sum of both use and non-use values; that is, TEV = direct use + indirect use + option + existence + bequest values (European Commission 2001).

18 The European Commission (2001) identifies conventional economic assessment techniques as: (i) conventional market techniques; (ii) revealed preference techniques; (iii) stated preference techniques. The stated preference approach is non-market-based.

19 Judicial challenges to the use of non-market-based approaches may be more common in Europe than in North America. One review of the literature (Carson 2000) indicates that stated preference (SP) methods have been in use for more than 40 years, during which time more than 2,000 SP studies had been conducted. They have been applied to a wide range of problems, including water quality, wilderness and wildlife preservation, air quality, health care and food safety. As noted by Carson, most modern SP studies are undertaken for the purpose of policy evaluation. Numerous federal and state agencies, governments and international organizations such as the World Bank now use this approach. In addition, Environment Canada, in co-operation with the US EPA and others, has constructed an online non-market valuations database, EVRI, to assist policy makers. As of March 2005 this database contained 757 SP studies, of which 290 focus on economic values associated with environmental commodities (www.evri. ca/english/tour.htm). Perhaps the best known application of SP was the NRDA of the infamous 1988 *Exxon Valdez* oil spill, following which demand for SP as a tool for assessing NRD increased dramatically. It is important to note, also, that US courts have upheld the use of contingent valuation in damage assessment and that both the Comprehensive Environmental Response Compensation and Liability Act and the Oil Pollution Act of 1990 allow for recovery of lost passive use (existence) values.

20 Complementary remediation consists of measures to compensate for lost resources value when primary remediation does not result in a full restoration (European Liability Directive).

21 Compensatory remediation consists of measures to compensate for interim losses in natural resources and services. They apply to the time span between the occurrence of the NRD and when the full effects of primary or complementary measures are in place, the time period over which damaged natural resources and/ or services are unable to perform their ecological functions or provide services to other natural resources or to the public. Compensatory remediation does not

include financial compensation to members of the public (European Liability Directive).

22 The US Department of the Interior's proposed regulations for NRD under the Comprehensive Environmental Response Compensation and Liability Act include similar compensation rules. The department describes the measure of damages as 'the cost of restoration, rehabilitation, replacement, and/or acquisition of the equivalent of the injured natural resources and the services those resources provide, *plus the compensable value of the services lost to the public for the time period from the discharge or release until the attainment of the restoration, rehabilitation, replacement and/or acquisition of equivalent of the resources and their services to the baseline*' (56 Fed. Reg. at 19,769 (proposed 43 CFR §11.80(b); US Environmental Protection Agency 2005; emphasis added).

23 This law established the Italian Ministry of the Environment.

24 For some 20 years Article 18 used the 'polluter pays' principle. More specific acts include Article 17 of Decree No. 22 (1997), which concerns clean-up issues, and Article 58 of Decree No. 152 (1999), which concerns water pollution protection.

25 The various elements of a NRD claim can be spread over different time periods, requiring a procedure that weights the costs that occur in different years so that they can be compared. Thus it is necessary to consider the appropriate discount (or compound) rate to apply. This choice has been actively debated and is relevant to NRD assessment uncertainty; however, we largely ignore it in our discussion.

26 S^* represents only the maximum potential sanction because of the insolvency protection problem, and because in civil and penal proceedings the amount of the adjudicated compensation claims can differ across courts or even, in some cases, be erased.

27 Thus compensatory remediation costs equal the monetary value of interim losses, and complementary remediation costs equal the monetary value of permanent losses.

28 This approach would underestimate qS^*, but it represents $\underline{S}$

29 In practice, NRD in context can be quite complex and it is necessary to analyse each service provided by each damaged resource. This demonstrates the criticality of a careful technical distinction of the NRD. Identifying precisely defined resources and services that have been damaged, and linking them with the community that has experienced their loss (utility), are essential for precise estimation of monetary values.

30 This is consistent with Article 174(3) of the European Union Treaty, which stipulates that, in preparing its policy on the environment, the community shall take account of the potential benefits and costs of action or lack of action.

31 This approach may be less appealing conceptually – it de-emphasizes the specifics of a site and its nexus with the NRD – but adapting pre-identified monetary parameters would be more practical in a judicial proceeding if the parameters could satisfy the need for standardization and concreteness.

32 Unfortunately, there are no systematic data characterizing the scope of the EUWM problem in Italy. However, roughly 30 per cent of the contaminated sites on the country's National Priority List entail landfills or waste stockpiles (APAT 2006). In addition, many of the sites with environmental damages involve NRD caused by illegal disposal of waste in inadequate landfills or the discharge of waste on to land (unlawful landfill).

33 Monetary assessment is usually required before technical analyses are completed. Therefore, due to lack of information, typically the costs of neither restorable nor non-restorable natural resources are part of $\underline{S}$. Although they can be roughly estimated *ex ante* in some cases, they usually constitute part of $\bar{S}$.

34 In addition, some external benefits, such as those from energy recovery, may exist.

35 Meta-analysis is a statistical technique for amalgamating, reviewing, summarizing and synthesizing previous quantitative or qualitative research. Where there is a

reasonable body of primary research studies, meta-analysis permits a wide variety of questions. Selected parts of the reported results of primary studies are entered into a database, and these meta-data are meta-analysed in similar ways to how data would be analysed in a primary study (first descriptively and then inferentially to test hypotheses).

References

Adams, M. and Steven, S. (1990) 'Zur Strafbarkeit des Versuchs', *Goltdammer's Archiv fur Strafrecht*, 137: 337–86.

Alberini, A. and Austin, D. (1999) 'Strict liability as a deterrent in toxic waste management: empirical evidence from accident and spill data', *Journal of Environmental Economics and Management*, 38: 20–48.

Alberton, M. (2003) 'Comparing Alternative Regulation Policies: An Environmental Law and Economics Approach', mimeo.

APAT (2006) *Il risarcimento del danno ambientale: aspetti teorici e operativi della valutazione economica*, Rome: APAT.

——(2002) *Il danno ambientale ex art. 18 L 349/86*, Rome: APAT.

Arora, S. and Gangopadhyay, S. (1995) 'Toward a theoretical model of emissions control', *Journal of Economic Behavior and Organization*, 28: 289–309.

Becker, G. S. (1968) 'Crime and punishment: an economic approach', *Journal of Political Economy*, 76: 169–217.

Blackman, A. and Bannister, G. J. (1998) 'Community pressure and clean technology in the informal sector: an econometric analysis of the adoption of propane by traditional Mexican brickmakers', *Journal of Environmental Economics and Management*, 35: 1–21.

Boyd, J. (2003) 'A market-based analysis of financial assurance issues associated with US natural resource damage liability', in M. Faure (ed.) *Deterrence, Insurability and Compensation in Environmental Liability: Future Developments in the European Union*, Vienna: Springer.

Brisson, I. and Pearce, D. (1995) 'Benefits Transfer for Disamenity from Waste Disposal', CSERGE Working Paper WM 95-06, London: University College London.

Calabresi, G. (1970) *The Cost of Accidents: A Legal and Economic Analysis*, New Haven CT: Yale University Press.

Carson, R. (2000) 'Contingent valuation: a user's guide', *Environmental Science and Technology*, 38: 1413–18.

Cortenraad, W. H. F. M. (1999) *The Corporate Paradox: Economic Realities of the Corporate Form of Organization*, Boston MA: Kluwer.

COWI (2000) *A Study on the Economic Valuation of Environmental Externalities from Landfill Disposal and Incineration of Waste*, Brussels: DG Environment, European Commission.

Cropper, M. L. and Oates, W. E. (1992) 'Environmental economics: a survey', *Journal of Economic Literature*, 30: 675–740.

Di Cocco, E. (1960) *La valutazione dei beni economici*, Bologna: Calderini.

European Commission (2001) *Study on the Valuation and Restoration of Damage to Natural Resources for the Purpose of Environmental Liability*, B4-3040/2000/265781/MAR/B3, Brussels: European Commission.

EEA (2007) *The Road from Landfill to Recycling: Common Destination, Different Routes*, Copenhagen: European Environment Agency.

Faure, M. G. and Visser, M. J. C. (2004) 'Law and economics of environmental crime', in H. Sjogren and G. Skogh (eds) *New Perspectives on Economic Crime*, Cheltenham: Edward Elgar.

Garrod, G. and Willis, K. G. (1999) *Economic Valuation of the Environment*, Cheltenham: Edward Elgar.

Germani, A. R. (2004) *Environmental Law and Economics in US and EU: A Common Ground?* Discussion Paper 45, London: SOAS, University of London.

Hausmann, H. and Wraakman, R. H. (1991) 'Toward unlimited shareholder liability for corporate torts', *Yale Law Journal*, 100: 1879–934.

Hawkins, K. (1984) *Environment and Enforcement*, Oxford: Oxford University Press.

Howe, C. (1990) 'Damage Handbook: A Uniform Framework and Measurement Guidelines for Damages from Natural and Related Man-made Hazards', draft report to the National Science Foundation, mimeo.

Khanna, M. and Anton, W. R. Q. (2002) 'Corporate environmental management: regulatory and market-based pressures', *Land Economics*, 78: 539–58.

Kolstad, C., Ulen, T. and Johnson, G. (1990) '*Ex post* liability for harm vs. *ex ante* safety regulation: substitutes or complements?', *American Economic Review*, 80: 888–901.

Kornhauser, L. A. and Revesz, R. L. (1994) 'Multi-defendant settlements under joint and several liability: the problem of insolvency', *Journal of Legal Studies*, 23: 517–42.

Landes, W. and Posner, R. (1987) *The Economic Structure of Tort Law*, Cambridge MA: Harvard University Press.

——(1984) 'Tort law as a regulatory regime for catastrophic personal injuries', *Journal of Legal Studies*, 13: 417–34.

Lyon, T. and Maxwell, J. (2004) *Corporate Environmentalism and Public Policy*, Cambridge MA: Harvard University Press.

McKean, R. (1980) 'Enforcement costs in environmental and safety regulation', *Policy Analysis*, 6: 269–90.

Michieli, I. and Michieli, M. (2002) *Trattato di estimo*, Bologna: Edagricole.

Monti, A. (2003) *Environmental Risks and Insurance: A Comparative Analysis of the Role of Insurance in the Management of Environment-related Risks*, Paris: OECD.

National Oceanic and Atmospheric Administration (2000) *Habitat Equivalency Analysis: An Overview*, Washington DC: NOAA Damage Assessment Restoration Program.

Ofiara, D. D. (2002) 'Natural resource damage assessments in the United States: rules and procedures for compensation from spills of hazardous substances and oil in waterways under US jurisdiction', *Marine Pollution Bulletin*, 44: 96–110.

Pigou, A. C. (1918) *The Economics of Welfare*, London: Macmillan.

Polinsky, A. M. (1980) 'Resolving nuisance disputes: the simple analytics of injunctive and damage remedies', *Stanford Law Review*, 32: 1075–112.

Polinsky, A. M. and Shavell, S. (2005) 'Economic Analysis of Law', Stanford Law and Economics Working Paper 316, Stanford CA: Stanford University.

Polinsky, M. and Shavell, S. (1991) 'A note on optimal fines when wealth varies among individuals', *American Economic Review*, 81: 618–21.

Posner, R. (1992) *Economic Analysis of Law*, Boston MA: Little Brown.

Richardson, G., Burrows, P. and Ogus, A. (1982) *Policing Pollution: A Study of Regulation and Enforcement*, Oxford: Clarendon Press.

Russell, C. S. (1990) 'Monitoring and enforcement', in P. Portney (ed.) *Public Policies for Environmental Protection*, Washington DC: Resources for the Future.

Russell, C., Harrington, W. and Vaughan, W. (1986) *Enforcing Pollution Control Laws*, Washington DC: Resources for the Future.

Segerson, K. and Miceli, T. (1998) 'Voluntary environmental agreements: good or bad news for environmental protection?', *Journal of Environmental Economics and Management*, 36: 109–30.

Segerson, K. and Tietenberg, T. (1992) 'The structure of penalties in environmental enforcement: an economic analysis', *Journal of Environmental Economics and Management*, 23: 179–200.

Shavell, S. (1987) *Economic Analysis of Accident Law*, Cambridge MA: Harvard University Press.

Stellin, G. and Candido, A. (2005) 'Gasoline spill in the Dolomites area: an application of indirect methods for environmental damage assessment', in E. De Francesco, L. Galletto and M. Thiene (eds) *Food, Agriculture and the Environment: Economic Issue*, Milan: Franco Angeli.

Tietenberg, T. (1989) 'Indivisible toxic torts: the economics of joint and several liability', *Land Economics*, 65: 305–19.

Touaty, M. and Giè, G. (2004) 'Synthèse des travaux français relatifs à l'évalutation des dommages', tenth Colloque de comptabilité nationale, Paris, mimeo.

US Environmental Protection Agency (2005) *Review and Evaluation of 'Identifying and Calculating Economic Benefit that goes beyond Avoided and/or Delayed Costs'*, Illegal Competitive Advantage Economic Benefit Advisory Panel, Science Advisory Board, EPA-SAB-ADV-05-003, Washington DC: EPA.

World Bank (1998) *Economic Analysis and Environmental Assessment*, Environmental Assessment Sourcebook update, Washington DC: World Bank.

8 Separation of organic waste and composting

European policies and local choices

Massimiliano Volpi

The environmental impact of urban waste can be considerable, as witness the 'waste crises' in Italy,[1] the amounts of waste that are being produced, and the high priority being afforded to waste management in European environmental policy in framework programmes and in legislation. This chapter investigates the relationship between the level of organic waste separation and the diffusion of composting. This is one of the most important options for treating organic waste, which is a significant fraction of urban waste. Urban waste constitutes a large part of the waste produced by a country: in Italy it is 539 kg per person, which is about 22 per cent of all the waste produced in Italy. The organic fraction of urban waste is considered the most problematic, as it is produced in large amounts, it is malodorous, it produces biogas, and it leaches in landfills; it also reduces the heating value of waste going for incineration, which, in turn, reduces the efficiency of the combustion process and subsequent energy recovery. As organic waste constitutes approximately 30 per cent of the waste collected, its separate collection is believed to be necessary for Italy to reach the ambitious recycling targets set by European environmental policy.

Composting means the transformation of organic waste into fertilizer, which closes the carbon cycle loop by returning beneficial organic matter to the land. It facilitates the removal of organic material from the streams of waste going to landfills and incinerators, thereby saving space in landfills and reducing pollution. It is therefore an example of a sustainable treatment method for wastes.

The European Waste Directive, recognizing that the various systems of treatment for waste have different impacts on the environment, has established a hierarchy of technological options for waste management, with waste prevention at the top, followed by recycling and recovery. This hierarchy of technologies, where disposal is the least preferred option, is based on life cycle assessment (LCA) and political choice but has been challenged on several counts, including costs and benefits. However, composting and the separation of organic wastes score well in the most recent cost–benefit analysis. It seems, therefore, that composting is an interesting case for analysis, and especially as an example of how policies can influence the choices of local governments, which in turn influence the choice of treatment system.

This study is innovative in several respects. While most studies that have investigated the relation between adoption of environmental technology and regulation focus on the effects on firms, here we look at how regulation affects the choices of local governments. Analysing these choices is important because local governments are often directly involved in the management of environmental issues. In many cases, and when there are considerable externalities, local governments take the decision to directly manage these activities, rather than regulating the complex activities of private firms. Hence the decisions of local government are at least as important as those of regulated firms.[2] Local government decisions can be important in themselves or they can affect the choices of private firms: either way they will be important for promoting or inhibiting the diffusion of environmental innovation and influencing the interplay between competing technologies.

Another novelty of the study described in this chapter is its examination of the possibility that regulation can lead to the development of new markets; this occurs when regulation influences new entry, rather than the adoption of technology by existing firms. This aspect is not without consequences: it means that, if there is the potential for winners and losers, and if the winner are likely to be new entrants in the market, which are completely new firms, political support for regulations that open new markets may be limited. New regulation may be opposed by incumbent firms, with would-be new entrants in no position to support it. Any negative consequences for incumbents might outweigh the benefits from new entry. In the case of composting, regulation does not directly affect firms operating in the waste sector, rather it influences the industry input, made available by separate collection of organic waste. Thus it would seem that regulation has opened new opportunities for firms using a certain input, rather than restricting the set of choices, and has not encountered any major resistance from incumbents. The importance of entry and exit in determining the evolution of environmental technology was highlighted by Miller *et al.* (2003); since then, however, this aspect has received almost no attention. This chapter attempts to consider this wider dynamic.

The aim in this chapter is also to show that not only are firms sometimes slow to adopt new environmentally beneficial solutions, a fact that is well documented in the literature, but that this can also apply to local governments and municipalities. We show that setting clear targets for environmental quality could be one means to overcome this problem. Our analysis demonstrates that aspiring to achieve these targets has influenced the diffusion of composting in Italy and provides evidence that the market for composting could have been developed sooner because the technology is relatively simple and has existed for a long time. However, it was locked out owing to institutional factors.

The case of composting was chosen for several reasons. First, it is a clear example of an environmentally beneficial solution to waste problems. Moreover, the diffusion of composting has increased significantly. The change in regulation has resulted in the move from a situation where almost all waste was landfilled to one where a (relatively) high proportion of waste is being recycled.[3] This change in regulation provides an opportunity to investigate its effects. Further, it is possible to track the history of waste composting because the sector is heavily regulated and its actors are subject to disclosure rules, which means that the relevant data are available. Finally, as municipalities have a legal monopoly of the collection of waste in Italy, it is possible to show how the choices of institutions can affect the diffusion of environmental technologies, and that these choices are at least as important as those of firms.

The chapter is organized as follows. The next section describes the waste sector in Italy in order to provide the institutional setting. Then we present a review of the literature, and a description of the hypothesis being tested. A description of the econometric specification and the data base follows. After a comment about the main empirical findings, the final section concludes.

The industry under investigation

Urban waste represents a considerable share of all the waste produced in Italy: it constitutes 22.74 per cent of the 139,189,668t of total waste. In 2005, production of urban wastes was 31,663,548t, an average of 539 kg per inhabitant per year. Special waste (produced by firms) was 55,647,338t and a further 45,851,469t of waste came from the construction and demolition sector, giving a total for the productive sector of 107,526,129t. As a proportion of construction and demolition waste comes from residential works, the most meaningful comparison in distinguishing between domestic and industrial waste generation is between municipal and special waste: this gives a figure of 36.25 per cent urban (domestic) waste. It should also be remembered that urban waste is growing over time: in 1999 it was 28,363,913t. Thus the problem of how to treat waste in an environmentally sound way has also increased (APAT 2006).

The exact volume of organic waste in urban waste is unknown, but is estimated to be around 30 per cent of the total (APAT 2002b: 17). Composting transforms the organic fraction of urban waste into fertilizer by an aerobic process. This process has long been understood and practised at household level, as a way of disposing of biological waste and producing fertilizer (compost). Composting technology consists of grinding or chopping up organic waste, mixing it with woodchip or similar material, and piling this in an enclosed area where the initial biological reactions occur. There are two steps to composting. It is in the first phase, which may last for up to a month, that the most intense biological reactions take place. The waste needs to be mixed every few days to control the temperature and ensure flow of oxygen within the waste mix; lack of oxygen would result in bad smells and interruption of the process. It is also necessary to control the moisture content. In this first phase the most unstable compounds (sugars, starches and proteins) are degraded. Once the first phase is complete, other reactions begin, which take place more slowly and do not produce unpleasant odours, which means that they need to be mixed less frequently and can be stored in an area that is not enclosed. This phase takes about three months, and the resulting stabilized material is ready to be used as fertilizer. This brief description of the composting process demonstrates its simplicity and low cost per unit of input; these aspects are exploited in our analysis. It is clear, therefore, that composting technology can be described as technology for treating waste or for producing fertilizer. In this chapter the focus is on the waste treatment aspect, because the economic feasibility of composting depends much more on the tariff for waste treatment than on the price of the fertilizer, which is typically low.

Despite the principle of composting being relatively simple and well known, it is only recently that composting has become an option for industrial application. The main reason for this is that if composting is to produce good-quality fertilizer, high-quality inputs are required. Only organic waste can be composted; if other material is mixed with it this will reduce the quality of the fertilizer obtained or make it completely unusable.[4] Therefore, for composting to be practised on an industrial scale, large volumes of good-quality uncontaminated organic waste are required and this is feasible only where large-scale separated collection of waste is in place. In Italy the collection of urban waste is a legal monopoly of the municipalities, so whether or not separated collection is implemented is down to them. No other entity is allowed to collect urban waste in Italy. This dependence on the choices of local governments means that it is necessary to consider the legal framework of waste management, to fully understand the diffusion of the technology for composting.

In 1997 there was a major reform of waste legislation[5] which meant that responsibility for waste management was shared between central and local governments. Central government sets the general criteria for the management of waste, environmental standards, adoption of technical norms and regulation of waste transport. Regions are responsible for the management of urban waste, and their planning must be based on the requirements related to the treatment of waste. The regions are also responsible for regulating the separated collection of waste (within targets set at the national level) and authorizing the construction of new waste treatment plants. The provinces have the administrative and control functions, but it is the municipalities, which have the legal monopoly of the management and collection of municipal waste, that make decisions about waste separation.[6] This means that whether or not composting is viable in a certain area ultimately depends on the choices of the local government. Within the reform, minimum targets were set for the separation of waste at province level to increase over time: from 15 per cent of urban waste produced in 1999 to 25 per cent in 2001, up to a final target of 35 per cent in 2003. There was consensus among those concerned that the final target could be achieved only if separation of organic waste was taken seriously, as no other separated collection would yield sufficient results (APAT 2002b). This legal change provided the opportunity for waste to be composted, and we show how the diffusion of composting depended on how the law was implemented by the municipality, and the degree of regional co-operation.

Literature review

The present analysis is based on two main streams of literature. The first deals with the relation between regulation and technical change, an inherently dynamic issue. The second is concerned with issues related to waste policy efficiency, mostly within a static framework.

The relationship between technology and regulation involves both controversial and uncontroversial aspects. There is general agreement that environmental innovations diffuse slowly (Stoneman 2001b; Gerosky 2000; Jaffe and Stavins 1994). There are various reasons for the multiple market failures that hamper their diffusion: there are market failures on the environmental side and on the side of technological change (Jaffe *et al.* 2005). Empirical evidence confirms the theoretical expectations that environmental technologies often diffuse far more slowly than optimal investment economic models would predict (Diederen *et al.* 2003). Thus speeding up the diffusion of environmentally friendly technologies is assumed to have very large potential for alleviating environmental issues (Interlaboratory Working Group 1997; Kneese and Schultz 1978).

Related to this issue, there is a large literature on which instrument would best satisfy this aim; its results, however, tend to depend on assumptions. These theoretical contributions are reviewed in Requate (2005). Here the focus is on empirical analyses, which are rather scarce, but are more coherent: Kemp (1998) demonstrates how the level of charges influences the aggregate diffusion of wastewater treatment technologies. Kerr and Newell (2003) and Miller *et al.* (2003) focus on the behaviour of individual firms: they find that the stringency and form of regulation as well as firm size are important. Yarime (2002) shows that strict environmental regulation can influence the pattern of diffusion of technology, but that the firm's history can also influence its decisions. Finally, Maynard and Shortle (2001) analyse the effects of uncertainty and suggest that uncertainty slows down adoption, while regulation accelerates it. To summarize the conclusions from the empirical literature, economic instruments would seem to be more efficient than command and control, but regulation interacts with firms' characteristics and history.[7] Other studies have focused on how firms decide to adopt a technology rather than on which instruments speed up the process. This too is a large literature, which is reviewed in Stoneman (2001b) and Geroski (2000). Here we refer only to the studies that are most relevant to this chapter.

Several papers deal with the issue of competition between technologies, showing that, in the presence of increasing returns, the early stages of diffusion are the most relevant, as this is when there are *windows of opportunity* (Farrell and Saloner 1985, 1986; Katz and Shapiro 1985, 1986; Colombo and Mosconi 1995; Geroski 2000; Farrell and Klemperer 2007). The literature on competing technologies does not evaluate whether the winning technology is better or worse than the competing ones. The lock-in literature, however, which is closely related, tries to explain why sub-optimal technologies may have been chosen in the first place and may persist (Arthur 1988; 1989; Cowan and Gunby 1996; Menanteau and Lefebvre 2000). Within the lock-in literature the work of Walker (2000) deserves special mention. Walker shows how the decisions of public actors can become a source of lock-in. This thesis is close to one presented in this chapter, which argues that local governments could have adopted separated collection of waste much earlier, and that their choices slowed down the diffusion of composting, a technology already available. This chapter tries to bridge the gap between the adoption and entry literature; the latter stream is relevant, in particular because it proposes that market entry is connected to market size: the larger the market, the more entrants can be expected (Thompson 1986; Dunne *et al.* 1988; Mitchell 1989; Geroski and Murphin 1991; Lilien and Yoon 1990; Geroski 1995; Sinha and Noble 2005).

A more controversial issue is the cost of the regulation for firms. Porter's (Porter and Van der Linde 1995) contentious hypothesis proposes that even regulated firms can take advantage of regulation and ultimately be better off, as they will discover new ways of doing things which prior to regulation they had not considered. Porter's hypothesis hinges on three assumptions: that firms have unrealized opportunities; that regulation can spur them to realize these cost-saving opportunities; and that the cost savings are sufficient to compensate for the costs associated with regulation. Most authors do not agree with this and provide evidence of the real costs of regulation. List *et al.* (2003), for example, highlight how clean air regulation, as well as reducing emissions, reduced the number of new regulated plants in US counties with strong clean air regulations, compared with counties with less stringent regulation. Also, Becker (2005) and Greenstone (2002) demonstrate that in regulated sectors there is reduced rate of new business start-ups. Other papers have tried to assess directly the expenses imposed on firms as a consequence of regulation, and find evidence of moderate costs. Isaksson (2005) found that firms responded to a tax on nitrogen emissions with actions that were not very costly and achieved emission reductions: the regulation provided the motivation to optimize in areas that firms had been ignoring. The empirical evidence in favour of the Porter hypothesis, therefore, seems weak, consisting of only a few case studies beside those cited by Porter himself (Klaassen *et al.* 2005).

This chapter does not aim to discuss Porter's hypothesis in depth; this literature survey is included to demonstrate that all the papers focus on *existing* firms or sectors. While, strictly speaking, it is to these firms and sectors that the Porter hypothesis should apply, such an approach might be restrictive in that it does not include the economic benefits outside the regulated sector, such as sectors producing scrubbers. And if the objective is to decide whether or not environmental regulation is beneficial, these benefits should be included. This chapter shows that the new waste regulation led to the creation of a new market. These benefits, which are outside the directly regulated market, should be taken into account alongside the environmental benefits.

The cost–benefit waste literature is also relevant to the analysis in this chapter. Much of it questions the meaningfulness of the technology hierarchy (Goddard 1995). Goddard, in particular, suggests that the waste crisis should be responded to with economic rather than engineering instruments, that is, by charging polluters rather than establishing ill founded recycling targets. He claims that the 'waste crisis' has occurred because of government's failure to establish a market for waste, generated by the zero prices for its collection, which in turn leads to excessive production of wastes. Other papers that take a cost–benefit perspective focus on the costs of recycling (Ibenholt and Lindhjem 2002) or on the choice between landfill and incinerating (Djikgraaf and Vollerbergh 2003; Eshet *et al.* 2006), providing estimates for the costs of these options, including external costs.

The approach in the cost–benefit literature is generally static, in the sense that it generally responds to the question of whether a certain technology is cost-effective when compared with others, at a certain time and in a given context. This is important information, as it is aimed at avoiding wasted resources on technologies that are neither competitive at the time of their evaluation nor are likely to become competitive at a later stage. It will be argued, though, that cost–benefit analysis evidence should not be used as the only criterion against which to judge a prospective new technology: provided that the results do not show a technology to be at too much of a disadvantage, evaluations should be repeated, as the results may change over time as the technology evolves. We will show this to be case for composting technology. One of the first cost–benefit analyses of composting (Renkow and Rubin 1998) suggested that, except for a few local situations where landfill costs were especially high, municipal solid waste composting was not cost-efficient in the US. Renkow and Rubin estimated the financial cost of composting at $53/ton on average, while landfill was estimated to cost $34/ ton (figures in 1995 US dollars). They predicted, therefore, that composting would remain geographically limited (at least in the US). A later analysis for Europe (Eunomia 2002) reversed this conclusion, finding the cost of landfill had increased to a level where composting was justified. The Eunomia study estimated the financial costs and externalities associated with the technologies required to manage biodegradable waste for European countries. The data for Italy, which are obviously the most relevant to the analysis in this chapter, show the financial costs of landfill (measured as a gate fee) to be in the range €50–€70/t, while the gate fee for composting is in the range €35–€60/t, to which €15/t should be added to cover the slightly higher collection costs for separated waste,[8] making the cost of composting €35–€75/t, which is still lower than landfill. The data also show that, assuming a discount rate of 3 per cent and state-of-the-art landfills, the external costs of landfill are in the range €6.56–€17.46/t. These assumptions are conservative; the exact figure will depend on which elements are included in the calculations. Assuming the same discount rate, the net external costs of composting are estimated to be in the range €11.80–€12.52/t: these are basically due to the carbon dioxide emissions caused by degradation of the waste. (In a landfill degradation is slow, which explains why the external costs of landfills are lower if the future is discounted.) The externalities for landfill and composting are therefore of the same order and do not affect the conclusion that composting is cost-competitive. Composting becomes even more competitive when it is compared with incinerating, which is estimated to cost €100–€200/t, and to have typically higher externality costs. (For France, based on a 3 per cent discount, these are calculated to be in the range €14.18–€93.55/t; depending on the assumptions made, the figures for Italy are similar.) It is interesting to compare these estimates with those proposed in an extensive review of landfill and incineration costs by Eshet *et al.* (2006) and the costs of separating out other materials, such as liquid board container from a study by Ibenholt and Lindhjem (2002).

The literature on landfills and incinerators reviewed in Eshet *et al.* (2006) proposes a range of US\$0.94–\$44/ton at 2003 prices, for landfill externalities, which is quite a wide variation. Eshet *et al.*'s preferred estimate is US\$15/ton, not far from the figure cited in Eunomia's analysis.

Finally, Ibenholt and Lindhjem's (2002) estimates are interesting, as they show that the full cost of recycling Tetrapaks (from household recycling) to be in the range €600–€805/t, including €111/t in time costs and €77/t in resource costs. These figures should be compared with €130/t for incineration with energy recovery or, respectively, €259/t and €304/t for incineration without energy recovery or landfill. While the authors admit that the latter two figures may be overestimated, as the corresponding external costs are high at respectively €86/t and €139/t, these options are still cheaper than recycling. The lesson from this analysis is that, compared with other forms of recycling, composting is a cheap option, which should afford it priority where high standards of separated collection are established, as mandated in European legislation.

The model

We measure the diffusion of composting with regional plants capacity and analyse how the choices of local governments to separately collect organic waste affected this variable. We control for other variables which we assume could potentially influence the diffusion of composting, in particular the number of pre-existing landfills and incinerators, and the growth in the population

We opted for a panel-based analysis, where the unit of observation is the Italian regions, which had the main responsibility for the option to collect separated waste and to implement national policy in the period 1999–2005. A panel approach allows us to control for unobservable factors, provided they are assumed to be time-invariant, and also to obtain more precise estimates (Cameron and Trivedi 2005). This approach has a long tradition in studies of the effects of environmental regulation (Hassett and Metcalf 1995; Greenstone 2002; Brunnenmeier and Cohen 2003; Berkhout *et al.* 2004; Earnhart 2004; Lange and Bellas 2005). The econometric specification will be discussed more in depth in next section.

Diffusion of composting is measured by treatment capacity. Treatment capacity is deemed to be the most appropriate proxy for the possibilities within a region for treating organic waste. It is considered to be better than number of plants because composting plants can be quite heterogeneous in terms of size. It is also better than amount of waste treated, which takes no account of entrepreneurs' expectations about the growth of the composting market.

The amount and quality of organic waste that is separated at source are the main variable of interest. It directly influences the technical feasibility of composting biological waste. If the material to be composted is polluted with other waste matter, a cost is incurred for their separation. This cost increases with the percentage of extraneous material, and separation of this extraneous material is feasible only up to low levels of non-organic materials. If the source of organic waste input were to be derived from *ex post* mechanical separation of mixed municipal wastes, as happened in the past, it would not be possible to obtain a useful fertilizer from the composting process:[9] The output would be treated as waste and disposed of in landfills. So, in order for composting to be a viable option, good-quality, source-separated, organic waste is a prerequisite (APAT 2002b). The amount of waste collected separately also represents the potential demand for waste treatment, hence it is thought to be the main determinant of the opportunity to enter the market. Potential demand is stressed more in the entry literature than in the literature on the adoption of technologies (Thompson 1986; Mitchell 1989; Geroski and Murphin 1991; Lilien and Yoon 1992; Sinha and Noble 2005). Including it in the model is a step toward the unification of these two streams of literature.

The amount of separately collected organic waste for each region is also the main policy variable. It is a variable that depends on the decisions of the municipalities, which, as previously described, have the monopoly on waste collection, implemented according to the rules set at regional level. As composting depends heavily on these decisions, the significance of this variable would indirectly prove that environmental regulations and the actions of institutions also provide opportunities for developing new markets, not only constraints on the choices of regulated firms. Separate collection of organic wastes is expected to increase as a result of the change in national regulation, which sets targets for collection of separated waste. This increased availability of input, in turn, will allow the composting industry to develop, removing the main obstacle to its earlier development. Hence separated collection of organic waste is expected to positively influence composting capacity and in turn to be influenced by the changes in national regulation.

The control variables in our analysis have more indirect effects. Abundant landfill capacity is likely to mean a cheap market for the disposal of wastes. Landfill is a relatively low-cost option. Hence abundant landfill capacity is likely to inhibit the diffusion of composting. Capacity of landfills is measured in terms of number of active plants, as data on residual capacities of landfills are poor. The data show a decreasing trend for number of landfills; finding locations for new landfills is becoming more and more difficult, mostly due to public opposition. Moreover, small existing landfills are closing as they become exhausted, and are not being replaced because the investments required to comply with modern landfill standards are too high, while *emergency landfills* (small temporary landfills built by order of the city mayor for emergency reasons) have also decreased, due to exhaustion and increasing limits on the powers of local mayors, so we expect a negative effect of the number of landfills on composting, but a relatively small one, as most of the closing landfills are small in size. Incineration capacity could interact with composting in even more subtle ways and with uncertain effects. On the one hand, a high incineration capacity might mean that there is an incentive to incinerate waste that could have been composted, because incinerators are built to run at a certain capacity, with whatever feedstock is available. Moreover, most incinerators are substantially subsidized via the payments they receive for the electricity they produce. During the period of our analysis, this electricity was classed as renewable energy, and these payments made incineration an attractive option. Competing with a subsidized incumbent would obviously lower the rate of diffusion of composting (Favoino *et al.* 1998). On the other hand, it might be that incinerating technology and composting would interact positively at lower incineration capacities, because incinerators run more efficiently on dry feedstock. Thus removing the organic fraction would improve combustion, increase temperatures and, hence, increase the amount of electricity produced.[10] So incineration and composting could be competitors or complements. Capacity of incinerators is also measured by the number of plants, which is deemed to be reasonable, as there is not much variation in their capacities.

Finally population is included as an explanatory variable. The size of the region's population can have two effects. On the one hand, a larger population produces more waste; on the other hand, in a more highly populated area there are likely to be more problems related to acceptance of a composting plant, which can produce bad smells. So this variable could have a positive or a negative effect. However, as the amount of organic waste currently being produced is controlled for, the first effect would prevail only if it influenced expectations about future organic waste generation. So we expect the negative effect to dominate.

The variables included in the model and their expected sign are summarized in Table 8.1.

Table 8.1 Variables included in the model and their expected effect on composting

Variable	Expected sign
Amount of separated organic waste	+
Population of the region	−
Capacity of landfills	−
Capacity of incinerators	+/−

Econometric specification

The model can be written as:

$$(1)\ \text{capacity}_{it} = \eta_i + \beta_1 \text{orgw}_{it} + \beta_2 \text{inhab}_{it} + \beta_3 \text{lag\_numb\_land}_{it}$$
$$+ \beta_4 \text{lag\_numb\_inc}_{it} + u_{it}$$

where capacity$_{it}$ is the total capacity of composting plants for year t and region i; orgw$_{it}$ is the amount of organic waste collected at time t; inhab$_{it}$ is the number of inhabitants of the region for year t; lag_numb_land$_{it}$ is the lagged value for the number of landfills for the year before, (the number at t-1) and lag_numb_inc$_{it}$ is the lagged value for the number of incinerators. η_i is a region fixed effect, which differs among regions but is assumed to be constant over time. This fixed effect should capture any unobserved regional effect. In this context, unobserved effects could include the commitment of the regional and local governments to a green policy and the environmental orientation of citizens, or the managerial ability of regional governments in providing the best conditions for the localization of composting capacity.

Lagged values are applied to both landfills and incinerators, as we assume that it will be the number of incumbent plants that will determine the choice of composting capacity at the current time. Moreover, this reduces endogeneity problems, as the lagged values can be considered to be pre-determined. However, these coefficients should be interpreted with some care because lagged variables, although reducing endogeneity, do not remove it completely.

In considering whether to use a fixed or random effects model we decided that the fixed effects specification was preferable as it would better capture any unobserved heterogeneity and would be consistent even if unobserved heterogeneity were correlated with the explanatory variables, something that is deemed likely in the present context.

An important econometric consideration in terms of our model is the treatment of potential endogeneity. Time-invariant heterogeneity, which may be a potential source of endogeneity, is controlled for by using a fixed-effects model. However, there may also be time-variant unobservables simulta-neously affecting both separate collection of organic waste and composting capacity (the problem of *simultaneity*). That separated organic waste is likely to be endogenous to the process of diffusion is clear if we consider that it is the municipalities that are responsible for choosing whether or not to sepa-rate organic waste, but their choices will also take into consideration the present and future treatment opportunities open to them. A possible solution to the endogeneity problem is the use of an Instrumental Variables (IV) estimation strategy. IV is equivalent to finding one or more *good instruments*, which, in our specific case, would be one or more variables correlated with separate organic waste collection, but which do not have a direct effect on composting capacity. Finding good instruments is often far from simple, but in this case there is a very good candidate. This is the amount of separated waste other than organic material (mostly glass, paper, bulk material), which is dependent on the political willingness of the municipality to separately collect waste, on the waste collection system, on the willingness of the population to separate its waste, and on the urbanization of the munici-pality – which will also influence the ease (and costs) of accomplishing separation of waste. This instrument is likely to be correlated with the instrumented variable, as it should, and it would be reasonable to regard it as theoretically uncorrelated with the explained variable, since there is no apparent reason why collection of separated non-organic waste, which is not an input for composting, should affect composting capacity. Together with the amount of non-organic material, dummy variables with the value 1 for the years starting with those set for achieving the separated waste collection targets, are also included. The logic for this is that after 2001 and 2003 there was a greater incentive to collect organic waste. The IV estimate was con-ducted by a two-stage least squares approach, along the lines suggested by Mullahy (1997). The first stage estimation outputs, together with the tests on the instruments are reported in Appendices 8.1–2.

The model was tested for over-identification restrictions, and the instru-ments were found to be valid (see Appendix 8.2). This was as expected; on theoretical grounds, it is reasonable to expect that, for each region, the same factors will influence the amount of separate collection for glass, paper and other materials as influence the separate collection of organic waste. The literature on the recycling behaviour of households supports this view, find-ing that the main determinants tend to be the same across materials, and identifying these as availability of drop-off and kerbside recycling options, and as being related to socio-economic variables, such as income, education and population density (Jenkins *et al.* 2000).

Data sources

The data used for the analysis are panel data on the total treatment capacity of composting plants in the Italian regions for 1999–2005. Treatment capacity is the maximum capacity, in tonnes per year, at which the plant is authorized to operate, and represents a proxy for the diffusion of composting. Information on treatment capacity is readily available, as plants intending to treat waste have to obtain authorization for the maximum quantity of waste that can be treated at a specific plant. Plants with capacity of less that 1,000 t/yr were excluded from the analysis; these are very small plants for treating garden and agricultural wastes, not municipal waste.[11] Inactive plants were also dropped, as inactivity was found always to be associated with later exit from the market, and there was no evidence of restart up of mothballed plants.

The data on composting capacity come from waste reports for the years 1996–2005 (*Rapporto rifiuti*) published by Agenzia Protezione Ambiente e Territorio (APAT), the national environmental agency. These reports also provide data on population, amount of total waste produced, and volumes of separated organic and non-organic waste. The data are at province level, and were aggregated at the regional level because, as we showed previously, it is the regions that play the major role in deciding about the implementation of waste legislation. Before conducting our analysis, a survey of composting firms was made, which provided evidence that composting plants generally operate on a regional scale, that is, the waste input comes from the province where the plant is located, and the wider area.

The waste reports also provide information on other treatment technologies for waste, which might be competing with composting. In particular, they report the characteristics and location of each authorized landfill and incineration plant. These data provide information on the quantities that each plant is authorized to treat, on what volume of waste was treated per year and (in the case of landfills) on residual capacity. The data on residual capacity of landfills were found to not always be reliable; however, data on the number of all (kinds of) plants were of good quality and reliable after 1999, so we decided to use these. Table 8.2 summarizes the data used.

Figure 8.1 shows the evolution of composting capacity and separate collection of waste, aggregated at national level. It is clear that the capacity and collection of organic waste grew in tandem, starting from a common point, but that capacity grew much more than the amount of organic waste being separated. This might be due to the fact that increases in the collection of organic waste led to an increase in the expected future collection of this material and, hence, to high levels of capacity. In fact, spare capacity has low costs, as shown previously, because the technology is simple and relatively cheap. Also, it should be noted that the growth of separate collection of other materials (glass, paper and other minor fractions) is highly correlated to the growth of organic waste. This suggests that separated collections of waste, organic or not, show an increasing trend. Finally, if the amount of organic waste estimated in urban waste is compared to the amount of separately collected waste, it is clear that there is potential for growth of separated collection, as not all organic waste is being covered, and composting capacity has not reached its maximum potential.

Table 8.2 Data summary

Acronym	Variable description	Mean	Std dev.	Min.	Max.
Inhabitants	No. of inhabitants	2,889,125	2,299,883	119,546	9,475,202
Total wastes	Total waste in tons	1,509,053	1,200,374	69,427	4,791,122
Total separated wastes	Total separated waste in tons	302,073	426,851	3,107	2,021,732
Organic waste (Orgw)	Organic separated waste in tons	93,935	158,798	0	700,865
Capacity	Capacity of composting plant in tons	218,748	241,440	0	889,141
Lag_numb_inc	No. of incinerating plants lagged by one year	2.18	3.36	0	14
Lag_numb_land	No. of landfills lagged one year	28.90	31.76	1	213
ob01	Dummy variable: 1 for years after 2001	0.83	0.37	0	1
ob03	Dummy variable: 1 for years after 2003	0.50	0.50	0	1

Source: Author's elaboration based on APAT's Waste Reports, various years.

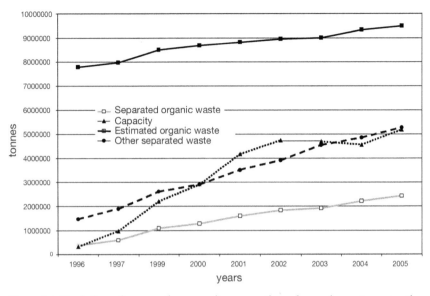

Figure 8.1 Evolution of composting capacity, separation of organic waste, separation of other waste, and estimated amount of organic waste in remaining waste

The results

The results of the robust fixed effects model that are presented in Table 8.3 provide support for the hypothesis of a significant effect on composting capacity of the amount of organic waste that is separated.[12] The coefficient of organic waste suggests that for every tonne of organic waste collected, 2,145 t of increased capacity is generated. At first sight this might seem to be too high an estimate, but a look at the original data confirms it. Indeed, Figure 8.1 showed that capacity increased more quickly than collection of organic waste, at a level approximately twice that for organic waste collected. Every tonne of organic waste that is separately collected probably creates the expectation of further future growth.

Moreover, it can be argued that the costs of excess composting capacity are quite low. As pointed out previously, most of the machinery involved is used for a very short time; therefore, treating larger amounts of material uses the same capital equipment, run for longer.[13] What is most influential in determining capital costs is the space requirement; the biological process takes time and the waste has to be stored. So the estimated coefficient is deemed to be within a credible range. The results from first stage estimate, which are used to control for the potential endogeneity of organic waste, are provided in Appendix 8.1. Organic waste was instrumented with the amounts of other separately collected waste and with time dummies for those years for which targets for separated collection were defined,[14] as discussed

Table 8.3 Determinants of composting capacity: instrumental variable estimation

Acronym	Variable description	Coeff.	P > |t|
Orgw	Amount of separately collected organic waste	2.15***	0.000
Lag_num_land	No. of landfills, lagged one year	−1,349.67**	0.045
Lag_num_inc	No. of incinerators, lagged one year	−24,541.05**	0.046
Inhabitants	No. of inhabitants	−0.76***	0.000

Note: Dependent variable: regional composting capacity. Estimation is corrected for heteroscedasticity; the instrumented variable is Orgw. It is instrumented with volume of other separately collected waste and dummy variable for policy indicators. 120 observations, over six years. Centred $R^2 = 0.3675$; uncentred $R^2 = 0.3675$. ***Significant at 1 per cent; **significant at 5 per cent.

in the section on the econometric specification of the model. All these variables were found to be significant, with the initial effects of the legislative reform stronger than its later effect, and with a significant effect of the amounts of separately collected non-organic waste on separately collected organic wastes. Tests for weak instruments were conducted, but no evidence of their presence was found, and in fact the instruments seem to work quite well.

The possibility of a negative relationship between the number of landfills and incinerators available in the previous year and a decrease in the capacity of composting firms is confirmed, although this result should be taken with care and not interpreted to mean a causal relationship. Although lagging the variables for landfills and incinerators makes them at least predetermined, it does not make them strictly exogenous. So this result should be considered as suggestive of a possible relationship, but should not be taken as a precise causal relationship. However, the hypothesis in Favoino *et al.* (1998), that incinerators could adversely affect the development of composting, does not seem to be falsified. Nonetheless, it should be stressed that the main interest of the analysis is in the relationship between collection of organic waste and diffusion of composting, whose coefficient can be interpreted in a causal way.

Another clear trend is that capacity decreases with increasing population. There are several possible explanations for this result. The first is that increasing population results in increased density, which in turn makes it more difficult to find a suitable site for composting plants (due to increased public opposition). Yet, since the analysis is at regional level, it is difficult to believe that there is nowhere in the region suitable for locating a plant. A similar, but more likely, explanation is that plants in more populated regions are smaller capacity than is presently needed, on the basis that larger plants will face stronger opposition. Another explanation is provided by Jenkins *et al.* (2000) who found that as population density increased, people were less willing to separately collect yard (garden) waste (so-called 'green' waste, mostly lawn cuttings), which is a significant fraction of organic wastes. So, again, increasing population reduces expectations about the future.

Conclusion

We aimed to test whether the choices of local government affect the diffusion of new technology in relation to composting. In our case, these choices were influenced by a change in national regulation of the waste sector, which posed ambitious targets.

We found clear evidence that the choices of local governments about waste separation did affect the diffusion of composting, and in significant ways. A prerequisite for the development of composting capacity requires that local governments (first regions, then provinces and municipalities) act to implement separated collection of organic waste. As local authorities have a legal monopoly on the choice of whether or not to conduct separated waste collections, there is no other actor involved. Our results were strengthened by the findings in the literature on separated collection of waste, which show that people's willingness to separate their waste is greatly increased if it is facilitated by availability of drop-off or kerbside collection schemes. As these schemes can only be provided by local governments, at least under current Italian legislation, this further proves that the actions of local governments, besides their regulatory role are important.[15]

This conclusion has important implications for policy. First, our finding that the actions of local governments directly affect the diffusion of environmental technologies is an important reminder that governments (local or not) have other responsibilities than regulation. They can take direct action. The literature on the diffusion of environmental technologies overlooks this important role of government, choosing instead to focus only on its regulatory role. However, especially in the Italian context, central and local governments directly (or indirectly) manage a number of activities that affect environmental quality and diffusion of environmental technologies, municipal waste being just one of them. Infrastructure and waste water treatment plants are other important examples of activities that have a considerable impact on the environment and where the public sector plays a vital – and often an exclusive – role. Further investigation of the influence of (mostly local) government direct actions on the diffusion of environmental technologies is needed. This is the most important conclusion to be drawn from our analysis, in terms of its policy relevance; it has been well established, but is frequently ignored.

A second finding from the analysis is that regulation can affect the opening of new markets, as in the case of composting. This finding seems clear, based on our data. It would indicate that these benefits should be included in any evaluation of regulatory policy, together with costs imposed on polluting sectors. This should be standard in cost–benefits analysis, but in some cases, it seems to have been forgotten, for example, in the case of the contentious Porter hypothesis. In discussing the doubtful conclusion that regulation can end up in a *net* gain, even for regulated firms, it seems that the *economic* benefits of regulation to other, non-regulated firms, are sometimes forgotten or underestimated, as are the environmental benefits.[16] While these findings do not contribute directly to the debate on the Porter hypothesis, which concerns *existing* firms which are *regulated*, our analysis attempts to counterbalance the conclusions of those papers which, in trying to demonstrate that the Porter hypothesis is false, point to the existence of considerable costs from regulation, by considering the regulated sector *only*, and ignoring those sectors that might benefit from that regulation. While this strategy could be defended as a way to disprove the Porter hypothesis, it leaves the reader with a probably unduly pessimistic attitude to regulation, as it focuses on the costs imposed and ignores the environmental and any other economic benefits. Of course, a possible objection to the claim that regulation helps to develop new markets and that this should be accounted for, is that there could simply be a *business stealing* effect, whereby the market gained by composting is lost to landfills and incinerators. This view, however, is seen as only partially correct, as organic waste also mean increasing costs to the traditional treatment sector, because of the technical problems it causes, which we discussed. So, if the cost of composting organic waste is lower than that for treatment in landfill, which in all likelihood is the case, there is at least a partial net economic gain which should be accounted for.

Despite the importance of the actions of local governments, the analysis suggests that local governments *could* be an important source of lock-in. This is not a suggestion that can be fully proved by this study, as it would require counterfactual analysis. Yet, there are several elements suggesting that, in the past, the choices of local government have acted as a barrier to earlier diffusion of composting. One element is the cost of separately collecting garbage. The costs of separated collections are not significantly higher than costs of collecting mixed wastes, as the collection of organic wastes produces savings in terms of the amount of residual waste to be collected (EUNOMIA 2002; APAT 2006). So it seems legitimate to doubt that separated collection was not chosen for cost reasons related to actual collection. Another element is that, before separated collection took off, there were some early attempts to compost mixed waste after mechanical separation, all of which failed. The reason for these failures was that, despite the equipment used being more complex and expensive than a typical composting plant today, the quality of the fertilizer obtained was extremely low, and, for all practical purposes, was no more than stabilized waste. The low quality of the fertilizer was based on the low quality of the input.

Finally, we have provided some preliminary evidence that the interaction of technologies can be important in this context. This needs to be ascertained by future analyses, in which the possible endogeneity of landfill and incineration capacity are completely controlled for, but there are elements in our analysis that suggest that the hypothesis of an interaction between technologies cannot be completely dismissed: more landfills and more incinerators seem to reduce composting capacity.

To conclude, we would suggest that the relationship between regulation and diffusion of technologies should be analysed more broadly than simply considering the effects of laws on firms. Governments (central and local) play a considerable role in influencing markets and technologies, a role that is not limited to regulation, but which also depends on the choices made for those sectors subject to direct intervention. This chapter shows how crucial it is to study the often overlooked role of government.

Appendices

First stage estimation: determinants of separated organic waste collection

Acronym	Variable description	Coeff.	$P > |t|$
Lag_num_land	No. of landfills, lagged one year	89,21	0.414
Lag_num_inc	No. of incinerators, lagged one year	5,164.06	0.157
Inhabitants	No. of inhabitants	0.17	0.008
Nonorgw	Non-organic separately collected waste (tons)	0.39	0.000
Ob01	Dummy variable: 1 for years after 2001	11,456,92	0.038
Ob03	Dummy variable: 1 for years after 2003	-7,411.37	0.021

Note: Dependent variable is separate collection of organic wastes; estimation is robust to heteroscedasticity; number of observations is 120; centred R^2 is 0.7821; partial R^2 of excluded instruments is 0.5723. Included instruments: lag_num_disc lag_num_inc abitanti rdno ob01 ob03.

Tests of instruments' validity

Test	Type of statistic	Value of statistic	p value
Anderson–Rubin Wald	$F(3,94)$	14.81	0.0000
Anderson–Rubin Wald	$\chi^2 (3)$	47.26	0.0000
Stock–Wright LM S statistic	$\chi^2 (3)$	0.464583	0.0136
Hansen J statistic (over-identification test of all instruments)	$\chi^2 (2)$	0.765	0.6820

Note: Under-identification, weak identification and weak-identification: robust test statistics. Heteroscedasticity: robust. Instrumented variable: Orgw. Included instruments: lag_num_land lag_num_inc abitanti; excluded instruments: rdno ob01 ob03. 120 observations.

Acknowledgements

This chapter would have not been possible without the help received from many colleagues. It benefited hugely from discussions with René Kemp, who taught me a lot about the relationship between technical change and environmental policy, gave me the important opportunity to visit MERIT and supported me both during my visit to Maastricht, and afterwards. I am particularly grateful to the editors of this volume, Massimiliano Mazzanti and Anna Montini. The econometric analysis has also benefited from suggestions from Massimiliano Bratti, my supervisor in the last phase of my PhD. Finally, I am deeply indebted to Anna Variato, my former supervisor, who encouraged me to engage in a research career and constantly supported me throughout the process. All remaining mistakes are my own.

Notes

1 That in Naples being the best known.
2 Other examples include waste water treatment, and decisions about the development of infrastructures.
3 Of the 31.7 million t of urban waste produced in Italy in 2005, 24.3 per cent was recycled, 22.6 per cent was stabilized and 10.2 per cent was incinerated. In 1997, of the 26.6 million t produced, only 9.4 per cent was recycled, 6.6 per cent was incinerated and 1.2 per cent was treated some other way.
4 In the 1970s and 1980s attempts were made to produce compost from waste, but without source separation; they all failed (personal communication with M. Centemero, technical co-ordinator of Italian Composting Association).
5 D.Lgs. 22/97, also known as the Ronchi Decree.
6 Note that this legal monopoly existed before the reform, so municipalities had the option to implement separated waste collection before it was required by law.
7 Jaffe *et al.* (2003), Vollebergh (2007) and Kemp and Volpi (2008) provide comprehensive surveys.
8 The reason for this low figure is that separate collection of organic waste facilitates less frequent collection of the dry fraction: as the risks of unpleasant smells are reduced, collection of unsorted waste can be less frequent, resulting in cost savings.
9 This process was pursued in the past and ended in failure: mechanically separated organic waste contains too many impurities.
10 It should be noted that a reduction in the amount of biological waste in incinerator feedstock could also be obtained via mechanical separation of non-source-separated waste. This would be viable if there were no interest in the quality of the organic waste, and if it could be disposed of easily. This would reduce the positive interactions between composting and incinerating.
11 This was pointed out by M. Centemero, who estimated 20,000 t/yr to be an efficient technical size for a plant treating municipal waste (M. Centemero, personal communication)
12 We also tested models that included regional GDP, but this variable was found not to be significant, either when used as an instrument or when used as an explanatory variable. This is probably due to the high correlation with separate non-organic waste collection and separate organic waste collection, respectively.
13 Strictly speaking, this is true only of windrow composting, which is the most common in Italy. It is not true of in-vessel technologies.
14 The model was estimated including these dummies in the composting equation; they were found not to be significant. This means that it was not possible to run any tests for instrument validity.
15 Of course, regulation and action are connected, but the point here is that regulation is not directed only at firms; sometimes national regulation can be directed at local governments. As our analysis shows, these effects can be interesting.
16 This is probably more likely when the firms that might benefit from the regulation have not been born.

References

APAT (2006) *Rapporto rifiuti 2006*, Rome.

——(2005) *Rapporto rifiuti 2005*, Rome.

——(2004) *Rapporto rifiuti 2004*, Rome.

——(2003) *Rapporto rifiuti 2003*, Rome.

——(2002a) *Rapporto rifiuti 2002*, Rome.

——(2002b) *Il recupero di sostanza organica dai rifiuti per la produzione di ammendanti di qualità*, Rome.

——(2001) *Rapporto rifiuti 2001*, Rome.

Arthur, B. (1989) 'Competing technologies, increasing returns and lock-in by historical events', *Economic Journal*, 99: 116–31.

——(1988) 'Competing technologies: an overview', in G. Dosi, C. Freeman, R. Nelson, G. Silverberg and L. Soete (eds) *Technical Change and Economic Theory*, London: Pinter Publishers.

Becker, R. A. (2005) 'Air pollution abatement costs under the Clean Air Act: evidence from the PACE survey', *Journal of Environmental Economics and Management*, 50: 144–69.

Berkhout, P. H. G., Ferrer-i-Carbonell, A. and Muskens, A. (2004) 'The *ex post* impact of an energy tax on an household energy demand', *Energy Economics*, 26: 297–317.

Brunnenmeier, S. B. and Cohen, M. A. (2003) 'Determinants of environmental innovation in US manufacturing industries', *Journal of Environmental Economics and Management*, 45: 278–93.

Cameron, C. A. and Trivedi, P. K. (2005) *Microeconometrics: Methods and Applications*. Cambridge: Cambridge University Press.

Colombo, M. and Mosconi, R. (1995) 'Complementarity and cumulative learning effects in the early diffusion of multiple technologies', *Journal of Industrial Economics*, 42: 13–47.

Cowan, R. and Gunby, P. (1996) 'Sprayed to death: path dependence, lock-in and pest control strategy', *Economic Journal*, 106: 521–42.

Diederen, P., van Tongeren, F. and van der Veen, H. (2003) 'Returns on investment in energy-saving technologies under energy price uncertainty in Dutch greenhouse horticulture', *Environmental and Resource Economics*, 24: 379–94.

Djikgraaf, E. and Vollerbergh, H. R. J. (2003) 'Burn or bury? A social cost comparison of final waste disposal methods', *Ecological Economics*, 50: 233–47.

Dunne, T., Roberts, M. and Samuelson, L. (1988) 'Patterns of firm entry and exit in the US manufacturing industries', *Rand Journal of Economics*, 19: 495–515

Earnhart, D. (2004) 'Panel data analysis of regulatory factors shaping environmental performance', *Review of Economics and Statistics*, 86: 391–401.

Eshet, T., Ayalon, O., and Shechter M. (2006) 'Valuation of externalities of selected waste management alternatives: a comparative review and analysis', *Resources, Conservation and Recycling*, 46: 335–64.

Eunomia (2002) 'Economic Analysis of Options for Managing Biodegradable Municipal Wastes', http://ec.europa.eu/environment/waste/compost/index.htm.

Farrell, J. and Klemperer, P. (2007) 'Coordination and lock-in: competition with switching costs and network effects', in M. Armstrong and R. Porter (eds) *Handbook of Industrial Organization*, Vol. III, Amsterdam: Elsevier.

Farrel, J. and Saloner, G. (1986) 'Installed base and compatibility: innovation, product preannouncement and predation', *American Economic Review*, 76: 940–55.

——(1985) 'Standardization, compatibility and innovation', *Rand Journal of Economics*, 16: 71–83.

Favoino, E., Centemero, M., Ricci, M. and Tornavacca, A. (1998) 'The Development of Biological Treatment in Italy: Programs for Source Separation, Features and Trends of Composting Facilities and the Role of Biological Treatment of Rest-waste', mimeo.

Geroski, P. A. (2000) 'Models of technological diffusion', *Research Policy*, 29: 603–25.

——(1995) 'What do we know about entry?' *International Journal of Industrial Organization*, 13: 421–40.

Geroski, P. A. and Murphin, A. (1991) 'Entry and industry revolution: the UK car industry, 1958–1983', *Applied Economics*, 23: 799–810.

Goddard, H. C. (1995) 'The benefits and costs of alternative solid waste management policies', *Resources, Conservation and Recycling*, 13: 183–213.

Greenstone, M. (2002) 'The impacts of environmental regulations on industrial activities: evidence from the 1970 and 1977 Clean Air Act amendments and the census of manufacturers', *Journal of Political Economy*, 110: 1175–219.

Hasset, K. A. and Metcalf, G. E. (1995) 'Energy tax credit and residential conservation investment: evidence from panel data', *Journal of Public Economic*, 57: 201–17.

Ibenholt, K. and Lindhjem, H. (2002) 'Costs and benefits of recycling liquid board containers', *Journal of Consumer Policy*, 26: 301–25.

Interlaboratory Working Group (1997) 'Scenarios of US Carbon Reductions: Potential Impacts of Energy-efficient and Low-carbon Technologies by 2010 and Beyond', Oak Ridge TN and Berkeley CA: Oak Ridge National Laboratory and Lawrence Berkeley National Laboratory, ORNL-444 and LBNL-40533, http://enduse.lbl.gov/projects/5lab.html.

Isaksson, L. H. (2005) 'Abatement costs in response to the Swedish charge on nitrogen oxide emissions', *Journal of Environmental Economics and Management*, 50: 102–20.

Jaffe, A. B. and Stavins, R. N. (1994) 'The energy paradox and the diffusion of conservation technology', *Resource and Energy Economics*, 16: 91–122.

Jaffe, A. B., Newell, R. and Stavins, R. N. (2005) 'The tale of two failures: technology and environmental policy', *Ecological Economics*, 54: 164–74.

——(2003) 'Technological change and the environment', in K. Mahler and J. Vincent (eds) *Handbook of Environmental Economics*, Vol. I, Amsterdam: Elsevier.

Jenkins, R., Martinez, S. A., Palmer, K. and Podolsky, M. J. (2000) 'The Determinants of Household Recycling: a Material Specific Analysis of Recycling Program Features and Unit Pricing', Resource for the Future discussion paper, Washington DC: Resource for the Future.

Katz, M. and Shapiro, C. (1986) 'Technology adoption in the presence of network externalities', *Journal of Political Economy*, 94: 822–41.

——(1985) 'Network externalities, competition and compatibility', *American Economic Review*, 75: 424–40.

Kemp, R. (1998) 'The diffusion of biological waste-water treatment plants in the Dutch food and beverage industry', *Environmental and Resource Economics*, 12: 113–36.

Kemp, R. and Volpi, M. (2008) 'The diffusion of clean technologies: a review with suggestions for future diffusion analysis', *Journal of Cleaner Production*, 16: 14–21.

Kerr, S. and Newell, R. G. (2003) 'Policy-induced technology adoption: evidence from the US lead phase-out', *Journal of Industrial Economics*, 51: 317–43.

Klaassen, G., Miketa, A., Larsen, K. and Sundqvist, T. (2005) 'The impact of R&D on innovation for wind energy in Denmark, Germany and the United Kingdom', *Ecological Economics* 54: 164–74.

Kneese, A. V. and Schultz, C. L. (1978) *Pollution, Prices and Public Policy*, Washington DC: Brookings Institution.

Lange, I. and Bellas, A. (2005) 'Technological change for sulfur dioxide scrubbers under market-based regulation', *Land Economics*, 81: 546–56.

Lilien, G. and Yoon, E. (1990) 'The timing of competitive market entry: an exploratory study of new industrial products', *Management Science*, 36: 568–85.

List, J. A., Millimet, D. L., Fredriksson, P. G. and McHone, W. W. (2003) 'Effects of environmental regulations on manufacturing plant births: evidence from a propensity score matching estimator', *Review of Economics and Statistics*, 85: 944–52.

Maynard, L. and Shortle, J. (2001) 'Determinants of cleaner technology investment in the US bleached kraft pulp industry', *Land Economics*, 77: 561–76.

Menanteau, P. and Lefebvre, M. (2000) 'Competing technologies and the diffusion of innovations: the emergence of energy-efficient lamps in the residential sector', *Research Policy*, 29: 375–89.

Miller, N., Snyder, L. and Stavins, R. (2003) 'The effects of environmental regulation on technology diffusion: the case of chlorine manufacturing', *American Economic Review*, 93: 431–35.

Mitchell, W. (1989) 'Whether and when? Probability and timing of incumbents' entry into emerging industrial subfields', *Administrative Science Quarterly*, 34: 208–30.

Mullahy, J. (1997) 'Instrumental variable estimation of count data models: applications to model of cigarette smoking behaviour', *Review of Economics and Statistics*, 79: 586–93.

Porter, M. and Van der Linde, C. (1995) 'Toward a new conception of environment–competiveness relationship', *Journal of Economic Perspectives*, 9: 97–118.

Renkow, M. and Rubin, A. R. (1998) 'Does municipal solid waste composting make sense?' *Journal of Environmental Management*, 53: 339–47.

Requate, T. (2005) 'Dynamic incentives by environmental policy: a survey', *Ecological Economics*, 54: 175–95.

Sinha, R. and Noble, C. (2005) 'A model of market entry in emerging technology markets', *IEEE Transactions on Engineering Management*, 52 (2): 186–98.

Stoneman, P. (2001a) *Financial Factors and the Inter-firm Diffusion of New Technology: A Real Option Approach*, UNU-Intech Working Paper 8.

——(2001b) *The Economics of Technical Diffusion*, Oxford: Blackwell.

Thompson, R. (1986) 'Entry and market characteristics: a logit study of newspaper launching in the Republic of Ireland', *Journal of Economic Studies*, 13: 14–22.

Vollebergh, H. R. J. (2007) *Differential Impact of Environmental Policy Instruments on Technological Change: A Review of Empirical Literature*, Tinbergen Institute Discussion Papers 42/3, Amsterdam: Tinbergen Institute.

Walker, W. (2000) 'Entrapment in large technological systems: institutional commitment and power relationships', *Research Policy*, 29: 833–46.

Yarime, M. (2002) 'From End-of-pipe Technology to Clean Technology: Effects of Environmental Regulation on Technological Change in the Chlor-alkali Industry in Japan and Western Europe', Ph.D. thesis, Maastricht University, mimeo.

Index

absolute delinking 7, 17, 133, 134;
    waste generation and disposal,
    drivers of 38, 41, 42, 43, 54, 56; waste
    management instruments and 107,
    109, 111, 112, 116
Adams, M. and Steven, S. 156
Agenzia Protezione Ambiente e
    Territorio (APAT) 127, 129, 163, 164,
    178n32, 184, 186, 190, 194, 195, 199
Agras, J. and Chapman, D. 98
Alberini, A. and Austin, D. 175–76n5
Alberton, M. 154
Alpay, S. et al. 66n33, 149n8
Andersen, F.M. and Larsen, L. 74
Andersen, F.M. et al. 34, 40, 72, 74,
    109, 110, 127, 129
Andersen, Frits Møller 4, 7, 72–89
Anderson, Cindy 175
Andre, F. and Cerda, E. 49, 128
Andreoni, J. and Levinson, A. 29n3,
    38–39, 64n7
APAT (see Agenzia Protezione
    Ambiente e Territorio)
Arora, S. and Gangopadhyay, S.
    176–77n15
Arthur, B. 187
Australia 102
Austria 46, 82, 102
avoided cost method (ACM) 163, 164,
    165, 166, 169, 170, 171, 173
Ayres, R.U. et al. 29n1

Baiocchi, G. and Di Falco, S. 20
Baltagi, B. 93
Baltagi, B. et al. 30n15
Basel Convention 93, 103
Becker, G.S. 156, 176n7
Becker, R.A. 187
Beede, D.N. and Bloom, D. 40, 91, 92

Belgium 46, 82, 102, 129
Berglund, C. and Soderholm, P. 66n33,
    149n8
Berglund, C. et al. 92, 93
Berkhout, P.H.G. et al. 190
Berrens, R. et al. 40
biodegradable municipal waste (BMW)
    3, 64n5, 72, 79–80, 86, 87, 88
Blackman, A. and Bannister, G.J.
    176–77n15
Bluffstone, R. and Deshazo, J.R. 65n24
Boyd, J. 164
Bradford, D. et al. 21
Bratti, Massimiliano 201
Breusch-Pagan test 97
Bringezu, S. et al. 29n5, 107
Brisson, I. and Pearce, D. 63n3, 149n2,
    171
Brock, W. and Taylor, S. 39
Brunnenmeier, S.B. and Cohen, M.A.
    190
Bruno, G.S.F. 67n42
Brunvoll, A. and Ibenholt, K. 74
Bulgaria 78, 82
Burnley, S. 42–43

Cagatay, S. and Mihci, H. 65n18,
    66n33, 114, 149n8
Calabresi, G. 157
Calcott, P. and Walls, M. 128
Callan, S. and Thomas, J. 66n33, 110,
    149n8
Cameron, C.A. and Trivedi, P.K. 190
Canada 102, 177n19
Caplan, A. et al. 63n3, 149n2
Carraro, C. et al. 30n10
Carson, R. 177n19
Centemero, M. 201n4, 201n11
Chavas, J.P. 39

Chimeli, A. and Braden, J. 29n3, 39
Cianflone, Tiziana 9, 154–79
closed loops strategies 63n2
Cole, M. 39, 44
Cole, M. *et al.* 21, 40, 42, 44, 64n7,
    66n33, 92, 114, 149n3, 149n8
Colombo, M. and Mosconi, R. 187
compensatory remediation 177–78n21,
    177n20
composting 5, 8, 10, 11, 35, 36, 47, 50,
    110, 126; landfill diversion through
    126, 129, 149n4; organic waste
    separation and 182–86, 187, 188, 189,
    190–91, 192–97, 198–99, 201n10
Cook-Weisberg test 97
Copeland, B.R. and Taylor, M.S. 39,
    64n7, 64n8
Cortenraad, W.H.F.M. 157
cost-benefit analysis (CBA) 5, 9, 10, 37,
    128, 155, 182, 188, 198
cost recovery 112, 113, 122n15, 133,
    134, 138, 142, 148
Cowan, R. and Gunby, P. 187
COWI (EC Study on the Economic
    Valuation of Environmental
    Externalities from Landfill Disposal
    and Incineration of Waste) 171
Cropper, M.L. and Oates, W.E. 154, 160
Culas, R. and Dutta, D. 98
Czech Republic 65n23, 82

damage assessment, contingent
    valuation in 177n19
Dasgupta, S. *et al.* 30n13
Daskalopoulos, E. *et al.* 128
Davies, B. and Doble, M. 128
De Bruyn, S. *et al.* 30n11, 98
decentralized waste management
    (DWM) 48, 56–57, 121
decoupling *see* delinking
defensive (or mitigation) cost method
    (DCM) 163–64, 165, 166, 169, 170,
    173
DEFRA 15, 108
delinking 1, 2, 3, 9; and EKCs for waste
    indicators in Europe 15–29, 108–21;
    indicators, popularity of 34, 107;
    structural integration of 4; trends in
    6, 37–63, 127–48; *see also* absolute
    delinking; relative delinking
Denmark 46, 74, 82, 102, 129
Department for the Environment, Food
    and Rural Affairs (DEFRA, UK) 15,
    108

Department of Trade and Industry
    (DTI, UK) 15
dependent variable(s), choice of 30n14
Di Cocco, E. 164
Di Toppa, Paola 175
Diederen, P. *et al.* 186
Dijkgraaf, E. and Gradus, P. 131
Dijkgraaf, E. and Vollebergh, H. 35, 59,
    63n3, 149n2, 188
Dinda, S. 30n13, 44, 64n7, 149n3
drivers (EU), waste generation and
    disposal 34–67; absolute delinking
    indicators 34; age index as control
    variable 47; descriptive statistics 45;
    dynamic models 61–62; empirical
    analysis 37–38, 51–62; empirical
    model and data 37, 44–51;
    environmental impacts of landfill
    36–37; environmental policy index
    48; estimation procedures, empirical
    analysis 51; EU-25, MSW generation
    52–54; EU-15 an EU-10, MSW
    generation compared 54–55;
    incinerated waste 50–51, 58–60;
    landfill, EU predominance of 36;
    landfill diversion 49–50; landfilled
    waste, EU-25 55–57; landfilled waste,
    EU-15 and EU-10 compared 57–58;
    methodological issues, empirical
    analysis 44–45, 51; model extensions
    60–62; policy proxies 47–48;
    population density, impact of 47, 49;
    R & D intensity 51; relative delinking
    indicators 34; results of empirical
    analysis 62–63; slope heterogeneity
    60–61; variables 46; waste accounting
    35–36; waste generation 46–48; waste
    indicators, EKC and delinking 38–44;
    waste management, EU groupings
    35; waste prevention 46–47, 48, 52,
    62, 63, 63n2, 65n19; waste-related
    studies, literature survey 40–41,
    43–44; waste trends 34–35, 43
DTI (Dept of Trade and Industry, UK)
    15
Dunne, T. *et al.* 187
Durbin-Watson (DW) statistic 75, 76,
    77, 78

EAP (Environmental Action
    Programme) 72, 79, 88
Earnhart, D. 190
Eastern European countries 23, 46, 50,
    54, 65n23, 78, 82, 84, 102

EC (European Commission) 2, 16, 23,
34, 72, 82–83, 163, 164, 167, 171,
177n18
econometric panel studies 30n15
economic drivers 129, 135, 150n13;
waste generation and disposal and
43, 47, 50, 56, 62; waste management
instruments and 107, 108, 109, 110,
117, 119, 120; waste prevention and
16, 17, 21, 22, 23, 26, 28; *see also*
socio-economic drivers
economic efficiency 107
EEA (European Environmental
Agency) 2, 3, 4, 5; environmental
liabilities 155, 176n6; landfill
diversion 126, 129, 149n1; MSW
generation, disposal and recycling 94,
102, 103n1; municipal waste, GHG
emissions and 72, 89; waste
generation drivers 34–35, 36, 63n1,
64n5; waste indicators 15, 29, 30n20;
waste management instruments 109
effectiveness 3, 5, 7, 11, 26, 28, 29, 42,
48, 56, 120, 138; of environmental
liability regimes 155; of landfill
taxation 128, 145, 148; policy
effectiveness 8, 13, 37, 43, 108, 113,
126, 128; of regulatory deterrence 156
efficiency: of combustion process 182;
comparison, EU-15 and EU-10
54–55; delinking and waste-efficiency
gains 28; economic efficiency,
improvements in 107; environmental
efficiency 2, 19, 26, 34, 157;
evaluation of 5; objective of
European liability regime 159, 168;
Pigouvian efficiency, objectives of
154–55; of policy implementation 35,
48, 186; resource efficiency 2, 3, 15,
16–17, 34; technological efficiency 17;
see also policy evaluation
Ehrlich, P.R. 29n7
EIONET 64n14
El Fadel, M. *et al.* 36
Eliste, P. and Fredriksson, P.G. 65n18
EKC (*see* environmental Kuznets curve)
emissions trading scheme (ETS) 4
empirical model, socio-economic and
policy drivers of MSW generation
34–38; analysis 51–62; comparison,
EU-15 and EU-10, MSW generation
54–55; data 44–51; dynamics,
introduction of 60–62; estimation
procedures 51; EU-25, MSW

generation 52–53; EU-15 and EU-10,
MSW generation 54–55; incinerated
waste 50–51, 58–60; landfill diversion
49–50; landfilled waste, comparison
EU-15 and EU-10 57–58; landfilled
waste, EU-25 55–57; methodology
51; model and data 44–51; MSW
generation 52–55; research
hypothesis, descriptive statistics and
45; slope heterogeneity 60–62;
variables 46; waste generation 46–48;
waste indicators, EKC and delinking,
recent evidence 38–44
empirical model, waste generation and
disposal 126–28, 128–29, 129–48;
conclusion 147–48; data sources
129–31; evidence 132–47; framework
129–32; model specification 131–32;
panel analysis, unbalanced 143–45;
provincial analysis 139–40; regional
analysis 132–39; research hypothesis
129–31; sample bias, verification of
relevance 145–47; semi-log balanced
specifications 140–42; state of the art
128–29; variables, dependent and
independent 133–34
empirical model, waste indicators and
delinking 107–8, 108–21; conclusions,
policy implications 120–21; data sets
109–12; evidence 114–20; Kuznets
curve model 113–14; policy proxies,
inclusion of 113–14; provincial level
evidence 114–17; regional level
evidence 117–20; tourist hotspots,
correction for 114; variables,
dependent and independent 111–12
end of life vehicles (ELV) 4, 23, 30, 48
energy recovery 4, 36, 82, 87, 178n34,
182, 189
Environment Canada 177n19
Environmental Action Programme
(EAP) 72, 79, 88
environmental damage 10, 154–55, 157,
162, 164, 174, 176n8, 178n32
environmental Kuznets curve (EKC) 1,
2, 3, 6, 7, 8, 92, 98; delinking and, for
European waste indicators 15–29,
30–31n21, 30n10; landfill diversion
127, 145, 147, 148, 149n3, 149n8;
municipal waste generation, drivers
and management instruments 107,
108–9, 113–14, 116–17, 119, 120,
121n7, 122n19; socio-economic and
policy drivers, EU waste generation

and disposal 34, 38–44, 50, 60, 62, 64n8, 64n13, 65n23, 65n26, 66n33, 67n39
environmental liabilities from landfill, assessment of 154–78; avoided cost method (ACM) 164–65, 166; benefit transfer 167; compensation objective 157, 172, 174; competing valuation frameworks 172–73; cost-based valuation approaches 164, 166, 173; data, robustness of 170–71; defensive (or mitigation) cost method (DCM) 164–65, 166; deterrence objective 157, 159–60, 167–72; economic valuation of NRD 167; economic valuation uncertainties 166; efficiency objective 159, 168; environmental liability regime 158; environmentally undesirable behaviour (EUB) 154, 155, 156–60, 160, 166, 173, 175, 176–77n15, 176n9; EUWM (Environmentally Undesirable Waste Management) 155, 156; exogenous uncertainties 155, 157, 158; externalities of waste generation 167–68; feasibility of restoration 164; judicial protocols (and disposals), standardization of 174–75; legal waste management, appropriate use of 167–68; liability regimes 154, 155, 156, 157–58, 167–72; literature on deterrence 155–56, 157; natural recoverability of NRD 164, 165, 168–69, 169; non-natural recoverability of NRD 165, 169, 170; NRD (Natural Resources Damage) 154, 155, 157–58; penalty structures 157; polluters, limited liability shield for 157; preference approaches 167; private costs, external costs and 171–72; remediation cost method (RCM) 164–65; resource damage, double counting of 174; resource recoverability/restorability 163–67; sanction for EUWM, estimation of components of 168–72, 173; soil damage 171; standardization in NRD assessment 158–59, 160–67, 173–74; status quo, restoration to 159; surrogate cost method (SCM) 164–65, 166; technical approach to NRDA 161–63; technical uncertainties 168; uncertainty 155, 157, 158, 168; water damage 171

environmental policy 7, 108, 117, 155, 157, 200; European policy 37, 182; *ex-post* policy 114; waste generation and disposal, empirical analysis and 48, 52–53, 56–57, 59, 65n18, 66n33, 128, 131–32, 135, 140, 149n8
Environmental Protection Agency (EPA, US) 95, 176n14, 177n19
environmental sustainability index (ESI) 22
environmentally undesirable behaviour (EUB) 10; illegal waste disposal, deterrence of 167, 168, 172, 176–77n15; liabilities from landfill, assessment of 154, 155, 156–60, 160, 166, 173, 175, 176–77n15, 176n9
environmentally undesirable waste management (EUWM) 155, 156, 157, 167, 168, 171, 172, 174, 178n32
EPA (Environmental Protection Agency, US) 95, 176n14, 177n19, 178n22
Eshet, T. *et al.* 36, 63n3, 149n2, 188, 189
Estonia 46, 82
Estrella fit measure 145
EU-10 7, 34, 40, 43, 49, 51, 52, 62, 64n4, 64n6, 66n30, 66n31, 109; comparison with EU-15 52, 54–55, 57–58, 66n31
EU-15 4, 6, 7, 40, 51, 52, 64n4, 66n34, 72, 78, 80, 109, 122n13; comparison with EU-10 52, 54–55, 57–58, 66n31; landfill diversion 49; municipal waste, baseline projection 83–85; packaging waste generated 23, 24; waste incineration 50; waste trends for 34–36
EU-25 6, 23, 35, 45, 51, 64n4, 65n24, 67n39, 94, 122n13; landfilled waste 55–57; MSW generation 52–54
EUB *see* environmentally undesirable behaviour
EUNOMIA 188–89, 199
European Environment Information and Observation Network (EIONET) 48, 64n14
European Environmental Agency (EEA) 2, 3, 4, 5, 15, 29, 30n20, 34, 35, 36, 63n1, 64n5, 64n14, 72, 89, 102, 103n1, 109, 126, 129, 149n1, 155, 176n6
Eurostat 29n5, 30n20, 44, 80, 94, 108, 109, 128

EUWM (environmentally undesirable waste management) 155, 156, 157, 167, 168, 171, 172, 174, 178n32
EVRI (Environmental Valuation Reference Inventory) 177n19
Expected Utility (EUT) 156, 158, 159, 176n9

Farrell, J. and Klemperer, P. 187
Farrell, J. and Saloner, G. 187
Faure, M.G. and Visser, M.J.C. 176–77n15
Favoino, E. *et al.* 191, 197
Femia, A. *et al.* 29n5
Ferrara, I. and Missios, P. 43
Finland 23, 46, 67n36, 82, 102
Fischer-Kowalski, M. and Amann, C. 38, 40, 42
Fonkych, K. and Lempert, R. 121n7
France 7, 23, 34, 46, 78, 82, 102, 109, 189
Fredriksson, P. 65n17

Galeotti, M. 64n7
Galeotti, M. *et al.* 20
Gallagher, L. *et al.* 37
Garrod, G. and Willis, K.G. 164
Germani, A.R. 154, 157, 175–76n5
Germany 38, 46, 50, 57, 59, 64n6, 78, 82, 86, 98, 102, 121
Geroski, P.A. 186, 187
Geroski, P.A. and Murphin, A. 187, 190
Goddard, H.C. 188
Greece 23, 46, 58, 59, 65n25, 82, 86, 102
greenhouse gas (GHG) emissions 1, 15, 37, 107, 171; generation, management and 72–89
Greenstone, M. 187, 190
Grossman, G.M. and Krueger, A.B. 29n2, 38
Gruebler, A. *et al.* 29n1, 30n10
Guerin, D. *et al.* 102, 103n1

Harbaugh, W. *et al.* 21, 39
Hassett, K.A. and Metcalf, G.E. 190
Hausman test 26, 27, 28, 51, 96, 135, 136, 137, 140, 141, 144
Hausmann, H. and Wraakman, R.H. 157
Hawkins, K. 157
Heckman model (two-stage) 139, 145, 146, 147
Hedal, Nanja 89
Holz-Eakin, D. and Selden, T.M. 29n2, 38

Howe, C. 164
Huhtala, A. 35
Hungary 46, 63, 65n24, 78, 82, 84, 102

Ibenholt, K. and Lindhjem, H. 188, 189
Iceland 23, 27, 102
impact, population, affluence, technology (IPAT) 1, 16; delinking analysis in 17–18; EKC analysis in 18–20
IMR (inverse Mills ratio) 146, 147
incineration 1, 2, 3, 4, 5, 6, 7, 8, 23, 35, 36, 37, 38, 45, 46, 49, 50, 58, 59, 60, 62, 63n1, 64n15, 65n22, 66n28, 67n37, 80, 81, 82, 86, 87, 92, 98, 102, 126, 127, 129, 138, 142, 143, 145, 148, 182, 189, 191, 194, 199
Incineration Directive (2000/76/EC) 23, 45, 47–48, 51, 56, 64n5
innovation 4, 10, 18, 30n10, 48, 49, 70, 138, 183, 186
integrated pollution prevention and control (IPPC) 23
inter-country differences, drivers of MSW generation, disposal and recycling 91–103; community or household level studies 91; conclusion and policy implications 101–2; countries analysed 102; data and sources 94; demographic determinants of waste generation rates 97; descriptive statistics 95; economic determinants of waste generation rates 97; fixed effects (FE) estimator 93, 96, 99, 100; landfills, proportion of deposits in 97–99, 101–2; models and data 93–94; MSW generation 94–97; 'not in my back yard' (NIMBY) 91; OECD cross-sectional time series data 91; panel data analysis and discussion 94–101; per capita waste generation 97; prices and/or taxes, role of 98; random effects (RE) 93, 96, 97, 99, 100; recycled paper and glass, proportion of 99–101, 102; tipping fees 98; variables included in analysis 91; variance on variables, analysis of 95; waste generation and management, literature review 92–93; waste legislation and policy index (POLDX) 93, 94, 95, 96, 97, 98, 99, 100, 101, 102, 103n2
Intergovernmental Panel on Climate Change (IPCC) 72, 80–81

Interlaboratory Working Group 186
International Institute for Applied
    Systems Analysis (IIASA) 29n1
IPCC (see Intergovernmental Panel on
    Climate Change)
IPPC (integrated pollution prevention
    and control) 23
Ireland 23, 46, 58, 59, 78, 82, 86, 102
Isaksson, L.H. 187
Italy 4, 5, 7, 8, 9, 10, 11, 82, 102;
    central and north-west Italy 116;
    environmental liabilities, assessment
    of 154–78; landfill diversion,
    embedding of 126–50; municipal
    waste generation drivers, waste
    management and 107–23; northern
    Italy 110, 120, 126; organic waste,
    separation and composting of 182–2–1;
    southern Italy 1, 116; waste and
    water management, long-run change
    in 122n15, 122n19; waste generation
    and disposal, drivers of 34, 41, 42,
    46, 49, 57, 59, 63, 66n34 107–23,
    126–50, 154–78, 182
IVM Institute for Environmental
    Studies, Amsterdam 128

Jacobsen, H. *et al.* 2, 25, 29n6, 34,
    64n12
Jaffe, A.B. and Stavins, R.N. 186
Jaffe, A.B. *et al.* 30n10, 186, 201n7
Japan 102
Jenkins, R. *et al.* 63n3, 193, 197
Johnstone, N. and Labonne, J. 40, 42,
    91, 92, 95, 113, 116, 122n10
*Journal of Environment and
    Development* 66n32

Kaldor-Hicks Paretian improvements
    37
Karousakis, Katia 7, 41, 42, 91–103
Katz, M. and Shapiro, C. 187
Kelly, D. 29n3
Kemp, R. and Volpi, M 201n7
Kemp, René 186, 200
Kerr, S. and Newell, R.G. 186
Khanna, M. and Anton, W.R.Q.
    176–77n15
Khanna, N. and Plassmann, F. 22
Kinnamon, T. and Fullerton, D. 91, 92
Kiviet, J.F. 67n42
Klaassen, G. *et al.* 187
Kneese, A.V. and Schultz, C.L. 186
Kolstad, C. *et al.* 175n3

Korea 102
Kornhauser, L.A. and Revesz, R.L. 157
Kuznets, Simon S. 15, 20, 44
Kyoto Protocol (and targets) 4, 80

Landes, W. and Posner, R. 157
Landfill Directive (1999/31/EC) 3, 5, 6,
    9, 23, 38, 42, 43, 45, 48, 49, 52, 56,
    61, 64n5, 64n6, 72, 79, 80, 86, 88,
    126, 127, 128, 172, 176n6; dual aims
    of 64n5; effectiveness of 64n6
landfill diversion 1, 3, 4, 7, 8, 9;
    embedding of, evidence from Italy
    126–50; waste generation and
    disposal, drivers of 37, 43, 47, 49–51,
    56, 57, 59, 60, 62, 65n19, 65n22,
    67n43
landfill diversion, embedding of 126–50;
    baseline specifications for research
    135–36; data sources 129–31;
    delinking, landfill trends and 147–48;
    empirical evidence 132–47; empirical
    framework 129–32; landfill siting and
    diversion 145–47; landfill taxation
    148; lock-in effects 138;
    methodological issues 139; model for
    research 131–32; provincial analysis
    139–40, 147–48; regional analysis
    132–39, 147–48; research hypothesis
    129–31; sample bias, verification of
    relevance 145–47; semi-log balanced
    specifications 140–42; socio-economic
    levers, relevance of 136, 138;
    unbalanced panel analysis 143–45;
    variables, dependent and independent
    133–34; waste generation and
    disposal, state of the art 128–29;
    waste management dynamics 138–39;
    waste management implements 142,
    148; waste per capita (1999–2005) 137
landfill externalities 9, 149n6, 189
landfill taxation 8, 9, 29, 42, 43, 91, 94,
    98, 100, 102, 103n1, 121n2, 127, 128,
    131, 134, 135, 138, 139, 142, 143,
    145, 147, 148, 149n9; nominal landfill
    tax 103n3; real landfill tax 8, 98, 99,
    100, 101, 102
landfilling 66n31, 67n39, 135, 143,
    150n14
Lang, J.C. 43, 56
Lange, I. and Bellas, A. 190
Larsen, Helge 4, 7, 72–89
Latvia 23, 46, 82
Leigh, R. 21–22, 41

Liability Directive (2004/35/EC) 10,
154, 161, 162, 177–78n21, 177n20
Lieb, C.M. 22, 109
life cycle assessment (LCA) 3, 81, 182
Lilien, G. and Yoon, E. 187, 190
Lim, J. 92
Lindmark, M. 98
List, J.A. *et al.* 187
Lithuania 46, 65n23, 82
Luxembourg 46, 58, 59, 60, 82, 102
Lyon, T. and Maxwell, J. 176–77n15

McKean, R. 157
Malta 27, 46, 82
Markandya, A. *et al.* 21
Martin, A. and Scott, I. 30n19, 43
Martin, J.M. 29n1
material recovery 35, 36, 42, 93, 99,
121, 126, 129, 150n13
Matsunaga, K. and Themelis, N.J.
95–96
Maynard, L. and Shortle, J. 186
Mazzanti, M. and Zoboli, R. 6, 30n18,
41, 42, 48, 108, 127
Mazzanti, M. *et al.* 41, 42
Mazzanti, M., Musolesi, A. and
Zoboli, R. 39
Mazzanti, Massimiliano 6, 8, 9, 15–30,
34–67, 107–23, 126–50, 201
Mazzanti M. *et al.* 66n34
McFadden fit measure 145
Menanteau, P. and Lefebvre, M. 187
meta-analysis 172, 178–79n35
Mexico 102
Michieli, I. and Michieli, M. 164
Miller, N. *et al.* 183, 186
Millimet, D. *et al.* 20
Miranda, M.L. *et al.* 63n3, 149n2
Mitchell, W. 187, 190
Moll, S. *et al.* 29n5
Monti, A. 154, 160
Montini, Anna 8, 107–23, 126–50, 201
Morris, J. *et al.* 42
Mullahy, J. 193
municipal solid waste (MSW) 4, 5, 6, 7;
disposal, generation and recycling,
drivers of 91, 92, 93, 94, 95, 96, 97,
98, 99, 101, 103n2; generation and
disposal, drivers of 34, 37, 40–42,
45–46, 48–49, 51–61, 64n12, 64n15,
65n19, 65n23, 66n27, 66n33; landfill
diversion of 129, 131, 133, 134, 135,
139, 140; management and GHG
emissions 74–79, 79–80, 80–88; waste

generation, socio-economic drivers
and management instruments 107,
109, 111, 112, 113, 117, 121n5
municipal waste, generation, drivers
and management in Italy 107–23;
conclusions and policy implications
120–21; data sets 109–10; empirical
analysis, regional and provincial
levels 109–14; empirical evidence
114–20; geographic dummies,
inclusion of 116; methodological
issues 113–14; policy proxies 113,
117; regional level evidence 117–20;
relative delinking 116–17; tourist
hotspots 114, 116; variables,
dependent and independent 111–12;
waste indicators and delinking,
empirical evidence 107–8, 108–9;
waste tariffs 108, 110, 117, 120; waste
taxes 108, 110; WKC empirical
model 113–14
municipal waste, GHG emissions and
72–89; baseline projection 73, 82–88;
biodegradable 86; delinking from
economic development 88;
developments in 83–84; emissions
from landfill and incineration 81,
86–87; EU Environmental Action
Programme (EAP) 72; GHG
emissions, estimation from MSW
management 80–82, 88–89; global
warming 87; IPCC
(Intergovernmental Panel on Climate
Change) 72, 80–81; Landfill Directive
(1999/31/EC) 72, 79–80, 86, 88;
landfill diversion 88; management of
85–86; model for waste generation
73–80; MSW, estimation results
74–79; MSW, European waste policy
and management 79–80; net GHG
emissions, forecast for 88–89; per
capita differences in 84; Projection of
European Waste Amounts (PEWA)
73–74; relative delinking 84–85

National Oceanic and Atmospheric
Administration (NOAA) 164
natural resource damage assessment
(NRDA) 158, 160–61, 163, 165, 166,
168, 171–72, 173, 174, 177n19;
technical approach to NRDA 161–63
natural resources damage (NRD) 154–55,
156, 157–60; economic valuation of
NRD 167; illegal waste disposal,

deterrence by liability regimes 167–72; natural recoverability of NRD 164, 165, 168–69, 169; non-natural recoverability of NRD 165, 169, 170; standardizing assessments 160–67; US proposed regulations for 178n22
Netherlands 46, 82, 98, 102, 129
New Zealand 102
Nicolli, Francesco 6, 9, 34–67, 126–50
NIMBY ('not in my back-yard') 91
Norway 23, 102
not in my back-yard (see NIMBY)
NRD (see natural resource damage)
NRDA (see natural resource damage assessment)

OECD (Organization for Economic Cooperation and Development) 2, 7, 15, 16, 30n16, 30n20, 34, 42, 82, 108, 121n5, 122n10; inter-country differences, MSW generation, disposal and recycling 91, 99–101, 101–2, 103n1
Ofiara, D.D. 164
opportunity cost 9, 111; landfill diversion and 127, 133, 134, 135, 138, 140, 143, 148; waste generation and disposal, drivers of 37, 47, 49, 50, 56, 57, 66n31
organic waste, separation and composting of 182–201; amount of separated organic waste 190–92; competition between technologies 186–87; composting 182, 185; composting capacity, determinants of 197–98; cost-benefit analysis 187, 188–89; cost of regulation for firms 187; data sources 193–95; determinants of waste collection 200; econometric specification 192–98; endogeneity, treatment of potential for 192–93; environment-competitiveness relationship, Porter's hypothesis on 187, 198–99; European Waste Directive 182, 185–86; findings from analysis 198–99; incineration capacity 191, 192; industry under investigation 184–86; lagged values, application of 192; landfill capacity 191, 192; life cycle assessment (LCA) 182; literature review 186–89; local government choices, diffusion of composting and 198; lock-in, local government as source for 199; model,

panel-based analysis 189–92; over-identification restrictions 193; policy implications 198–200; population 191, 192; regulation, opening of new markets and 198–99; results of analysis 196–98; study on, innovative nature of 183; technologies, interaction of 199; treatment capacity 190; urban waste, environmental impact of 182, 184–85; variables included in model 190–92; 'waste crises' in Italy 182
Ozawa, T. 43, 56, 128

Packaging and Packaging Waste Directive (1994/62/EC) 30n20, 79
Packaging and Packaging Waste Directive (2004/12/EC) 28
packaging waste 6, 41, 42, 48, 74, 79, 93, 95, 108–9; waste indicators in Europe 15, 16, 22, 23, 24, 25, 26, 28, 29, 30n20
Pearce, D.W. 5, 35, 36, 37, 48, 108, 120, 128
PEWA (see Protection of European Waste Amounts)
Phillips, P.S. *et al.* 128
Pigou, A.C. 154
Poland 23, 46, 65n23, 78, 82, 84, 102
policy analysis, outcomes of 122n16
policy evaluation 2, 3, 7, 15, 29n6, 177n19; environmental policy 114; landfill policy 127; waste disposal 34, 38, 39, 42, 62
policy indexes 51, 57, 60, 61, 62, 65n20, 91; environmental 7, 48, 52, 59, 149n8; landfill policy index 62; synthetic policy index 49, 65n19; time-variant policy index 42; waste legislation and policy index 91, 93, 94, 97, 100, 102, 103n1; waste strategy policy index 45
Polinsky, A.M. 157
Polinsky, A.M. and Shavell, S. 156, 176n10
polychlorinated biphenyls (PCB) 23
Porter, M. and Van den Linde, C. 187; environment-competitiveness relationship, hypothesis on 187, 198–99
Portugal 46, 59, 67n36, 82, 102
Posner, R. 156
Powell, J. and Brisson, I. 63n3, 149n2
Prais-Winsten correction technique 114, 122n10

projections 7, 34, 72, 78–79, 83, 89, 97, 101, 109
Protection of European Waste Amounts (PEWA) 73
provincial analysis: empirical model, waste generation and disposal 139–40; landfill diversion, embedding of 139–40, 147–48; municipal waste, generation, drivers and management in Italy 109–14, 114–17

Quadrio Curzio, A. and Pellizzari, F. 30n10
Quadrio Curzio, A. and Zoboli, R. 30n10
Quadrio Curzio, A. *et al.* 30n10

Ray, G. 30n10
R & D (research and development) 38, 45, 49, 50, 51, 59–60, 62, 63, 67n39
recovery: cost recovery 112, 113, 122n15, 133, 134, 138, 142, 148; energy recovery 4, 36, 82, 87, 178n34, 182, 189; material recovery 35, 36, 42, 93, 99, 121, 126, 129, 150n13
recycling 1, 4, 5, 6, 7, 8, 10, 155; inter-country differences 91–103; landfill diversion and 126, 127, 129, 138, 143; municipal waste, GHG emissions and 73, 79, 80, 81–82, 85–86, 87, 89; organic waste and composting 182, 184, 188–89, 193, 201n3; waste generation and disposal, drivers of 35, 36, 37, 38, 42, 43, 48, 50, 52, 57, 59, 63, 64n15; waste indicators in Europe 23, 28, 29; waste management instruments 114, 116, 117, 121
regional analysis: empirical model, waste generation and disposal 132–39; landfill diversion, embedding of 132–39, 147–48; municipal waste, generation, drivers and management in Italy 109–14, 117–20
Reinhart, D. 92
Reitveld, P. and van Woudenberg, S. 103n4
relative delinking 2, 6, 7, 107, 108–9, 116; waste generation and disposal, drivers of 34, 41, 42, 47, 52, 62; waste indicators in Europe 15, 16, 17, 19, 26, 27, 28
relative re-linking 17
Renkow, M. and Rubin, A.R. 188

Requate, T. 186
restoration costs 10, 162, 165; RCM (restoration cost method) 163, 164
Richardson, G. *et al.* 157
Romania 82
Rosenberg, N. 30n10
Rothman, D. 25, 30n17, 64n12
Russell, C. *et al.* 157
Russell, C.S. 157

SCM (see surrogate cost method)
Segerson, K. and Miceli, T. 176–77n15
Selden, D.H. and Song, D. 29n2
Seok Lim, J. and Missios, P. 149n2
Seppala, T. *et al.* 41
Shafik, N. and Bandyopadhyay, S. 92
Shavell, S. 154, 157, 175n3
Shobee, S. 30n21
Sinha, R. and Noble, C. 187, 190
Skovgaard, M. *et al.* 72, 81, 82, 87
Skovgaard, Mette 4, 7, 72–89
Slovakia 23, 46, 65n23, 82
Slovenia 46, 65n23, 82
socio-economic drivers 9, 44, 62; waste management instruments and 107, 117, 120
Solow growth model 39
Spain 46, 59, 78, 82, 102, 121
Stellin, G. and Candido, A. 161, 163
Stern, D. 15, 25, 30n13, 39, 44, 64n7, 113, 149n3
Sterner, T. and Bartelings, H. 43
Stoneman, P. 186
surrogate cost method (SCM) 163, 164
Swamy linear regression model 51, 60, 61
Sweden 46, 82, 98, 102, 129

Taseli, B. 43
Ten Kate, A. 29n2
Terry, N. 92
TEV (see total economic value)
Thompson, R. 187, 190
Tietenberg, T. 157
Torras, M. and Boyce, J. 65n26
total economic value (TEV) 160, 163, 177n17
Touaty, M. and Giè, G. 164
TP (turning point) 135, 143; municipal waste generation, drivers and management instruments 108, 114, 116, 117, 119, 120, 122n17; waste generation and disposal, drivers of 40, 41, 47, 54, 55, 56, 57, 58, 59, 60,

61; waste indicators in Europe 15, 18, 25, 29, 30n16

Turkey 43, 102

Turner, K. *et al.* 128

turning point *see* TP

United Kingdom (UK) 7, 34, 42, 43, 46, 76, 82, 86, 98, 102, 109, 128, 138, 145

United Nations (UN): Environment Program 103n1; Framework Convention on Climate Change (UNFCCC) 80, 81, 82, 87

United States (US) 15, 22, 40, 41, 92, 95, 98, 102, 108, 121, 164, 176n14, 177n19, 178n22, 187, 188

Villanueva, Alejandro 89

Villanueva, V. *et al.* 81

Vollebergh, H. and Dijkgraaf, E. 37

Vollebergh, H. and Kemfert, C. 38

Vollebergh, H.R. 201n7

Volpi, Massimiliano 10, 182–201

Walker, W. 187

Wang, P. *et al.* 22, 41

waste collection 1, 83, 87; municipal waste generation, drivers and management instruments 113, 119, 120, 123n24; organic waste and composting 190, 193, 198, 200, 201n6, 201n12; waste generation and disposal, drivers of 47, 52, 54, 57, 64n12, 64n15

waste disposal 1, 4, 7, 8, 11, 13, 28, 72, 113, 114; environmental liabilities 155, 167–72; landfill diversion 128, 135–36; MSW generation, disposal and recycling 91, 97, 98; waste generation and disposal, drivers of 37, 42, 54, 56, 57, 59, 62

waste electrical and electronic equipment (WEEE) 5, 23

waste generation (WG) 1, 2, 3, 4, 6, 7, 8, 9, 11, 23, 24, 29; drivers (EU), waste generation and disposal 34–67; empirical model, waste generation and disposal 126–28, 128–29, 129–48; environmental liabilities and 155, 168, 176n6; inter-country differences, drivers of MSW generation, disposal and recycling 91–103; municipal waste, generation, drivers and management in Italy 107–23; municipal waste, GHG emissions and

72, 74, 75, 78, 84, 85, 86, 88; municipal waste, socio-economic drivers and management instruments 107–10, 112–14, 116, 117, 119, 120–21, 123n23; organic waste and composting 184, 191; waste indicators in Europe 23, 24, 29

waste hierarchy 28, 36, 126, 176n6

waste indicators (EU), delinking and EKCs for 15–30; aspects of delinking and EKC analysis 17–19; benefits and costs 18–19; best policy strategy 19–20; data, nature and quality of 21; delinking analysis, framework for 16–20; delinking trends 15–16; economic efficiency 17–18; EKC and delinking, research on 15–16; EKC estimation, key issues 20–22; empirical results 25–28; environmental performance index 21; EU waste legislation 22–23; horizontal waste legislation 22–23; IPAT model 16–20; methodological issues 24–25; municipal waste, empirical results 27–28, 28–29; packaging waste, empirical results 25–26, 28–29; packaging waste, trends in 23; quantitative analysis 16; relative delinking 17; waste and material flows 21–22; waste indicators and delinking, EU evidence 22–25, 28–29

waste Kuznets curve *see* WKC

waste management 1, 3, 4, 5, 9, 11; environmental liabilities and 167, 171, 176n6; EUWM (Environmentally Undesirable Waste Management) 155; generation, disposal and recycling of, drivers of 91, 93, 95, 97, 100, 101, 103n1; instruments for (and approaches to) 108, 109, 110, 111, 112, 113, 114, 116, 117, 120, 121n2, 122n19; and landfill diversion 126, 127, 128–29, 130, 133–34, 138–39, 142, 143, 145, 147, 148, 149n8, 149n10; municipal waste and GHG emissions 72, 85–86, 89; organic waste, composting and 182, 185; waste generation and disposal, drivers of 35, 37, 39, 42, 43, 45, 47, 48, 52, 54, 55, 57, 63, 64n9, 65n18, 65n24, 66n33; waste indicators in Europe 22; *see also* decentralized waste management (DWM)

waste management instruments 9, 42, 43–44, 107–23, 142, 148
waste mix 184
waste policy: action on 66n27; adoption of 8–9; analysis of 42, 108; changes in 22; commitment to 57, 113; decentralization of 48, 59, 113; efficiency of 91, 186; EU strategy on 16, 22, 63, 64n5, 72, 79–80; history of 16, 28; innovation in 120; and legislation index (POLDX) 98, 102; packaging waste policy (EU) 26
waste prevention 9, 16, 28, 93, 113, 117, 121, 182; targets for 9, 28, 63, 65n19; waste generation and disposal, drivers of 46–47, 48, 52, 62, 63, 63n2, 65n19
waste strategy 45, 126
waste tariffs 108, 110, 111, 113, 117, 130, 132, 133, 134, 138, 142, 143
waste tax 108, 110, 111, 113, 117, 130, 132, 133, 134

waste trends 4, 7, 91, 127, 129; municipal waste generation, drivers and management instruments 109, 110, 114; waste generation and disposal, drivers of 34, 37, 44, 62, 64n9, 66n29
Wernstedt, Kris 9, 154–79
WKC (waste Kuznets curve) 37, 38, 40, 42, 43, 44, 46, 47, 48, 50, 52, 55, 62, 128
Wooldridge test 97
World Bank 38, 42, 94, 103n3, 108, 164, 177n19
WRI (World Resources Institute) 97, 101

Yandle, B. *et al.* 29n4
Yang, H.L. and Innes, R. 43
Yarime, M. 186

Zoboli, Roberto 6, 8, 9, 15–30, 34–67, 107–23